411 SAT
CRITICAL READING
QUESTIONS

411 SAT
CRITICAL READING
QUESTIONS

LEARNINGEXPRESS®

NEW YORK

Library of Congress Cataloging-in-Publication Data:
  411 SAT critical reading questions.
      p. cm.
  ISBN 1-57685-561-9
  1. Reading comprehension—Examinations—Study guides.   2. Reading
comprehension—Problems, exercises, etc.   3. Reading—Examinations—
Study guides.   4. SAT (Educational test)—Study guides.
  I. LearningExpress (Organization)   II. Title.
  LB1050.45.A13 2006
  428.0076—dc22

                                                    2006007207

Printed in the United States of America

9 8 7 6 5 4 3 2 1

ISBN 1-57685-561-9

For information on LearningExpress, other LearningExpress products, or bulk sales,
please write to us at:
    LearningExpress
    55 Broadway
    8th Floor
    New York, NY 10006

Or visit us at:
    www.learnatest.com

Contents

INTRODUCTION 1

PRETEST 5

CHAPTER 1   Sentence Completion Questions 17

CHAPTER 2   Passage-Length Questions 43

CHAPTER 3   Short-Passage Questions 129

POSTTEST 147

411 SAT
CRITICAL READING
QUESTIONS

Introduction ▶

Preparing for the SAT can at first seem like a daunting task (*daunting* = intimidating . . . remember that word for later). Four out of every five colleges and universities around the country require that students take the SAT in order to be considered for admission. Although other factors are taken into consideration during the admission process (including high school grade point average, extracurricular activities, and personal essays), SAT scores are still considered an extremely useful tool for gauging a student's scholastic abilities.

The SAT includes three sections: Math, Writing, and Critical Reading. Each section is scored independently on a scale of 200–800. The purpose of this book is to help students prepare for the Critical Reading section. The exercises and practice tests in this book are intended to help you practice the skills that will be most useful when taking the actual SAT.

▶ What to Expect

The actual questions on the SAT change from year to year, so there is no way of knowing exactly which questions will be included on any individual test. However, there are only two types of questions that appear in the Critical Reading section: sentence completion and passage-based reading. Using this book will improve your ability to *recognize* the types of questions that appear on the exam and *reason out* the correct answers.

Sentence Completion
The sentence completion questions test your:

- knowledge of word definitions and/or connotations
- understanding of the ways in which sentences fit together

There are generally between five and eight sentence completion questions per Critical Reading section, with a total of 19 sentence completion questions spread out over the length of the SAT. Sentence completion questions can either feature one word answer choices or paired answer choices. For this kind of question, studying word definitions and understanding sentence context are key.

Passage-Based Reading

There are three different kinds of passage-based reading questions:

- Vocabulary in Context: Similar to sentence completion questions, vocabulary-in-context questions test your ability to understand words and find appropriate synonyms based on sentence context.
- Literal Comprehension: Literal comprehension questions test your ability to find specific information that is directly stated in the passage.
- Extended Reasoning: Extended reasoning questions test your ability to analyze and interpret information from the passage to synthesize ideas and come to new conclusions.

Within the passage-based reading section, there are two different kinds of passages—short and long passages.

- Short passages are generally 100–400 words long, with two to five questions. The questions for short passages tend to be extended reasoning questions, centering on crucial ideas in the passage, such as key phrases, main ideas, and author's point of view.
- Long passages are generally 600–850 words in length. These passages are followed by six or more questions drawn from any of the three types of passage-based reading questions.

Both short passages and long passages can either consist of one passage or paired passages. Paired passages are on a shared issue or theme, and test takers are generally asked to compare and contrast. There is a total of 48 passage-based reading questions spread out over the length of the SAT.

▶ Test-Taking Strategies for the Critical Reading Section

The SAT Critical Reading section differs slightly from the Math section in that, with math, rules can be learned and applied to find definitive answers. Although each question in the Critical Reading section will have only one correct answer, there are no formulas that can be used to find the single correct answer, and sometimes, more than one answer choice can be reasonably argued. The most important thing to keep in mind when taking the Critical Reading section is this: *The SAT does not test your ability to creatively justify your answer.* Sometimes, you will see answer choices that could make sense with a creative interpretation of the sentence or passage; however, the SAT allows only one correct answer choice for each question. Therefore, the best strategy you can use on the Critical Reading section is to find the *most likely* answer choice, according to the parameters established by the sentence or passage.

What does this mean in a practical sense? Here is an example, using a sentence completion question:

The forlorn child _____ when he realized he would not get the Christmas toy he had requested.
a. sulked
b. danced
c. giggled
d. exhaled
e. slept

The correct answer here is answer choice **a**, *sulked*. It is entirely possible that the forlorn child danced, giggled, exhaled, or slept when he realized he would not get his Christmas toy. Each of the answers is grammatically correct and could potentially make sense if a subsequent sentence indicated a different motivation for the child. However, in this case, all you have to go on is the context provided by the sentence, and given that the child is "forlorn" and did not get something he wanted, the *best* assumption is that the child sulked.

Because critical reading requires that you make judgments based on the available information, many people find the Critical Reading section to be the most difficult part of the SAT. The exercises in this book are intended to familiarize you with the common types of reasoning you will be expected to do when taking the actual SAT. You may not be able to say with 100% certainty, for example, what intended effect an author had when writing a passage, but given five answer choices, you should be able to pick the choice that most closely aligns with the clues within the passage.

Here are some strategies you can use to come to the correct conclusions:

1. **Read each sentence or passage carefully.** First, read each sentence or passage carefully to get an overview of the sentence or passage. What is the author trying to say? What words seem most important? As you are reading, feel free to highlight or circle information in your test booklet that seems as though it may be pertinent later.
2. **Read each question carefully, then return to the passage to find the context.** Don't just rely on your memory to find the correct answer choices. If a question points you to a specific sentence or specific lines within the passage, reread that section to make sure you have the best information.
3. **Use the process of elimination.** In any given question set, there are usually only two or three

answer choices that are reasonable. Eliminate the most incorrect answer choices first. Then, looking back to the answer choices and the passage or sentence, narrow the remaining choices down to the one most likely answer choice.

4. **When in doubt, make an educated guess.** After you have eliminated all incorrect answer choices, you may be left with a few answer choices that seem correct. Statistics have shown that your first instinct will be correct more often than not. Make the best educated guess based on the information available, and if you truly cannot decide the best answer, do not overthink the question; go with your gut instinct.
5. **Use your time wisely.** The SAT is a timed test. Your score is based on the number of questions you answer correctly minus a percentage of incorrect answers. Blank answers do not count for or against your score. In extremely difficult questions, therefore, it is better not to answer at all than to answer incorrectly. Instead of wasting valuable time puzzling over extremely difficult questions, it is wise to move on and return to those questions when you have time.

Immediately following this introduction is a pretest that will help you gauge your current level of ability. Take the pretest first, and then read the answer key to determine where you need the most help. After that, there are three chapters featuring questions similar to those found on the SAT. Completing these exercises and checking your answers against the answer keys will help you understand how questions are constructed on the SAT. When you are finished with these three chapters, take the posttest and see how much your scores have improved.

Study hard, remember to get plenty of rest before the actual test, and good luck!

Pretest ▶

To find out how well you already know what you will be tested on during the SAT Critical Reading section, take a brief 25-question pretest. Even though you won't have to do this test on a time limit (like you will the SAT), do it as fast as you can. On the official test, you will have only 35 minutes to do 60 questions. At that rate, this one should only take you about 15 minutes or less. When you stop working, make sure to check your answers.

PRETEST

1.	ⓐ ⓑ ⓒ ⓓ ⓔ		**11.**	ⓐ ⓑ ⓒ ⓓ ⓔ		**21.**	ⓐ ⓑ ⓒ ⓓ ⓔ
2.	ⓐ ⓑ ⓒ ⓓ ⓔ		**12.**	ⓐ ⓑ ⓒ ⓓ ⓔ		**22.**	ⓐ ⓑ ⓒ ⓓ ⓔ
3.	ⓐ ⓑ ⓒ ⓓ ⓔ		**13.**	ⓐ ⓑ ⓒ ⓓ ⓔ		**23.**	ⓐ ⓑ ⓒ ⓓ ⓔ
4.	ⓐ ⓑ ⓒ ⓓ ⓔ		**14.**	ⓐ ⓑ ⓒ ⓓ ⓔ		**24.**	ⓐ ⓑ ⓒ ⓓ ⓔ
5.	ⓐ ⓑ ⓒ ⓓ ⓔ		**15.**	ⓐ ⓑ ⓒ ⓓ ⓔ		**25.**	ⓐ ⓑ ⓒ ⓓ ⓔ
6.	ⓐ ⓑ ⓒ ⓓ ⓔ		**16.**	ⓐ ⓑ ⓒ ⓓ ⓔ			
7.	ⓐ ⓑ ⓒ ⓓ ⓔ		**17.**	ⓐ ⓑ ⓒ ⓓ ⓔ			
8.	ⓐ ⓑ ⓒ ⓓ ⓔ		**18.**	ⓐ ⓑ ⓒ ⓓ ⓔ			
9.	ⓐ ⓑ ⓒ ⓓ ⓔ		**19.**	ⓐ ⓑ ⓒ ⓓ ⓔ			
10.	ⓐ ⓑ ⓒ ⓓ ⓔ		**20.**	ⓐ ⓑ ⓒ ⓓ ⓔ			

▶ Sentence Completion

In each of the following sentences, one or two words have been omitted (indicated by a blank). Choose the word(s) from the answer choices provided that makes the most sense in the context of the sentence.

1. I thought Jackie's valedictorian speech was unnecessarily cruel; I saw no reason for her to _____ the administration as much as she did.
   a. implicate
   b. malign
   c. expiate
   d. involve
   e. evade

2. Although some of his classmates were _____ by the play's engaging script, Gautum thought the overall production was slow and _____.
   a. perplexed . . . turgid
   b. perturbed . . . melodramatic
   c. stifled . . . ponderous
   d. riveted . . . tedious
   e. intrigued . . . salacious

3. When submitting a manuscript, please provide a brief, _____ synopsis of the plot.
   a. succinct
   b. vivid
   c. ecstatic
   d. dense
   e. extensive

4. The homeless _____ could not find a job, so he was forced to _____ on the street to make ends meet.
   a. pensioner . . . loiter
   b. sybarite . . . ruminate
   c. scoundrel . . . abide
   d. mendicant . . . advocate
   e. vagrant . . . supplicate

5. The sweet, _____ song of a canary drifted along the wind.
   a. eccentric
   b. evanescent
   c. erratic
   d. erudite
   e. euphonious

6. Although the documents appeared _____ upon a cursory glance, under professional inspection, they were determined to be _____.
   a. legitimate . . . fraudulent
   b. impressive . . . devious
   c. luminous . . . obtuse
   d. immutable . . . ductile
   e. authentic . . . evasive

7. Darren should really _____ Shauna's hurt feelings if he expects to get back in her good graces.
   a. clarify
   b. satiate
   c. obfuscate
   d. mollify
   e. contest

▶ Short-Passage Questions

Read the passage and the questions that follow it. As you form your answers, be sure to base them on what is stated in the passage or the inferences you can make from the passage.

Wondering what to do with that old Atari home video game in the attic? It's on the wish list of the Computer Museum of America, in San Diego, California, which hopes you will donate it to their holdings. The museum was founded in 1983 to amass and preserve historic computer equipment such as calculators, card punches, and typewriters, and now it owns one of the world's largest collections. In addition, it has archives of computer-related magazines, manuals, and books that are available to students, authors, researchers, and others for historical research. Although many doubted the need to preserve modern technology when the museum was founded, technology becomes outmoded so quickly nowadays that the founders of the museum are now seen as remarkably prescient.

8. All of the following are probably part of the collection of the Computer Museum of America EXCEPT
   a. adding machines.
   b. old computers.
   c. operation manuals for calculators.
   d. card punch machines.
   e. kitchen scales.

9. What term paper topic could probably be researched at the Computer Museum of America?
   a. Alexander Graham Bell's contributions to American society
   b. IBM's contribution to the development of the modern computer
   c. more than just paintings: the museums of California
   d. how email is affecting our ability to communicate effectively
   e. why video games are harmful to our nation's youth

10. The author suggests that
   a. the museum is mainly used by students and professors doing historical research.
   b. the Computer Museum of America contains the world's largest archive of outdated technology.
   c. in 1983, many did not predict that computer technology would evolve as quickly as it has.
   d. the museum primarily focuses on old video game systems and other computerized entertainment devices.
   e. the museum's founders did not anticipate the crucial role the museum would serve in preserving technology.

▶ Passage-Length Questions

Read the passage and the questions that follow it. As you form your answers, be sure to base them on what is stated in the passage or the inferences you can make from the passage.

The following selection explains the origins and development of the modern shopping mall.

Line

Today's shopping mall has its antecedents in historical marketplaces such as Greek agoras, European piazzas, and Asian bazaars. The purpose of these sites, as of the shopping mall, is both economic and social. People go not only to buy and sell wares, but also to be seen, catch up on news, and be part of the human drama. Both the marketplace and its descendant, the mall, might also contain restaurants, banks, theaters,

(5)   and professional offices.

The mall is the product of the creation of suburbs. Although villages outside of cities have existed since antiquity, it was the technological and transportation advances of the nineteenth century that gave rise to a conscious exodus of the population away from crowded, industrialized cities toward quieter, more rural towns. Since the suburbs typically have no centralized marketplace, shopping centers or malls

(10)   were designed to fill the needs of the changing community, providing retail stores and services to an increasing suburban population.

The shopping mall differs from its ancient counterparts in a number of important ways. While piazzas and bazaars were open-air venues, the modern mall is usually enclosed. Since the suburbs are spread out geographically, shoppers drive to the mall, which means that parking areas must be an integral part of a mall's

(15)   design. Ancient marketplaces were often set up in public spaces, but shopping malls are designed, built, and maintained by a separate management firm as a unit. The first shopping mall was built by J.C. Nichols in 1922 near Kansas City, Missouri. The Country Club Plaza was designed to be an automobile-centered plaza, as its patrons drove their own cars to it, rather than take mass transportation, as was often the case for city shoppers. It was constructed according to a unified plan, rather than as a random group of stores. Nichols's

(20)   company owned and operated the mall, leasing space to a variety of tenants.

The first enclosed mall was the Galleria Vittoria Emanuele in Milan, Italy, in 1865–1877. Inspired by its design, Victor Gruen took the shopping and dining experience of the Galleria to a new level when he created the Southdale Center Mall in 1956. Located in a suburb of Minneapolis, it was intended to be a substitute for the traditional city center. The 95-acre, two-level structure had a constant, climate-controlled

(25)   temperature of 72°, and included shops, restaurants, a school, a post office, and a skating rink. Works of art, decorative lighting, fountains, tropical plants, and flowers were placed throughout the mall. Southdale afforded people the opportunity to experience the pleasures of urban life while being protected from the harsh Minnesota weather.

In the 1980s, giant megamalls were developed. The 5.3-million-square-foot West Edmonton Mall in

(30)   Alberta, Canada, opened in 1981, with over 800 stores, 110 eating establishments, a hotel, an amusement park, a miniature-golf course, a church, a zoo, and a 438-foot-long lake. Often referred to as the "eighth wonder of the world," the West Edmonton Mall is the number-one tourist attraction in the area, and it will soon be expanded to include more retail space, including a facility for sports, trade shows, and conventions. While Canada has had the distinction of being home to the largest of the megamalls for over 20 years,

(35)   that honor will soon go to Dubai, where the Mall of Arabia is being completed at a cost of over $5 billion.

The largest enclosed megamall in the United States is Bloomington, Minneapolis's Mall of America, which employs over 12,000 people. It has over 500 retail stores, an amusement park that includes an indoor roller coaster, a walk-through aquarium, a college, and a wedding chapel. The mall contributes over $1 billion each year to the economy of the state of Minnesota. Its owners have proposed numerous expan-

(40)   sion projects, but have been hampered by safety concerns because of the mall's proximity to an airport.

11. What is NOT a probable reason for the proposed expansion of the Mall of America?
   a. so it can contribute more to the economy of its state
   b. to keep it closer in size to the other megamalls
   c. so it can employ more people
   d. to attract more tourists
   e. to compete for visitors with the Mall of Arabia

12. The statement that people went to marketplaces to be part of the human drama (lines 3–4) suggests that people
   a. prefer to shop anonymously.
   b. like to act on stage rather than shop.
   c. seem to be more emotional in groups.
   d. like to be in a community, interacting with one another.
   e. prefer to be entertained rather than shop for necessities.

13. In line 1, *antecedents* most nearly means
   a. designers.
   b. planners.
   c. predecessors.
   d. role models.
   e. teachers.

14. All of the following questions can be explicitly answered on the basis of the passage EXCEPT
   a. Who designed Minneapolis's Mall of America?
   b. Why was the Country Club Plaza automobile-centered?
   c. What are three examples of historical marketplaces?
   d. Where is the Galleria Vittoria Emanuele?
   e. What is the Edmonton Mall often referred to as?

15. How was the Country Club Plaza different from an urban shopping district?
   a. It consisted of many more stores.
   b. It was built by one company that leased space and oversaw operations.
   c. It was enclosed.
   d. It had both retail stores and restaurants, and offered areas for community programs.
   e. It was based on an Italian design.

16. According to the passage, how did Southdale expand the notion of the shopping mall?
   a. It added an amusement park.
   b. It was unheated.
   c. It was the first to rise above two stories.
   d. It was designed with more parking spaces than any previous shopping mall.
   e. It was intended to be a substitute for the traditional city center.

17. According to paragraph 5, which is the only activity visitors to the West Edmonton Mall cannot enjoy?
   a. staying in a hotel
   b. gambling in a casino
   c. visiting animals in a zoo
   d. playing miniature golf
   e. riding an amusement park ride

18. When the author states in lines 26–28 that Southdale afforded people the opportunity to experience the pleasures of urban life, she means that they could
   a. perform necessary and leisurely activities in one location.
   b. have a greater variety of retailers to choose from.
   c. see more artwork and botanicals than they would in a city.
   d. be entertained as they would be in a city.
   e. have taller buildings in their landscape.

The selection that follows is based on an excerpt from a history of the game of Monopoly.

Line

In 1904, the U.S. Patent Office granted a patent for a board game called "The Landlord's Game," which was invented by a Virginia Quaker named Lizzie Magie. Magie was a follower of Henry George, who started a tax movement that supported the theory that the renting of land and real estate produced an unearned increase in land values that profited a few individuals (landlords) rather than the majority of the people
(5) (tenants). George proposed a single federal tax based on land ownership; he believed this tax would weaken the ability to form monopolies, encourage equal opportunity, and narrow the gap between rich and poor.

Lizzie Magie wanted to spread the word about George's proposal, making it more understandable to a majority of people who were basically unfamiliar with economics. As a result, she invented a board game that would serve as a teaching device. The Landlord's Game was intended to explain the evils of
(10) monopolies, showing that they repressed the possibility for equal opportunity. Her instructions read in part: "The object of this game is not only to afford amusement to players, but to illustrate to them how, under the present or prevailing system of land tenure, the landlord has an advantage over other enterprisers, and also how the single tax would discourage speculation."

The board for the game was painted with 40 spaces around its perimeter, including four railroads,
(15) two utilities, 22 rental properties, and a jail. There were other squares directing players to go to jail, pay a luxury tax, and park. All properties were available for rent, rather than purchase. Magie's invention became very popular, spreading through word of mouth, and altering slightly as it did. Since it was not manufactured by Magie, the boards and game pieces were homemade. Rules were explained and trans-muted, from one group of friends to another. There is evidence to suggest that The Landlord's Game was
(20) played at Princeton, Harvard, and the University of Pennsylvania.

In 1924, Magie approached George Parker (president of Parker Brothers) to see if he was interested in purchasing the rights to her game. Parker turned her down, saying that it was too political. The game increased in popularity, migrating north to New York state, west to Michigan, and as far south as Texas. By the early 1930s, it reached Charles Darrow in Philadelphia. In 1935, claiming to be the inventor, Darrow got
(25) a patent for the game and approached Parker Brothers. This time, the company loved it, swallowed Darrow's prevarication, and not only purchased his patent, but also paid him royalties for every game sold. The game quickly became Parker Brothers' best-seller and made the company, and Darrow, millions of dollars.

When Parker Brothers found out that Darrow was not the true inventor of the game, they wanted to protect their rights to the successful game, so they went back to Lizzie Magie, now Mrs. Elizabeth Magie
(30) Phillips of Clarendon, Virginia. She agreed to a payment of $500 for her patent, with no royalties, so she could stay true to the original intent of her game's invention. She therefore required in return that Parker Brothers manufacture and market The Landlord's Game in addition to Monopoly. However, only a few hundred games were ever produced. Monopoly went on to become the world's best-selling board game, with an objective that is the exact opposite of the one Magie intended: "The idea of the game is to buy and
(35) rent or sell property so profitably that one becomes the wealthiest player and eventually monopolist. The game is one of shrewd and amusing trading and excitement."

19. In line 10, what does *repressed the possibility for equal opportunity* mean?
   a. Monopolies led to slavery.
   b. Monopolies were responsible for the single tax problems.
   c. Monopolies made it impossible for poorer people to follow Henry George.
   d. Monopolies were responsible for Lizzie Magie's $500 payment and Charles Darrow's millions.
   e. Monopolies made it impossible for poorer people to have the same chances as the wealthy.

20. How does the objective of The Landlord's Game differ from that of Monopoly?
   a. In The Landlord's Game, you can only rent the properties, but in Monopoly, you may buy them.
   b. The Landlord's Game illustrates the inequality of the landlord-tenant system, while Monopoly encourages players to become landlords and become wealthy at the expense of others.
   c. The Landlord's Game teaches the problems of capitalism, and Monopoly teaches the value of money.
   d. The Landlord's Game was a way for Quakers to understand the economic theories of Henry George, and Monopoly explains the evolutionary theories of Charles Darrow.
   e. In The Landlord's Game, players try to land on as many railroads and utilities as possible, but in Monopoly they try to avoid them.

21. In lines 25–26, what does *swallowed Darrow's prevarication* mean?
   a. ate his lunch
   b. believed his lie
   c. understood his problem
   d. played by his rules
   e. drank his champagne

22. In lines 18–19, the statement that the rules of The Landlord's Game were explained and transmuted relies on the notion that
   a. when people pass along information by word of mouth, the information changes.
   b. when people explain things to their friends, they take on adifferent appearance.
   c. friends rely on one another for vital information.
   d. it's not always easy to play by the rules.
   e. word of mouth is the best way to spread information.

23. In paragraph 4, the author implies that
   a. Parker Brothers bought the game from Charles Darrow.
   b. it is not difficult to get a patent for an idea you didn't invent.
   c. Monopoly made Parker Brothers and Darrow millions of dollars.
   d. Lizzie Magie tried to sell her game to George Parker.
   e. The Landlord's Game was popular with Quakers.

24. Why did Lizzie Magie sell her patent to Parker Brothers?
  a. so a large company would market her game and spread the word about Henry George's single tax theory
  b. so she could make money
  c. so The Landlord's Game could compete with Monopoly
  d. so the truth would be told about Charles Darrow
  e. so she would become famous

25. All of the following questions can be explicitly answered on the basis of the passage EXCEPT
  a. Why did Lizzie Magie invent The Landlord's Game?
  b. What was the object of The Landlord's Game?
  c. What were some of the properties on The Landlord's Game board?
  d. Who did Charles Darrow sell the game to?
  e. How did Parker Brothers find out that Charles Darrow didn't invent the game?

▶ Answers

1. b. The key to answering this question correctly is simply knowing the meaning of the five words. Of the five choices, **a** and **b** come closest to the correct answer. Between **a** and **b**, *malign*, or "speak evil of," is the best answer choice based on context.

2. d. Pay close attention to the adjectives in this sentence to find the correct answer choices. Based on the word *engaging*, the choice can immediately be narrowed down to **d** or **e**. The second part of the sentence seems to be looking for a word with the same connotation as *slow*; of the two answer choices, *tedious*, or "boring," fits more closely than *salacious*, or "bawdy."

3. a. The words *brief* and *synopsis* provide context clues that can be used to eliminate choices **d** and **e**. Based on these context clues, you can assume that the correct answer choice will have a similar connotation as *brief*; of the three remaining answer choices, the best answer is *succinct*, meaning "concise."

4. e. The key to finding the correct answer choice in this sentence is the phrase *to make ends meet*. As you know that the person described cannot find a job, he or she would most likely have to beg to get money. Based on this information, the best answer choice is **e.**

5. e. Context clues tell you that the best answer choice will describe a *sweet song*; therefore, *euphonious*, meaning "agreeableness of sound," is the best answer choice.

6. a. You can tell best from the sentence structure that the two words will be opposites; this narrows the choices down to **a, d,** and **e.** It is unlikely that documents would be determined to be *ductile*, or "flexible," so answer choice **d** can be ruled out. Between the remaining two answer choices, *fraudulent* would be a more likely choice to describe documents than *evasive*.

7. d. Based on context, you can tell that the correct answer choice will be a synonym for "soothe." Although **b** has a similar connotation as "soothe," *satiate* is closer to "satisfy"; therefore, **d** is the best answer choice.

8. e. Lines 7–10 mention calculators (adding machines), computers, card punches, and manuals. The only item not mentioned is kitchen scales.

9. b. The museum has a collection of computer-related magazines, manuals, and books (line 10). They would not contain information on the inventor of the telephone (choice **a**), other museums in California (choice **c**), the impact of e-mail on communication (choice **d**), or why video games are harmful (choice **e**). Since

IBM played, and continues to play, an important role in the development of computers and computer-related technology, it could most likely be researched at the museum.

10. c. In the last sentence, the author notes that the need for the museum was doubted by many at first, implying that many believed technology would not change quickly enough to necessitate an entire museum.

11. e. All of the other choices were mentioned in the last two paragraphs as positive impacts of megamalls. However, it is unlikely that a mall in Minnesota would be in direct competition for visitors with a mall located on the other side of the world.

12. d. Lines 2–4 explain that there was a social component to a trip to the marketplace. To be social means to be around others, suggesting that people sought out interaction with one another.

13. c. The prefix *ante-* means earlier, as does *pre-*. Additional context clues may be found in the first paragraph, which explains the similarities between historical marketplaces (those of long ago), and the malls of today, and in lines 4–5, which states the mall is a descendant of the marketplace.

14. a. This information is not given in the passage.

15. b. The answer is in lines 21–22: It was constructed according to a unified plan, rather than as a random group of stores. Nichols's company owned and operated the mall, leasing space to a variety of tenants.

16. e. Gruen took the shopping mall to the next level by intending it to take the place of a city center, with leisure and entertainment opportunities as well as shopping and dining.

17. b. All of the other choices are mentioned in the passage.

18. a. Lines 25–28 list some of Southdale's offerings, such as shops, restaurants, a school, a post office, a skating rink, works of art, and fountains. These are also available in a city and may be considered among the pleasures of urban life.

19. e. Look back to lines 5–6, where George's single tax proposal (the idea The Landlord's Game was meant to teach) is described as aiming to weaken the ability to form monopolies, encourage equal opportunity, and narrow the gap between rich and poor.

20. b. Don't be distracted by the other answers that contain true statements that are not, however, the objectives of the games. Note also that evolution was a theory of Charles Darwin, not Charles Darrow.

21. b. Lines 24–26 explain that Darrow fraudulently claimed to be the game's inventor (he was introduced to it before he got a patent as its inventor). Parker Brothers bought his patent believing that it was genuine, meaning that they believed Darrow's falsehood.

22. a. The answer is in lines 16–17. Having the game and its rules spread by word of mouth means it will alter slightly from one person to another.

23. b. To imply means to hint at rather than to state outright. The other choices are all directly stated in the paragraph, while **b** is implied.

24. a. She sold it to remain true to her original intent, which was to spread the word about George's single tax theory.

25. e. Parker Brothers found out that Darrow wasn't the inventor, but nowhere in the passage does it say how they learned the information.

Sentence Completion Questions

The following are examples of the sentence completion questions you will be tested on in the SAT Critical Reading section. Often, the sentences are long and difficult to follow, but with practice, you can learn to master them. There are 100 practice questions in this chapter, so by the time you get to the last one, you will be well prepared to tackle this type of Critical Reading question!

SENTENCE COMPLETION QUESTIONS

1.	ⓐ	ⓑ	ⓒ	ⓓ	ⓔ	36.	ⓐ	ⓑ	ⓒ	ⓓ	ⓔ	71.	ⓐ	ⓑ	ⓒ	ⓓ	ⓔ
2.	ⓐ	ⓑ	ⓒ	ⓓ	ⓔ	37.	ⓐ	ⓑ	ⓒ	ⓓ	ⓔ	72.	ⓐ	ⓑ	ⓒ	ⓓ	ⓔ
3.	ⓐ	ⓑ	ⓒ	ⓓ	ⓔ	38.	ⓐ	ⓑ	ⓒ	ⓓ	ⓔ	73.	ⓐ	ⓑ	ⓒ	ⓓ	ⓔ
4.	ⓐ	ⓑ	ⓒ	ⓓ	ⓔ	39.	ⓐ	ⓑ	ⓒ	ⓓ	ⓔ	74.	ⓐ	ⓑ	ⓒ	ⓓ	ⓔ
5.	ⓐ	ⓑ	ⓒ	ⓓ	ⓔ	40.	ⓐ	ⓑ	ⓒ	ⓓ	ⓔ	75.	ⓐ	ⓑ	ⓒ	ⓓ	ⓔ
6.	ⓐ	ⓑ	ⓒ	ⓓ	ⓔ	41.	ⓐ	ⓑ	ⓒ	ⓓ	ⓔ	76.	ⓐ	ⓑ	ⓒ	ⓓ	ⓔ
7.	ⓐ	ⓑ	ⓒ	ⓓ	ⓔ	42.	ⓐ	ⓑ	ⓒ	ⓓ	ⓔ	77.	ⓐ	ⓑ	ⓒ	ⓓ	ⓔ
8.	ⓐ	ⓑ	ⓒ	ⓓ	ⓔ	43.	ⓐ	ⓑ	ⓒ	ⓓ	ⓔ	78.	ⓐ	ⓑ	ⓒ	ⓓ	ⓔ
9.	ⓐ	ⓑ	ⓒ	ⓓ	ⓔ	44.	ⓐ	ⓑ	ⓒ	ⓓ	ⓔ	79.	ⓐ	ⓑ	ⓒ	ⓓ	ⓔ
10.	ⓐ	ⓑ	ⓒ	ⓓ	ⓔ	45.	ⓐ	ⓑ	ⓒ	ⓓ	ⓔ	80.	ⓐ	ⓑ	ⓒ	ⓓ	ⓔ
11.	ⓐ	ⓑ	ⓒ	ⓓ	ⓔ	46.	ⓐ	ⓑ	ⓒ	ⓓ	ⓔ	81.	ⓐ	ⓑ	ⓒ	ⓓ	ⓔ
12.	ⓐ	ⓑ	ⓒ	ⓓ	ⓔ	47.	ⓐ	ⓑ	ⓒ	ⓓ	ⓔ	82.	ⓐ	ⓑ	ⓒ	ⓓ	ⓔ
13.	ⓐ	ⓑ	ⓒ	ⓓ	ⓔ	48.	ⓐ	ⓑ	ⓒ	ⓓ	ⓔ	83.	ⓐ	ⓑ	ⓒ	ⓓ	ⓔ
14.	ⓐ	ⓑ	ⓒ	ⓓ	ⓔ	49.	ⓐ	ⓑ	ⓒ	ⓓ	ⓔ	84.	ⓐ	ⓑ	ⓒ	ⓓ	ⓔ
15.	ⓐ	ⓑ	ⓒ	ⓓ	ⓔ	50.	ⓐ	ⓑ	ⓒ	ⓓ	ⓔ	85.	ⓐ	ⓑ	ⓒ	ⓓ	ⓔ
16.	ⓐ	ⓑ	ⓒ	ⓓ	ⓔ	51.	ⓐ	ⓑ	ⓒ	ⓓ	ⓔ	86.	ⓐ	ⓑ	ⓒ	ⓓ	ⓔ
17.	ⓐ	ⓑ	ⓒ	ⓓ	ⓔ	52.	ⓐ	ⓑ	ⓒ	ⓓ	ⓔ	87.	ⓐ	ⓑ	ⓒ	ⓓ	ⓔ
18.	ⓐ	ⓑ	ⓒ	ⓓ	ⓔ	53.	ⓐ	ⓑ	ⓒ	ⓓ	ⓔ	88.	ⓐ	ⓑ	ⓒ	ⓓ	ⓔ
19.	ⓐ	ⓑ	ⓒ	ⓓ	ⓔ	54.	ⓐ	ⓑ	ⓒ	ⓓ	ⓔ	89.	ⓐ	ⓑ	ⓒ	ⓓ	ⓔ
20.	ⓐ	ⓑ	ⓒ	ⓓ	ⓔ	55.	ⓐ	ⓑ	ⓒ	ⓓ	ⓔ	90.	ⓐ	ⓑ	ⓒ	ⓓ	ⓔ
21.	ⓐ	ⓑ	ⓒ	ⓓ	ⓔ	56.	ⓐ	ⓑ	ⓒ	ⓓ	ⓔ	91.	ⓐ	ⓑ	ⓒ	ⓓ	ⓔ
22.	ⓐ	ⓑ	ⓒ	ⓓ	ⓔ	57.	ⓐ	ⓑ	ⓒ	ⓓ	ⓔ	92.	ⓐ	ⓑ	ⓒ	ⓓ	ⓔ
23.	ⓐ	ⓑ	ⓒ	ⓓ	ⓔ	58.	ⓐ	ⓑ	ⓒ	ⓓ	ⓔ	93.	ⓐ	ⓑ	ⓒ	ⓓ	ⓔ
24.	ⓐ	ⓑ	ⓒ	ⓓ	ⓔ	59.	ⓐ	ⓑ	ⓒ	ⓓ	ⓔ	94.	ⓐ	ⓑ	ⓒ	ⓓ	ⓔ
25.	ⓐ	ⓑ	ⓒ	ⓓ	ⓔ	60.	ⓐ	ⓑ	ⓒ	ⓓ	ⓔ	95.	ⓐ	ⓑ	ⓒ	ⓓ	ⓔ
26.	ⓐ	ⓑ	ⓒ	ⓓ	ⓔ	61.	ⓐ	ⓑ	ⓒ	ⓓ	ⓔ	96.	ⓐ	ⓑ	ⓒ	ⓓ	ⓔ
27.	ⓐ	ⓑ	ⓒ	ⓓ	ⓔ	62.	ⓐ	ⓑ	ⓒ	ⓓ	ⓔ	97.	ⓐ	ⓑ	ⓒ	ⓓ	ⓔ
28.	ⓐ	ⓑ	ⓒ	ⓓ	ⓔ	63.	ⓐ	ⓑ	ⓒ	ⓓ	ⓔ	98.	ⓐ	ⓑ	ⓒ	ⓓ	ⓔ
29.	ⓐ	ⓑ	ⓒ	ⓓ	ⓔ	64.	ⓐ	ⓑ	ⓒ	ⓓ	ⓔ	99.	ⓐ	ⓑ	ⓒ	ⓓ	ⓔ
30.	ⓐ	ⓑ	ⓒ	ⓓ	ⓔ	65.	ⓐ	ⓑ	ⓒ	ⓓ	ⓔ	100.	ⓐ	ⓑ	ⓒ	ⓓ	ⓔ
31.	ⓐ	ⓑ	ⓒ	ⓓ	ⓔ	66.	ⓐ	ⓑ	ⓒ	ⓓ	ⓔ						
32.	ⓐ	ⓑ	ⓒ	ⓓ	ⓔ	67.	ⓐ	ⓑ	ⓒ	ⓓ	ⓔ						
33.	ⓐ	ⓑ	ⓒ	ⓓ	ⓔ	68.	ⓐ	ⓑ	ⓒ	ⓓ	ⓔ						
34.	ⓐ	ⓑ	ⓒ	ⓓ	ⓔ	69.	ⓐ	ⓑ	ⓒ	ⓓ	ⓔ						
35.	ⓐ	ⓑ	ⓒ	ⓓ	ⓔ	70.	ⓐ	ⓑ	ⓒ	ⓓ	ⓔ						

1. Even though she's almost 80, my grandmother seems _____; she still plays golf three times a week and has an active social life.
   a. indefatigable
   b. persistent
   c. senile
   d. eccentric
   e. feeble

2. The defendant appeared to be _____ in his testimony, but under cross-examination, he revealed a more _____ temperament.
   a. brazen . . . dauntless
   b. candid . . . austere
   c. benign . . . caustic
   d. retroactive . . . propulsive
   e. disconsolate . . . forlorn

3. The prince fancied himself a dandy and insisted that his tailors outfit him in the latest Parisian fashions; privately, the other royals scoffed at his _____ attire.
   a. becoming
   b. foppish
   c. odious
   d. insipid
   e. macabre

4. "I believe I shall be _____ tonight and order the most _____ dessert on the menu," Esmeralda announced with a twinkle in her eye.
   a. decadent . . . sumptuous
   b. belligerent . . . lurid
   c. pragmatic . . . extravagant
   d. guileless . . . banal
   e. ostentatious . . . spartan

5. Some people feel insulted by Marco's _____ sense of humor, but I find him hilarious.
   a. optimistic
   b. urbane
   c. subversive
   d. whimsical
   e. sardonic

6. Edison was on the verge of _____ his invention when a _____ turn of events finally secured the funding he desperately needed.
   a. dismissing . . . cataclysmic
   b. patenting . . . ponderous
   c. completing . . . precarious
   d. envisioning . . . fortuitous
   e. abandoning . . . serendipitous

7. Penelope could tell that her suitors' _____ declarations of superiority were nothing but mere braggadocio.
   a. cacophonous
   b. benevolent
   c. requisite
   d. bombastic
   e. gregarious

8. The _____ of being known as a _____ was enough to make the gang member renounce his criminal past.
   a. honor . . . malcontent
   b. feasibility . . . misanthrope
   c. angst . . . philanthropist
   d. pretension . . . ruffian
   e. stigma . . . reprobate

9. The treasure hunter's interest was _____ by a small glimmer of gold at the bottom of the pit.
a. piqued
b. enhanced
c. deluded
d. obfuscated
e. stymied

10. Judge Travers dismissed the attorneys so he could _____ over the evidence in the _____ of his empty chambers.
a. ponder . . . confinement
b. pontificate . . . isolation
c. delight . . . gravity
d. ruminate . . . solitude
e. prosper . . . service

11. "I don't know how you can feel comfortable in this _____ apartment," said his girlfriend, eyeballing the peeling wallpaper and the stacks of magazines with disdain.
a. luxurious
b. refurbished
c. impractical
d. squalid
e. resplendent

12. With over 22 years of sales experience, my boss is a _____ veteran and an eager _____ to the younger salespeople.
a. notorious . . . proselytizer
b. consummate . . . figurehead
c. seasoned . . . mentor
d. presumptuous . . . pariah
e. lauded . . . colleague

13. Once the _____ courses have been completed, you are free to create a class schedule to your liking.
a. requisite
b. elective
c. vapid
d. superfluous
e. innocuous

14. Although the _____ doctor had just started his internship, he was already _____ by the amount of work required.
a. amateur . . . perplexed
b. novice . . . overwhelmed
c. incorrigible . . . appalled
d. naïve . . . negated
e. boisterous . . . energized

15. Indira's English professor was impressed by the grammatical _____ Indira displayed in her well-written paper.
a. fatuousness
b. condescension
c. acumen
d. bravado
e. deference

16. It was _____ to all of us that Pierre was trying to confuse us with his bizarre and _____ explanation of the night's events.
a. gratifying . . . meticulous
b. inconsequential . . . plausible
c. preposterous . . . pragmatic
d. valiant . . . astute
e. apparent . . . abstruse

17. Although the film was _____ a futuristic thriller, there was an underlying theme about our current political climate.
  a. ostensibly
  b. presumably
  c. persistently
  d. reprehensibly
  e. erroneously

18. If Calvin continues to ride his motorcycle in such an irresponsible and _____ manner, he will most certainly suffer a _____ accident.
  a. reprehensible . . . trivial
  b. reckless . . . debilitating
  c. conspicuous . . . revelatory
  d. hubristic . . . trifling
  e. refined . . . monumental

19. The gigantic sow astounded everyone at the fair with its _____ bulk.
  a. Brobdingnagian
  b. Lilliputian
  c. infinitesimal
  d. comely
  e. perspicacious

20. Many people admire the musician for his _____ efforts with African debt relief, although others point out that he only contributes a _____ amount of his vast personal income to the cause.
  a. dire . . . trivial
  b. presumptive . . . banal
  c. esteemed . . . fleeting
  d. philanthropic . . . meager
  e. astute . . . deceptive

21. Fashion seems to be changing so rapidly that magazines will often declare a look _____ just when it becomes trendy.
  a. benign
  b. passé
  c. austere
  d. arrant
  e. eminent

22. Spending time with Nolan can be tiresome and _____ because we are constantly having to _____ his massive ego with compliments.
  a. infuriating . . . foment
  b. fortuitous . . . massage
  c. nauseating . . . curtail
  d. exasperating . . . placate
  e. deprecating . . . endure

23. When the headlining band took the stage, the excitement in the room was _____ to everyone in the crowd.
  a. palpable
  b. clandestine
  c. flouted
  d. conspicuous
  e. harmonious

24. The old man was _____ with his fortune, refusing to give his children even a _____ to help them pay for college.
  a. lackadaisical . . . trove
  b. imperious . . . lien
  c. miserly . . . pittance
  d. incessant . . . modicum
  e. mischievous . . . memento

25. As a pacifist, I _____ all forms of violence.
   a. deride
   b. entreat
   c. descry
   d. endorse
   e. deplore

26. After three days of hunger, the travelers' appetites were finally _____ by a fertile grove of trees bearing _____ amounts of fruit.
   a. satiated . . . copious
   b. stifled . . . negligible
   c. deceived . . . cursory
   d. eradicated . . . stringent
   e. counteracted . . . noisome

27. The king furiously declared that the philosopher should be _____ by society for his anti-authoritarian views.
   a. embraced
   b. lauded
   c. reprimanded
   d. ostracized
   e. discredited

28. The gorgeously _____ voice of the soprano completely _____ the somewhat average voice of the tenor.
   a. cacophonous . . . derided
   b. grandiloquent . . . impeded
   c. mournful . . . emulated
   d. ebullient . . . contradicted
   e. mellifluous . . . overshadowed

29. The phrase *innocent until proven guilty* means the _____ of proof is on the prosecutor, not the defendant.
   a. suspicion
   b. corroboration
   c. diversion
   d. onus
   e. guile

30. The farmer erected a scarecrow to _____ birds from _____ his crops.
   a. cajole . . . obliterating
   b. deter . . . devouring
   c. compel . . . inciting
   d. deprive . . . repelling
   e. impede . . . impugning

31. We had to break the devastating news very gently to Jacquelyn for fear that she become _____.
   a. listless
   b. languid
   c. loquacious
   d. licentious
   e. lachrymose

32. Climbing Mount Everest may be a _____ prospect, but successful climbing expeditions in the past have proved that the peak is not _____.
   a. cogent . . . formidable
   b. tantalizing . . . frigid
   c. daunting . . . insurmountable
   d. dubious . . . mundane
   e. magisterial . . . pedestrian

33. Reagan hoped the bitter _____ between the United States and the Soviet Union could one day evolve into a close friendship.
a. avarice
b. enmity
c. infatuation
d. fervor
e. lassitude

34. Dr. Cook was _____ by the scientific community when it was discovered he completely _____ the results of his study, and therefore, his hypothesis was based on erroneous information.
a. discredited . . . fabricated
b. hailed . . . misdiagnosed
c. extolled . . . denounced
d. designated . . . embellished
e. impressed . . . implicated

35. Romeo and Juliet had to arrange _____ meetings, lest someone discover their secret love.
a. fraudulent
b. hypocritical
c. reverent
d. furtive
e. nefarious

36. Senator McCarthy's _____ obsession with Communism has been characterized as _____ by Professor Thomas Johnson, a well-known McCarthy critic.
a. singular . . . monomania
b. waning . . . zealotry
c. gullible . . . frivolous
d. eminent . . . impeccable
e. morbid . . . sage

37. General Wilkenson ordered his troops to charge at the invading forces and _____ them away from the vulnerable town.
a. sequester
b. incense
c. condense
d. chastise
e. repel

38. I have a feeling Dinaw is going to make a lot of money with his _____ business sense and his charming, _____ social abilities.
a. conservative . . . dogmatic
b. shrewd . . . gregarious
c. dexterous . . . frugal
d. egregious . . . mawkish
e. impetuous . . . obdurate

39. The promise of a new toy momentarily _____ the screaming child.
a. petrified
b. repulsed
c. abased
d. derided
e. pacified

40. The people in the saloon braced themselves when the _____ outlaw walked through the door; he was known to become violent and _____ when he was in a foul mood.
a. genial . . . disingenuous
b. loutish . . . convivial
c. depraved . . . obstreperous
d. egocentric . . . complaisant
e. hoary . . . geriatric

41. Everyone who learns to play the guitar must first learn the basic, _____ skills.
a. rudimentary
b. painstaking
c. diligent
d. eleemosynary
e. deductive

42. When we set out on the tracking expedition, we thought there was a _____ of _____ hogs in the American wilderness; however, we were surprised to come across a great many of the wild creatures on our trip.
a. wealth . . . fledgling
b. trove . . . mammoth
c. modicum . . . primordial
d. dearth . . . feral
e. paucity . . . primitive

43. I was impressed that the reporter was able to turn the confusing mass of facts into a _____ story.
a. coarse
b. fractious
c. perplexing
d. coherent
e. deranged

44. The crowd was somewhat _____ that the young violinist would not live up to the hype, but as soon as she began playing, her _____ talents were obvious.
a. resigned . . . meager
b. wary . . . prodigious
c. unremitting . . . negligible
d. baffled . . . modest
e. disconcerted . . . notorious

45. The answer choices are too similar for there to be a clear, _____ answer.
a. discernible
b. confounding
c. ample
d. profound
e. irrelevant

46. Rain continues to pound against the roof _____, and it seems as though the _____ may continue for hours.
a. incessantly . . . tranquility
b. sluggishly . . . mirage
c. placidly . . . folly
d. boisterously . . . repose
e. unremittingly . . . deluge

47. Jonathan was _____ by his mother for coming home three hours late.
a. approbated
b. eulogized
c. esteemed
d. berated
e. eradicated

48. I felt awful that I missed Dorene's birthday party, but my guilt was _____ when I realized she did not feel any _____.
a. resigned . . . deference
b. enhanced . . . pride
c. inferred . . . malice
d. assuaged . . . spite
e. reprimanded . . . optimism

49. The poorly researched paper was filled with _____ errors.
a. grievous
b. inconsequential
c. exquisite
d. credible
e. innovative

50. Mr. Brida's excruciating new novel is filled with trite, _____ dialogue, poorly conceived characters, and a completely _____ plot that stretches the boundaries of disbelief.

   a. memorable . . . factual

   b. inane . . . implausible

   c. frugal . . . comprehensible

   d. poignant . . . meritorious

   e. lavish . . . prudent

51. If it doesn't rain soon, the governor fears our state water reservoirs will be _____.

   a. depleted

   b. accentuated

   c. crystallized

   d. colossal

   e. ample

52. The _____, icy conditions of the Arctic make it _____ to all but the most well-adapted animals.

   a. iconic . . . dramatic

   b. overwrought . . . immaculate

   c. bleak . . . hospitable

   d. effervescent . . . dubious

   e. frigid . . . uninhabitable

53. I am quite proud of my father and I hope to _____ his brilliant career when I leave college.

   a. elicit

   b. embellish

   c. emulate

   d. emancipate

   e. eradicate

54. I might agree with this newspaper article if it presented a more cohesive argument; as it is, the first paragraph is filled with _____ information that has no _____ on the author's intended argument.

   a. scintillating . . . context

   b. fallacious . . . effect

   c. extraneous . . . bearing

   d. flamboyant . . . legacy

   e. latent . . . malevolence

55. The soldiers proved their _____ on the battlefield when they defeated the insurgent army.

   a. munificence

   b. mettle

   c. negligence

   d. petulance

   e. qualms

56. Doctors claim that poor eating habits and a lack of exercise have led to an _____ epidemic that is having _____ effects on the health of many Americans.

   a. encouraging . . . resilient

   b. obesity . . . detrimental

   c. epicurean . . . dwindling

   d. appetite . . . ambiguous

   e. emergent . . . nutritious

57. The law clerk had a difficult time deciphering the lawyer's _____ writing.

   a. ornamental

   b. indelible

   c. pompous

   d. illegible

   e. ostentatious

58. The mischievous Sawyer had a _____ for tomfoolery, and as a result, he was often _____ by his exasperated teachers.
  a. idiosyncrasy . . . exacerbated
  b. forbearance . . . fomented
  c. compunction . . . castigated
  d. disrespect . . . applauded
  e. penchant . . . reprimanded

59. On the spur of the moment, we decided to jump in the car and take an _____ trip to the desert.
  a. impromptu
  b. impassive
  c. illicit
  d. indolent
  e. inveterate

60. Once the important information that was _____ to my alibi had been established, it was clear that I did not deserve to be _____ in the crime and I was allowed to return to my family.
  a. inconsequential . . . exculpated
  b. frivolous . . . infused
  c. germane . . . implicated
  d. comparable . . . incited
  e. crucial . . . absconded

61. If we do not get this boat back to shore before the typhoon begins, our lives are certainly in _____ danger.
  a. imminent
  b. negligible
  c. passable
  d. inimitable
  e. moderate

62. A _____ cheer arose along the parade route as the World Series champions smiled and waved _____ to the adoring crowd.
  a. credible . . . exuberantly
  b. serendipitous . . . passionately
  c. precipitous . . . candidly
  d. boisterous . . . affably
  e. resounding . . . impassively

63. His _____ behavior at the dinner table disgusted all who had the misfortune of dining with him.
  a. precocious
  b. boorish
  c. sanguine
  d. banal
  e. avuncular

64. The magician _____ the audience with his marvelous slight-of-hand tricks; even the most _____ members of the crowd found themselves wondering, "How did he do that?"
  a. prepared . . . savvy
  b. resisted . . . reluctant
  c. perplexed . . . adamant
  d. befuddled . . . prominent
  e. bamboozled . . . canny

65. The owl's _____ sense of sight allows it to spot prey from an incredible distance.
  a. intrepid
  b. acute
  c. innate
  d. prescient
  e. immense

66. Many critics cynically believed that Fulton's attempts to make the first steam-powered boat were _____; however, his ground-breaking, _____ design soon proved the naysayers wrong.
a. presumptuous . . . meticulous
b. foolish . . . provincial
c. impressive . . . tenacious
d. folly . . . innovative
e. incidental . . . practical

67. It would be _____ to assume the world is flat with all the evidence to the contrary.
a. erroneous
b. imaginative
c. negligent
d. sanctimonious
e. prescient

68. He, like all the others, was stunned by the beautiful princess's _____ smile; her appearance was so _____ that people were often shocked speechless when she entered a room.
a. luxurious . . . startling
b. luminescent . . . intrusive
c. blatant . . . irresistible
d. saccharine . . . unobtrusive
e. alluring . . . striking

69. The riot police stood outside the convention hall just in case the protest erupted into _____.
a. fervor
b. catastrophe
c. bedlam
d. irrationality
e. mischievousness

70. Historians doubted the _____ of the "lost" Picasso painting, partly because the work did not seem true to Picasso's style and partly because the dealer had been known to be _____.
a. technique . . . tendentious
b. existence . . . nefarious
c. veracity . . . forthright
d. authenticity . . . deceptive
e. verisimilitude . . . illusory

71. Many experts on child-rearing endorse "time-outs" as an _____ way to discipline misbehaving children.
a. asinine
b. efficacious
c. ignominious
d. impassive
e. egregious

72. A gas leak forced the family to _____ their apartment; they had to leave so _____ they did not even have time to pack clothing.
a. release . . . conditionally
b. enhance . . . unnecessarily
c. exhume . . . hastily
d. vacate . . . expeditiously
e. desert . . . inconveniently

73. One of the great things about our democracy is that American citizens are allowed to voice their _____ when they do not agree with the government's policies.
a. affirmation
b. distaste
c. contradiction
d. predilection
e. dissent

74. Revolutionary plans were first _____ among the peasants, who wished to replace their cruel king with a more _____ leader.

   a. established . . . mercenary

   b. advanced . . . judicious

   c. fomented . . . benevolent

   d. instigated . . . craven

   e. evinced . . . meritorious

75. Carlos found the movie so _____ that he continued to feel immersed in the film's world for hours afterward.

   a. engrossing

   b. enlightening

   c. enchanting

   d. inventive

   e. intriguing

76. The professor spent many months doing _____ research to make sure his book was _____ accurate.

   a. exhaustive . . . factually

   b. preliminary . . . essentially

   c. extensive . . . passably

   d. painstaking . . . superficially

   e. cursory . . . defensibly

77. Jackie was certain the song would become a hit, but I was slightly more _____.

   a. optimistic

   b. spurious

   c. decisive

   d. ambiguous

   e. dubious

78. The team was forced to _____ the game when half the team became _____ with the flu.

   a. endure . . . defeated

   b. disown . . . infected

   c. contest . . . smitten

   d. abandon . . . emaciated

   e. forfeit . . . afflicted

79. The writer named his main character Hamlet in an obvious _____ to Shakespeare.

   a. homage

   b. paean

   c. ode

   d. proposition

   e. revision

80. Scouts were sent ahead to _____ the situation; they returned with the message that, although the enemy would not surrender, they were prepared to _____ to our demands.

   a. appraise . . . acquiesce

   b. denounce . . . cater

   c. deduce . . . ascribe

   d. assess . . . confess

   e. resist . . . succumb

81. The beautiful and moving message Sarah left in my yearbook was especially _____ in light of all we had been through together.

   a. adequate

   b. iridescent

   c. patronizing

   d. derogatory

   e. poignant

82. Sookie felt relaxed as she sat beside the lazy river, watching the _____, _____ waters drift along unhurriedly.
  a. intense . . . pristine
  b. serene . . . tranquil
  c. vast . . . quiescent
  d. timorous . . . cantankerous
  e. fervid . . . listless

83. "I'm having a difficult time deciding what to get for lunch," announced Tariq. "I'm _____ between the chicken sandwich and the Cobb salad."
  a. vacillating
  b. insinuating
  c. hesitating
  d. balking
  e. finessing

84. Many people think Renny is a child when they first meet her because of her _____ size and her _____ fashion sense.
  a. unfortunate . . . trendy
  b. Lilliputian . . . atrocious
  c. remarkable . . . austere
  d. diminutive . . . whimsical
  e. middling . . . pervasive

85. His _____ smile carried a hint of condescension.
  a. alluring
  b. reprehensible
  c. smug
  d. gleeful
  e. loutish

86. Although Dante is usually very _____, he can become quite agitated and _____ if he feels as though his human rights are being violated.
  a. eloquent . . . impervious
  b. composed . . . vociferous
  c. recalcitrant . . . lucid
  d. squeamish . . . perplexed
  e. urbane . . . pedestrian

87. Although I had never thought of my sister as beautiful, she looked positively _____ on her wedding day.
  a. reluctant
  b. radiant
  c. vivid
  d. frazzled
  e. resonant

88. The company could not afford to completely _____ to the demands of the union, but they knew they would have to _____ some of their demands if they hoped to avoid a strike.
  a. attune . . . condone
  b. subscribe . . . endure
  c. succumb . . . resist
  d. cede . . . appease
  e. hew . . . respect

89. Some electronics makers have a policy of planned _____, meaning they purposely build their products to stop working after a few years of usage.
   a. intransigence
   b. assignation
   c. inconvenience
   d. obsolescence
   e. consolation

90. After years as a _____ smoker, Elmira developed a _____ cough that caused her constant throat pain.
   a. habitual . . . chronic
   b. moderate . . . severe
   c. diligent . . . casual
   d. persistent . . . tentative
   e. furtive . . . caustic

91. The evil genius was busy cooking up a _____ plan to thwart the superhero's good intentions.
   a. conspiratorial
   b. derisive
   c. incidental
   d. nefarious
   e. conservative

92. I was impressed that my mother handled the difficult situation with such coolness and _____; my father would certainly be far more _____ when he saw the damage the hit-and-run driver had done to their car.
   a. temperance . . . astonished
   b. aplomb . . . distraught
   c. rigidity . . . versatile
   d. ardor . . . inscrutable
   e. constancy . . . melodramatic

93. Young school children can sometimes become _____ if you do not keep them busy.
   a. listless
   b. fervent
   c. tepid
   d. rancorous
   e. despicable

94. Although the old woman was wealthy enough to afford an _____ palace, she preferred the _____ of her simple cabin in the woods.
   a. abundant . . . privacy
   b. immense . . . severity
   c. extravagant . . . ostentation
   d. opulent . . . austerity
   e. enigmatic . . . gravity

95. Meeting with my old friend _____ long-forgotten memories of elementary school.
   a. resigned
   b. unsheathed
   c. divulged
   d. instituted
   e. evoked

96. The pleasant aroma of fresh-baked bread _____ the air, and I suddenly realized how _____ I had become from skipping breakfast and lunch.
   a. glazed . . . voracious
   b. permeated . . . ravenous
   c. infused . . . incredulous
   d. preceded . . . wanton
   e. aerated . . . feeble

97. Mr. Crane did not say anything about being fired from his last job because he did not want to _____ his chances of being hired by the new company.
   a. jeopardize
   b. stigmatize
   c. evade
   d. divulge
   e. scrutinize

98. My grandfather was a happy person with a _____ attitude toward life; when he found something amusing, he would double over in a _____ of laughter.
   a. stentorian . . . crescendo
   b. resplendent . . . seizure
   c. commendable . . . geyser
   d. possessive . . . tremor
   e. jovial . . . paroxysm

99. Desert-dwellers tend to be _____, moving from place to place as water sources dry up.
   a. listless
   b. nomadic
   c. conscientious
   d. spontaneous
   e. acerbic

100. Although Johnson claimed to be a loyal crew-member, the captain sensed that he had _____ motives; his suspicions were confirmed when he caught the traitor trying to convince the rest of the crew to _____.
   a. deranged . . . conspire
   b. inscrutable . . . pillage
   c. ulterior . . . revolt
   d. provocative . . . alit
   e. malignant . . . prevail

▶ Answers

1. a. The phrase *even though she's almost 80* indicates that the correct answer will seem contrary to what we would normally think of as being a quality of an elderly person. Therefore, choices **c** (*senile*) and **e** (*feeble*) are incorrect. Although the grandmother's behavior could be seen as unusual for an 80-year-old woman, it probably could not be characterized as **d**, *eccentric*. Answer **b**, *persistent*, is a possibility, but there is a better answer choice—choice **a**, *indefatigable*, meaning "untiring."

2. c. The structure of this sentence indicates that the blanks will be filled by two opposing answers; therefore, answer choices **a**, *brazen . . . dauntless* and **e**, *disconsolate . . . forlorn*, both pairs of synonyms, are incorrect. Choice **d**, *retroactive . . . propulsive*, simply doesn't make sense in the context of the sentence. Although a case could be made for choice **b**, *candid . . . austere*, choice

c, *benign . . . caustic*, makes the most sense in the context of the sentence.

3. b. Based on the word *scoffed*, you know that the prince's fashions were somewhat amusing to the other royals; therefore, the words *odious* (detestable) and *macabre* (frightening) are not the best choices. If the royals found the prince's fashions **a**, *becoming*, they probably would not scoff either, as becoming means flattering. Choice **d**, *insipid*, is almost correct, but it is not a word that is generally used to describe clothing. Therefore, the best answer choice is **b**, *foppish*, meaning "unduly and/or comically devoted to dress."

4. a. In some cases, the only key to getting the correct answer is to know what each word means. In choices **c**, **d**, and **e**, the two words contradict one another so that the sentence does not make sense. Choice **b** could work, but desserts are not generally described as *lurid*.

5. e. The correct answer choice for this sentence will give a clue as to why some people might be insulted by Marco's sense of humor. Therefore, the answer choice that makes the most sense is **e**, *sardonic*, meaning "scornfully or bitterly sarcastic."

6. e. The key phrase to pay attention to in this sentence is *finally secured the funding he desperately needed*. The sentence indicates that Edison was on the verge of taking drastic action if he did not receive funding. The only answer choices that fit this construction would be **a** and **e**. *Dismissing* and *abandoning* have a similar meaning, so you should look at the second word in the pair. A *cataclysmic* turn of events would be considered negative; therefore, the best answer choice is **e**.

7. d. The best answer choice will be synonymous with the phrase *mere braggadocio*; therefore, the best answer is **d**, *bombastic*, meaning "pompous speech."

8. e. Based on the structure of the sentence, the only answer choice that makes complete sense is **e**, *stigma . . . reprobate*.

9. a. A treasure hunter would most likely be interested by a glimmer of gold, so choices **c**, **d**, and **e** do not make sense in the context of the sentence. Answer choice **b** is almost correct, but the best word is answer choice **a**, *piqued*.

10. d. Choice **e** does not make sense in context, so that can be discounted immediately. One would not generally pontificate in isolation, so choice **b** is probably not the best choice. Likewise, a judge would probably not *delight* over evidence, so choice **c** can be discounted. This leaves choices **a** and **d**. Although choice **a** makes sense in context, *solitude* is a slightly better description of what the judge is seeking in his empty chambers than *confinement*.

11. d. The best answer choice will indicate how the girlfriend feels about the apartment. Answer choices **a**, *luxurious*, **b**, *refurbished*, and **e**, *resplendent*, all indicate that the apartment is nicer than the description would imply. Answer **c**, *impractical*, is a possible choice, but **d**, *squalid*, makes the most sense in context.

12. c. Looking at the first word in the pair, choices **a**, **b**, and **d** can be immediately discounted, as the adjectives *notorious*, *consummate* and *presumptuous* do not make sense in conjunction with *veteran*. This leaves choices **c** and **e**. Although the boss could be a *lauded* veteran, it is more likely that he would be an eager *mentor*, meaning "counselor," than an eager *colleague*, meaning "coworker."

13. a. Context of the sentence indicates that the courses are in opposition to *a class schedule to your liking*, so choice **b**, *elective*, can be ruled out. It is unlikely that any school system would require *vapid*, *superfluous*, or *innocuous* courses, so choices **c**, **d**, and **e** are not correct, leaving only choice **a**.

14. b. Assuming that the context clues are in place to help you find the correct answers, choices **c** and **e** can be discounted—the adjectives *incorrigible* and *boisterous* do not have anything to do with a doctor who has just started his internship. Of the three remaining answer choices, it makes the most sense that a *novice*, or "new," doctor would be *overwhelmed* by the amount of work required.

15. c. The hyphenated adjective *well-written* indicates that Indira had an impressive grasp of grammar; therefore, the best answer choice would be synonymous for mental ability, or *acumen*.

16. e. Based on the context of the sentence, you can tell that the second word will have a similar connotation as *bizarre*; therefore, **b**, *plausible*, **c**, *pragmatic*, and **d**, *astute* can be discounted. It is possible that a situation could exist in which people found a bizarre and *meticulous* explanation *gratifying*, but the object of the sentence completion portion of the test is to find the best answer choice; therefore, answer choice **e** makes the most sense.

17. a. The word *although* suggests that there is a difference between the underlying theme of the film and the way the film is presented. The only answer choice that makes sense is **a**, *ostensibly*, meaning "appearing as such."

18. b. The first part of the sentence indicates that the first word is similar to *irresponsible*; based on this information, choice **e** can be discounted. A motorcycle accident would most likely not be described as *trivial* or *trifling*, so choices **a** and **d** can be overruled. Between **b** and **c**, choice **b** is a better fit considering the context of the sentence.

19. a. The *gigantic sow astounded* fairgoers with its bulk, indicating that the correct answer choice will be an adjective meaning "great." Taken from Jonathan Swift's novel *Gulliver's Travels*, the word *Brobdingnagian* means "unusually large."

20. d. Choices **b** and **c** can be quickly ruled out because neither *fleeting* nor *banal* are appropriate words to describe an amount of money. Likewise, the word *deceptive* in choice **e** is not descriptive enough to explain how much of his personal income the musician contributes. The key word *although* indicates that the two parts of the sentence are in opposition, and the answer choice that makes the most sense according to this construction is choice **d**.

21. b. The sentence implies that the correct answer choice will be the opposite of *trendy*, and *passé*, meaning "out of fashion," is the best of the five choices.

22. d. The first part of the correct answer choice should be similar to the word *tiresome*; therefore, choices **b** and **e** can be ruled out. Compliments would enhance the ego of a person with an already massive ego, so choice **c** is

not the correct answer. Of the two remaining choices, choice **d** more accurately reflects the tone of the sentence.

23. a. The sentence indicates that the excitement is something everyone in the crowd felt; therefore, the best answer choice is **a**, *palpable*, meaning "tangible."

24. c. Based on context clues, you can tell that the first missing word will indicate a lack of generosity on the part of the old man; therefore, choices **a**, **d**, and **e** are not the best answer choices. A *lien* is "the right to take and hold or sell property," so the only possible answer choice left is **c**.

25. e. To answer this question correctly, you must first know the meaning of the word *pacifist*. The correct answer choice defines the word *pacifist*, which is someone who refuses to engage in violence; therefore, the best answer choice is **e**, *deplore*, meaning "hate."

26. a. If a group of hungry travelers found a fertile grove of trees with fruit, they would most likely eat their fill; therefore, choice **c** can be ruled out. The travelers would not find the fertile grove *noisome*, meaning obnoxious, and their appetites would not be stifled by *negligible*, or meager, amounts of fruit, so choices **b** and **e** are incorrect. The amount of fruit on a tree would most likely not be described as *stringent*, or strict, so the only possible answer choice is **a**.

27. d. An anti-authoritarian philosopher would hold views that were against the king, so choices **a** and **b** are incorrect. Although **c** and **e** could make sense, it is more likely that a *furious* king would call for the philosopher to be *ostracized*.

28. e. Choices **a** and **b** can be discounted immediately, as *cacophonous* and *grandiloquent* both have a negative connotation that does not make sense with the adjective *gorgeously*. Although the soprano's voice could be gorgeously mournful, a gorgeous voice would not *emulate*, or "attempt to be like" an average voice, so choice **c** is incorrect. Choice **d** is possible but somewhat awkward, leaving answer **e** as the best option.

29. d. In some ways, this type of question tests your knowledge of subject matter rather than your knowledge of vocabulary. *Innocent until proven guilty* means the burden, or *onus*, of proof is on the prosecutor, so choice **d** is the only possible answer.

30. b. As its name implies, a scarecrow frightens birds away from crops. The only answer choice in which both words adequately describe the purpose of a scarecrow is choice **b**.

31. e. Although it is possible that someone could have any of these responses to devastating news, sentence completion questions do not test your ability to imagine creative scenarios. Based on the context, it is most reasonable to assume that someone would become *lachrymose*, or "tearful," upon hearing devastating news.

32. c. The construction of this sentence suggests that the two missing words are in opposition. Although other individual words make sense in the blanks, the only answer choice with two fitting words is choice **c**.

33. b. The best answer choice will be opposed to the notion of *friendship*. Choices **c** and **d** can be ruled out, as *infatuation* and *fervor* can rarely be described as *bitter*. *Lassitude*, or "weariness," cannot really change into friendship, so **e** is not the best answer choice. Although *avarice*, meaning "jealousy," can be described as bitter, *enmity*, meaning "hatred," makes the most sense in the context of the sentence.

34. a. Based on the context of the second part of the sentence, the second blank will be a word that explains why Dr. Cook's hypothesis was based on erroneous information. Therefore, choices **c** and **e** are not correct. If a scientist's hypothesis was discovered to be wrong, he would most likely not be hailed by the scientific community, so choice **b** is incorrect. Between choices **a** and

d, it makes more sense to say that Dr. Cook was *discredited* than *designated*.

35. d. The word *secret* provides a context clue for the proper answer choice, and choice **d**, *furtive*, is synonymous with "secret."

36. a. The information that Professor Thomas Johnson is a critic of McCarthy indicates that his characterization of McCarthy will be negative; therefore, choices **d** and **e** can be ruled out. Of the remaining answer choices, **b** can be ruled out because a *waning*, or fading, obsession, would not be characterized as *zealotry*. Although answer choice **c** makes sense in context, choice **a** better fits the context of the sentence.

37. e. The correct answer choice would explain what an army would do to an invading force if it were to charge at them; of the five answer choices, *repel* most accurately fits the sentence.

38. b. Based on the second half of the sentence, the correct answer choice will have a similar connotation as *charming*. The only answer choice that fits in this context is **b**.

39. e. Although it is possible that a screaming child would be *petrified* or *repulsed* by the promise of a toy, chances are far more likely that the child would be *pacified*; therefore, answer choice **e** is the best choice.

40. c. Choices **a** and **d** can be ruled out immediately based on the context at the beginning of the sentence; an outlaw would most likely not be called *genial* (kind), and *egocentric* is too innocuous a word to describe an obviously dangerous man. The outlaw could be *hoary* (old) or *loutish* (boorish), but the best answer choice will match the connotation of the word *violent* in the second half of the sentence; therefore, choice **c** is the best answer choice.

41. a. The correct answer choice will be a word that means almost the same thing as *basic*; the only possible correct answer is **a**.

42. d. The key word *however* indicates that the second half of the sentence is in opposition to the first half of the sentence. If the people on the expedition were surprised to find many hogs in the wilderness, then choices **a** and **b** are clearly wrong. Of the three remaining answer choices, the best choice will describe a *wild creature*; therefore, the correct answer choice is **d**.

43. d. Based on context, the correct answer choice will be the opposite of *confusing*; the best answer choice is therefore *coherent*, meaning "clear."

44. b. The word *but* indicates that the young violinist did indeed *live up to the hype*; thus, it is unlikely that her talents could be described as *negligible*, *modest*, or *meager*. Of the two remaining answer choices, it is more likely that a crowd would be *wary* that the violinist would not live up the hype, rather than *disconcerted*.

45. a. The best answer choice will have the same connotation as *clear*. *Discernible*, meaning "easily perceived," is the best of the five choices.

46. e. Answer choices **b** and **c** can both be ruled out immediately, as rain would not pound *sluggishly* or *placidly*. A state of pounding rain would most likely not be described as *tranquil* or *repose*, so answer choice **e** is the clear choice.

47. d. Jonathan would probably not be *esteemed* (heralded) or *approbated* (sanctioned) by his mother for coming home late, so choices **a** and **c** are incorrect. *Eulogizing* him would suggest that he's dead, and *eradicating* him seems a harsh punishment, so this leaves only **d**.

48. d. The sentence's construction indicates that the speaker no longer *felt awful* after his or her realization; the only answer choice that stands in opposition to the first part of the sentence is choice **d**.

49. a. Although the errors in a paper could potentially be described as *inconsequential*, *exquisite*, *credible*, or *innovative*, chances are more likely that a poorly researched paper would include *grievous*, or severe, errors.

50. b. The key word *excruciating* indicates that the correct answer choice will have a negative connotation. The only answer choice that features two negative words is choice **b**.

51. a. Water reservoirs require rain in order to be full; in this sentence, the state is lacking rain. Without rain, the reservoirs would be *depleted*, or emptied.

52. e. The construction of this sentence indicates that the icy conditions have an effect on the animals in the Arctic. The only answer choice that supports a clear connection between the conditions in the Arctic and the results of those conditions is choice **e**.

53. c. Based on context clues, it appears that the speaker strives to be as good as his father; therefore, the best answer choice is **c**.

54. c. Based on the first part of the sentence, you know the correct answer choice will describe an article without a cohesive, or well-constructed argument. An article with *extraneous* information and with no *bearing* on the author's argument would not be cohesive; therefore, answer **c** is the correct answer choice.

55. b. The best answer would describe a positive attribute of soldiers; by the context, you can guess that the correct answer choice would have something to do with strength or courage. Therefore, the best answer is a synonym for courage, or *mettle*.

56. b. Based on the first part of the sentence, you can assume that the epidemic would have a negative effect on health. The only answer choice that describes a negative effect on health is choice **b**.

57. d. Although writing could potentially be described as *ornamental*, *indelible*, or *ostentatious*, the best answer choice would fit the context of the sentence. Writing that would be difficult to decipher would most likely be *illegible*.

58. e. Based on the key word *exasperated*, you can tell that the second word will describe actions taken by exasperated teachers. The two options that match these criteria are choices **c** and **e**. *Compunction* means "pangs of guilt," so **e** is the best answer choice.

59. a. Although answer choice **c** is a possibility, the only answer choice that fits the immediate context of the sentence is choice **a**.

60. c. The first part of the sentence establishes that the information is important, so choices **a** and **b** can be eliminated. The sentence does not invite a comparison between *important information* and *alibi*, so choice **d** can be eliminated. *Absconded* means "stolen away with," so the best answer choice is **c**.

61. a. *Negligible, passable,* and *moderate* all describe small or unimportant amounts of danger so **b**, **c**, and **e** are incorrect. Although danger could potentially be described as *inimitable* or "impossible to imitate," the best answer choice is **a**, *imminent*.

62. d. A cheer from a crowd could best be described as *boisterous* or *resounding*, so you can eliminate **a**, **b**, and **c**. The World Series champions would more likely be waving *affably* than *impassively*, so **e** is the best answer choice.

63. b. Context clues in the sentence indicate that the correct answer choice will have a negative connotation. Although a *banal*, or trite, dinner guest might not be pleasant, the only answer choice that describes a disgusting dinner guest is **b**, *boorish*.

64. e. The second part of the sentence indicates that the magician fooled the audience; therefore, answer choices **a** and **b** can be eliminated. Answer choices **c** and **d** are grammatically correct, but the answer choice that best fits both parts of the sentence is **e**.

65. b. A sense of sight could not be described as *immense* or *intrepid*, so choices **a** and **e** can be eliminated. For the owl's sight to be *prescient*, it would have to be able to see into the future, so **d** is incorrect. Although the owl's sense of sight is *innate*, or part of its being, the best answer choice describes the sense of sight; therefore, **c** is the best answer choice.

66. d. Choices **a** and **e** can be discounted based on the word *cynically* in the first half of the sentence— cynical critics would not find Fulton's attempts *impressive* or *incidental*. *Provincial* means "unsophisticated," so choice **b** can be ruled out. Of the two remaining answer choices, the key word *groundbreaking* should tell you that **d** is the best choice, based on context clues.

67. a. *Sanctimonious* (self-righteous) and *prescient* (foreseeing) can be rejected based on the context of the sentence. *Negligent* is not the best choice either, as that implies negative consequences that would not necessarily occur if one assumed the world was flat. Between *imaginative* and *erroneous*, it makes more sense to say that one would be *erroneous*, or wrong, to assume the world is flat.

68. e. Based on the second words in the pairs, **a**, **b**, and **d** can be eliminated—*startling* has a slightly negative connotation, *intrusive* implies that the princess's presence is undesirable, and *unobtrusive* implies that the princess would not be noticed. Of the two choices left, it is far more likely that the smile of a beautiful princess would be described as *alluring*.

69. c. The key words in this sentence are *riot police*. Choice **b**, *catastrophe*, comes close to the correct word, but the best of these five choices is **c**, *bedlam*, meaning "an anarchic situation."

70. d. The quotation marks around the word *lost* imply that there is a question as to whether Picasso created the "lost" painting, so this means that **c**, **d**, or **e** are the most likely choices. *Veracity* is closer in meaning to "true" than "genuine," so **c** can be rejected. Of the two remaining choices, a dishonest person would more likely be referred to as *deceptive* than *illusory*, so **d** is the best answer choice.

71. b. The word *endorse* tells you that the correct answer choice will be a word with a positive connotation. The only choice that fits into the context of the sentence is *efficacious*, meaning "efficient."

72. d. If a family had a gas leak in their apartment, they would most likely have to *vacate* or *desert* their apartment, so the correct answer choice is either **d** or **e**. Although it would be inconvenient to have to *desert* an apartment, the sentence implies that the family had to leave quickly, so the best answer choice is **d**.

73. e. Based on context clues, you know that **a** is incorrect, as *affirmation* implies agreement. *Predilection* means choice, and *contradiction*, although close to the correct word, does not fit the sentence as well as other answer choices. Although *distaste* and *dissent* both make sense, *dissent* is more appropriate given the context of the sentence.

74. c. Based on the second part of the sentence, you can tell the correct answer will be in opposition to *cruel*; therefore, choices **a** and **d** can be eliminated. Choice **e** can be eliminated next, because *evinced* is synonymous with "shown" and does not make much sense in the sentence. Of the remaining two choices, *fomented* is a better fit grammatically, and *benevolent* forms a better contrast with *cruel* than *judicious*.

75. a. Although all five choices fit the sentence, the only word that explains why Carlos would continue to feel immersed in the film's world is **a**, *engrossing*.

76. a. Based on the first missing word, you can eliminate choice **e**—*cursory* research would be hastily done research. Choices **c** and **d** can be ruled out based on the second part of the sentence, as the professor would not spend many months making sure his book was

almost accurate. Between **a** and **b**, the words in choice **a** most accurately reflect the context of the sentence.

77. e. The sentence sets up an opposing relationship between Jackie's certainty and the word in the blank. Although *ambiguous* is almost correct, *dubious* implies a more negative connotation that better fits the context.

78. e. The word in the first blank is dependant upon the word in the second blank, so the second blank should be filled in first. Answer choice **c** can, therefore, be eliminated, as it contains an improper usage of the word *smitten*. Choices **a** and **b** can subsequently be ruled out, as it is doubtful the team would *endure* or *disown* the game when the players had the flu. Of the two remaining answer choices, choice **e** is more accurate, as it is impossible to tell by context whether the team members became *emaciated*, or frighteningly thin.

79. a. The sentence implies that the writer named his main character Hamlet as a tribute, and the word that most closely matches the meaning of tribute is **a**, *homage*.

80. a. The first step in determining the correct answer is figuring out why the scouts were sent; it is unlikely that scouts would be sent to *denounce* or *resist* a situation, so **b** and **e** are incorrect. An enemy would not *confess* to another's demands, so **d** can be ruled out. If the enemy agreed to *succumb* to the demands, it would imply they had surrendered, so choice **a** is the only remaining option.

81. e. A beautiful and moving message would not be considered *derogatory* or *patronizing*, so choices **c** and **d** are incorrect. *Iridescent* can sometimes mean beautiful, but it is not generally used to refer to language. *Adequate* means merely acceptable, so the correct answer choice is *poignant*, meaning "emotionally resonant."

82. b. The sentence indicates that the correct answer will correspond to the words *relaxed*, *lazy*, and *unhurriedly*. The only answer choice that meets these criteria is choice **b**.

83. a. Tariq says he is having a difficult time deciding what to get for lunch. The word that shows he is being torn between two choices is *vacillating*, meaning "swaying from one side to the other."

84. d. The most important idea in this sentence is that Renny is often mistaken for a child. Based on this information, the best answer choice would indicate that she is small, with childlike qualities. Although any of the choices would make grammatical sense, choice **d** best fits the context of the sentence.

85. c. The best answer choice will be a word that implies *condescension*. Although choice **b**, *reprehensible*, is a strong possibility, there is not enough information in the sentence to indicate that the speaker finds the person's smile detestable. Based on the information in the sentence, choice **c** is the best answer.

86. b. The key word *although* indicates that the correct answer choice will contain two opposing words, which makes **b** and **e** the only possible choices. Based on the context, **b** is the best answer choice.

87. b. Although someone might very well look *reluctant* or *frazzled* on her wedding day, the sentence indicates that the best answer choice will be a synonym for *beautiful*. Therefore, **b**, *radiant*, is the correct answer.

88. d. Based on context clues, you can tell that the first blank will be filled with a word meaning "give in," which narrows the options down to choices **c** and **d**. If a company hoped to avoid a strike, they would have to *appease* the union's demands rather than *resist* them, so the correct answer choice is **d**.

89. d. In this case, the only strategy to finding the correct answer choice is knowing the meaning of the words. *Obsolescence* means "the process of becoming useless," so choice **d** is the best answer choice.

90. a. The context of the sentence tells you that Elmira's cough is a constant source of pain; based on this information, choices **c** and **d** can be eliminated. Choice **b** can be eliminated next, as a *moderate* smoker would not be as likely to develop a *severe* cough as the other remaining answer choices. Finally, choice **e** can be eliminated. Although a *furtive* (secret) smoker might develop a *caustic* cough, given the context of the sentence, choice **a** is a better answer choice.

91. d. The sentence indicates that the correct answer will oppose the superhero's *good intentions*. Based on this criterion, *nefarious* is the only plausible answer choice.

92. b. The first part of the sentence indicates that the correct word will have the same connotation as *coolness*, which narrows the choice down between **a** and **b**. Of the two, *distraught* forms a better opposing relationship with *aplomb* than *astonished* does with *temperance*; therefore, the best answer choice is **b**.

93. a. Any of the word choices would be grammatically correct in the sentence; however, using logic, it is doubtful that young school children would become *tepid* (unenthusiastic) without activity or *fervent* (extremely emotional). Likewise, it would be harsh to assume that young children could become *rancorous* (disgusting) or *despicable* (evil). Of the five word choices, it is most likely that young children would become *listless*, or restless, if they were not entertained.

94. d. Choices **a** and **e** can be eliminated immediately—*abundant* is not a modifier that would be used to describe a palace, and *enigmatic* means puzzling. Choice **c** can be eliminated next, as an *ostentatious* cabin would be needlessly showy. Of the remaining two choices, a simple cabin would more likely be described as *austere* than *severe*; therefore, **d** is the best answer.

95. e. The sentence implies that the meeting brought back long-forgotten memories; of the five answer choices, **e**, *evoked*, best fits the context.

96. b. If someone skipped breakfast and lunch, they would most likely feel either *voracious*, *ravenous*, or *feeble*, so the choices can be quickly narrowed down to **a**, **b**, or **e**. Of the three remaining choices, the best word to describe how an aroma fills the air is *permeated*; therefore, the words in choice **b** best fit the two blank spaces.

97. a. The implication is that Mr. Crane might harm his chances of being hired if he divulged the previous firing; therefore, the best answer choice is **a**, *jeopardize*, meaning "endanger."

98. e. A happy person would have a positive attitude toward life; of the five answer choices, **e**, *jovial*, best describes a positive attitude. The second word, *paroxysm* (meaning fit), makes sense as well; therefore, **e** is the best answer choice.

99. b. Although desert dwellers might be classified as any of these words, the sentence is really looking for a word describing people who are constantly moving—the word that best fits this definition is **b**, *nomadic*.

100. c. The key word in this sentence is *traitor*; that tells you that Johnson was not as loyal as he claimed to be. Choice **a** is attractive, but the second word, *conspire*, does not necessarily indicate that Johnson would be convincing the crew to conspire against the captain. Choice **c** makes the most sense considering both of the missing words.

Passage-Length Questions

Read the following passages carefully and answer the questions that follow each passage. These 217 practice questions will be drawn from any of the three types of passage-based reading questions: vocabulary in context, literal comprehension, and extended reasoning.

PASSAGE-LENGTH QUESTIONS

1. ⓐ ⓑ ⓒ ⓓ ⓔ
2. ⓐ ⓑ ⓒ ⓓ ⓔ
3. ⓐ ⓑ ⓒ ⓓ ⓔ
4. ⓐ ⓑ ⓒ ⓓ ⓔ
5. ⓐ ⓑ ⓒ ⓓ ⓔ
6. ⓐ ⓑ ⓒ ⓓ ⓔ
7. ⓐ ⓑ ⓒ ⓓ ⓔ
8. ⓐ ⓑ ⓒ ⓓ ⓔ
9. ⓐ ⓑ ⓒ ⓓ ⓔ
10. ⓐ ⓑ ⓒ ⓓ ⓔ
11. ⓐ ⓑ ⓒ ⓓ ⓔ
12. ⓐ ⓑ ⓒ ⓓ ⓔ
13. ⓐ ⓑ ⓒ ⓓ ⓔ
14. ⓐ ⓑ ⓒ ⓓ ⓔ
15. ⓐ ⓑ ⓒ ⓓ ⓔ
16. ⓐ ⓑ ⓒ ⓓ ⓔ
17. ⓐ ⓑ ⓒ ⓓ ⓔ
18. ⓐ ⓑ ⓒ ⓓ ⓔ
19. ⓐ ⓑ ⓒ ⓓ ⓔ
20. ⓐ ⓑ ⓒ ⓓ ⓔ
21. ⓐ ⓑ ⓒ ⓓ ⓔ
22. ⓐ ⓑ ⓒ ⓓ ⓔ
23. ⓐ ⓑ ⓒ ⓓ ⓔ
24. ⓐ ⓑ ⓒ ⓓ ⓔ
25. ⓐ ⓑ ⓒ ⓓ ⓔ
26. ⓐ ⓑ ⓒ ⓓ ⓔ
27. ⓐ ⓑ ⓒ ⓓ ⓔ
28. ⓐ ⓑ ⓒ ⓓ ⓔ
29. ⓐ ⓑ ⓒ ⓓ ⓔ
30. ⓐ ⓑ ⓒ ⓓ ⓔ
31. ⓐ ⓑ ⓒ ⓓ ⓔ
32. ⓐ ⓑ ⓒ ⓓ ⓔ
33. ⓐ ⓑ ⓒ ⓓ ⓔ
34. ⓐ ⓑ ⓒ ⓓ ⓔ
35. ⓐ ⓑ ⓒ ⓓ ⓔ
36. ⓐ ⓑ ⓒ ⓓ ⓔ
37. ⓐ ⓑ ⓒ ⓓ ⓔ
38. ⓐ ⓑ ⓒ ⓓ ⓔ
39. ⓐ ⓑ ⓒ ⓓ ⓔ
40. ⓐ ⓑ ⓒ ⓓ ⓔ
41. ⓐ ⓑ ⓒ ⓓ ⓔ
42. ⓐ ⓑ ⓒ ⓓ ⓔ
43. ⓐ ⓑ ⓒ ⓓ ⓔ
44. ⓐ ⓑ ⓒ ⓓ ⓔ
45. ⓐ ⓑ ⓒ ⓓ ⓔ
46. ⓐ ⓑ ⓒ ⓓ ⓔ
47. ⓐ ⓑ ⓒ ⓓ ⓔ
48. ⓐ ⓑ ⓒ ⓓ ⓔ
49. ⓐ ⓑ ⓒ ⓓ ⓔ
50. ⓐ ⓑ ⓒ ⓓ ⓔ
51. ⓐ ⓑ ⓒ ⓓ ⓔ
52. ⓐ ⓑ ⓒ ⓓ ⓔ
53. ⓐ ⓑ ⓒ ⓓ ⓔ
54. ⓐ ⓑ ⓒ ⓓ ⓔ
55. ⓐ ⓑ ⓒ ⓓ ⓔ
56. ⓐ ⓑ ⓒ ⓓ ⓔ
57. ⓐ ⓑ ⓒ ⓓ ⓔ
58. ⓐ ⓑ ⓒ ⓓ ⓔ
59. ⓐ ⓑ ⓒ ⓓ ⓔ
60. ⓐ ⓑ ⓒ ⓓ ⓔ
61. ⓐ ⓑ ⓒ ⓓ ⓔ
62. ⓐ ⓑ ⓒ ⓓ ⓔ
63. ⓐ ⓑ ⓒ ⓓ ⓔ
64. ⓐ ⓑ ⓒ ⓓ ⓔ
65. ⓐ ⓑ ⓒ ⓓ ⓔ
66. ⓐ ⓑ ⓒ ⓓ ⓔ
67. ⓐ ⓑ ⓒ ⓓ ⓔ
68. ⓐ ⓑ ⓒ ⓓ ⓔ
69. ⓐ ⓑ ⓒ ⓓ ⓔ
70. ⓐ ⓑ ⓒ ⓓ ⓔ
71. ⓐ ⓑ ⓒ ⓓ ⓔ
72. ⓐ ⓑ ⓒ ⓓ ⓔ
73. ⓐ ⓑ ⓒ ⓓ ⓔ
74. ⓐ ⓑ ⓒ ⓓ ⓔ
75. ⓐ ⓑ ⓒ ⓓ ⓔ
76. ⓐ ⓑ ⓒ ⓓ ⓔ
77. ⓐ ⓑ ⓒ ⓓ ⓔ
78. ⓐ ⓑ ⓒ ⓓ ⓔ
79. ⓐ ⓑ ⓒ ⓓ ⓔ
80. ⓐ ⓑ ⓒ ⓓ ⓔ
81. ⓐ ⓑ ⓒ ⓓ ⓔ
82. ⓐ ⓑ ⓒ ⓓ ⓔ
83. ⓐ ⓑ ⓒ ⓓ ⓔ
84. ⓐ ⓑ ⓒ ⓓ ⓔ
85. ⓐ ⓑ ⓒ ⓓ ⓔ
86. ⓐ ⓑ ⓒ ⓓ ⓔ
87. ⓐ ⓑ ⓒ ⓓ ⓔ
88. ⓐ ⓑ ⓒ ⓓ ⓔ
89. ⓐ ⓑ ⓒ ⓓ ⓔ
90. ⓐ ⓑ ⓒ ⓓ ⓔ
91. ⓐ ⓑ ⓒ ⓓ ⓔ
92. ⓐ ⓑ ⓒ ⓓ ⓔ
93. ⓐ ⓑ ⓒ ⓓ ⓔ
94. ⓐ ⓑ ⓒ ⓓ ⓔ
95. ⓐ ⓑ ⓒ ⓓ ⓔ
96. ⓐ ⓑ ⓒ ⓓ ⓔ
97. ⓐ ⓑ ⓒ ⓓ ⓔ
98. ⓐ ⓑ ⓒ ⓓ ⓔ
99. ⓐ ⓑ ⓒ ⓓ ⓔ
100. ⓐ ⓑ ⓒ ⓓ ⓔ
101. ⓐ ⓑ ⓒ ⓓ ⓔ
102. ⓐ ⓑ ⓒ ⓓ ⓔ
103. ⓐ ⓑ ⓒ ⓓ ⓔ
104. ⓐ ⓑ ⓒ ⓓ ⓔ
105. ⓐ ⓑ ⓒ ⓓ ⓔ
106. ⓐ ⓑ ⓒ ⓓ ⓔ
107. ⓐ ⓑ ⓒ ⓓ ⓔ
108. ⓐ ⓑ ⓒ ⓓ ⓔ
109. ⓐ ⓑ ⓒ ⓓ ⓔ
110. ⓐ ⓑ ⓒ ⓓ ⓔ
111. ⓐ ⓑ ⓒ ⓓ ⓔ
112. ⓐ ⓑ ⓒ ⓓ ⓔ
113. ⓐ ⓑ ⓒ ⓓ ⓔ
114. ⓐ ⓑ ⓒ ⓓ ⓔ
115. ⓐ ⓑ ⓒ ⓓ ⓔ
116. ⓐ ⓑ ⓒ ⓓ ⓔ
117. ⓐ ⓑ ⓒ ⓓ ⓔ
118. ⓐ ⓑ ⓒ ⓓ ⓔ
119. ⓐ ⓑ ⓒ ⓓ ⓔ
120. ⓐ ⓑ ⓒ ⓓ ⓔ
121. ⓐ ⓑ ⓒ ⓓ ⓔ
122. ⓐ ⓑ ⓒ ⓓ ⓔ
123. ⓐ ⓑ ⓒ ⓓ ⓔ
124. ⓐ ⓑ ⓒ ⓓ ⓔ
125. ⓐ ⓑ ⓒ ⓓ ⓔ
126. ⓐ ⓑ ⓒ ⓓ ⓔ
127. ⓐ ⓑ ⓒ ⓓ ⓔ
128. ⓐ ⓑ ⓒ ⓓ ⓔ
129. ⓐ ⓑ ⓒ ⓓ ⓔ
130. ⓐ ⓑ ⓒ ⓓ ⓔ
131. ⓐ ⓑ ⓒ ⓓ ⓔ
132. ⓐ ⓑ ⓒ ⓓ ⓔ
133. ⓐ ⓑ ⓒ ⓓ ⓔ
134. ⓐ ⓑ ⓒ ⓓ ⓔ
135. ⓐ ⓑ ⓒ ⓓ ⓔ
136. ⓐ ⓑ ⓒ ⓓ ⓔ
137. ⓐ ⓑ ⓒ ⓓ ⓔ
138. ⓐ ⓑ ⓒ ⓓ ⓔ
139. ⓐ ⓑ ⓒ ⓓ ⓔ
140. ⓐ ⓑ ⓒ ⓓ ⓔ
141. ⓐ ⓑ ⓒ ⓓ ⓔ
142. ⓐ ⓑ ⓒ ⓓ ⓔ
143. ⓐ ⓑ ⓒ ⓓ ⓔ
144. ⓐ ⓑ ⓒ ⓓ ⓔ
145. ⓐ ⓑ ⓒ ⓓ ⓔ
146. ⓐ ⓑ ⓒ ⓓ ⓔ
147. ⓐ ⓑ ⓒ ⓓ ⓔ
148. ⓐ ⓑ ⓒ ⓓ ⓔ
149. ⓐ ⓑ ⓒ ⓓ ⓔ
150. ⓐ ⓑ ⓒ ⓓ ⓔ

151.	ⓐ	ⓑ	ⓒ	ⓓ	ⓔ
152.	ⓐ	ⓑ	ⓒ	ⓓ	ⓔ
153.	ⓐ	ⓑ	ⓒ	ⓓ	ⓔ
154.	ⓐ	ⓑ	ⓒ	ⓓ	ⓔ
155.	ⓐ	ⓑ	ⓒ	ⓓ	ⓔ
156.	ⓐ	ⓑ	ⓒ	ⓓ	ⓔ
157.	ⓐ	ⓑ	ⓒ	ⓓ	ⓔ
158.	ⓐ	ⓑ	ⓒ	ⓓ	ⓔ
159.	ⓐ	ⓑ	ⓒ	ⓓ	ⓔ
160.	ⓐ	ⓑ	ⓒ	ⓓ	ⓔ
161.	ⓐ	ⓑ	ⓒ	ⓓ	ⓔ
162.	ⓐ	ⓑ	ⓒ	ⓓ	ⓔ
163.	ⓐ	ⓑ	ⓒ	ⓓ	ⓔ
164.	ⓐ	ⓑ	ⓒ	ⓓ	ⓔ
165.	ⓐ	ⓑ	ⓒ	ⓓ	ⓔ
166.	ⓐ	ⓑ	ⓒ	ⓓ	ⓔ
167.	ⓐ	ⓑ	ⓒ	ⓓ	ⓔ
168.	ⓐ	ⓑ	ⓒ	ⓓ	ⓔ
169.	ⓐ	ⓑ	ⓒ	ⓓ	ⓔ
170.	ⓐ	ⓑ	ⓒ	ⓓ	ⓔ
171.	ⓐ	ⓑ	ⓒ	ⓓ	ⓔ
172.	ⓐ	ⓑ	ⓒ	ⓓ	ⓔ
173.	ⓐ	ⓑ	ⓒ	ⓓ	ⓔ

174.	ⓐ	ⓑ	ⓒ	ⓓ	ⓔ
175.	ⓐ	ⓑ	ⓒ	ⓓ	ⓔ
176.	ⓐ	ⓑ	ⓒ	ⓓ	ⓔ
177.	ⓐ	ⓑ	ⓒ	ⓓ	ⓔ
178.	ⓐ	ⓑ	ⓒ	ⓓ	ⓔ
179.	ⓐ	ⓑ	ⓒ	ⓓ	ⓔ
180.	ⓐ	ⓑ	ⓒ	ⓓ	ⓔ
181.	ⓐ	ⓑ	ⓒ	ⓓ	ⓔ
182.	ⓐ	ⓑ	ⓒ	ⓓ	ⓔ
183.	ⓐ	ⓑ	ⓒ	ⓓ	ⓔ
184.	ⓐ	ⓑ	ⓒ	ⓓ	ⓔ
185.	ⓐ	ⓑ	ⓒ	ⓓ	ⓔ
186.	ⓐ	ⓑ	ⓒ	ⓓ	ⓔ
187.	ⓐ	ⓑ	ⓒ	ⓓ	ⓔ
188.	ⓐ	ⓑ	ⓒ	ⓓ	ⓔ
189.	ⓐ	ⓑ	ⓒ	ⓓ	ⓔ
190.	ⓐ	ⓑ	ⓒ	ⓓ	ⓔ
191.	ⓐ	ⓑ	ⓒ	ⓓ	ⓔ
192.	ⓐ	ⓑ	ⓒ	ⓓ	ⓔ
193.	ⓐ	ⓑ	ⓒ	ⓓ	ⓔ
194.	ⓐ	ⓑ	ⓒ	ⓓ	ⓔ
195.	ⓐ	ⓑ	ⓒ	ⓓ	ⓔ
196.	ⓐ	ⓑ	ⓒ	ⓓ	ⓔ

197.	ⓐ	ⓑ	ⓒ	ⓓ	ⓔ
198.	ⓐ	ⓑ	ⓒ	ⓓ	ⓔ
199.	ⓐ	ⓑ	ⓒ	ⓓ	ⓔ
200.	ⓐ	ⓑ	ⓒ	ⓓ	ⓔ
201.	ⓐ	ⓑ	ⓒ	ⓓ	ⓔ
202.	ⓐ	ⓑ	ⓒ	ⓓ	ⓔ
203.	ⓐ	ⓑ	ⓒ	ⓓ	ⓔ
204.	ⓐ	ⓑ	ⓒ	ⓓ	ⓔ
205.	ⓐ	ⓑ	ⓒ	ⓓ	ⓔ
206.	ⓐ	ⓑ	ⓒ	ⓓ	ⓔ
207.	ⓐ	ⓑ	ⓒ	ⓓ	ⓔ
208.	ⓐ	ⓑ	ⓒ	ⓓ	ⓔ
209.	ⓐ	ⓑ	ⓒ	ⓓ	ⓔ
210.	ⓐ	ⓑ	ⓒ	ⓓ	ⓔ
211.	ⓐ	ⓑ	ⓒ	ⓓ	ⓔ
212.	ⓐ	ⓑ	ⓒ	ⓓ	ⓔ
213.	ⓐ	ⓑ	ⓒ	ⓓ	ⓔ
214.	ⓐ	ⓑ	ⓒ	ⓓ	ⓔ
215.	ⓐ	ⓑ	ⓒ	ⓓ	ⓔ
216.	ⓐ	ⓑ	ⓒ	ⓓ	ⓔ
217.	ⓐ	ⓑ	ⓒ	ⓓ	ⓔ

Questions 1–8 are based on the following passage.

The following selection explains the origins of sushi *and its popularity in the United States.*

Line

Burgers, fries, pizza, raw fish. Raw fish? Fast food in America is changing. *Sushi*, the thousand-year-old Japanese delicacy, was once thought of in this country as unpalatable and too exotic. But tastes have changed, for a number of reasons. Beginning in the 1970s, Americans became increasingly more aware of diet and health issues, and began rejecting their traditional red-meat diets in favor of healthier, lower-

(5) fat choices such as fish, poultry, whole grains, rice, and vegetables. The way food was prepared began to change, too; rather than frying food, people started opting for broiled, steamed, and raw versions. Sushi, a combination of rice and fish, fit the bill. In addition, that same decade saw Japan become an important global economic force, and companies began flocking to the country to do business. All things Japanese, including décor, clothing, and cuisine, became popular.

(10) Sushi started small in the United States, in a handful of restaurants in big cities. But it caught on. Today, sushi consumption in American restaurants is 40% greater than it was in the late 1990s, according to the National Restaurant Association. The concession stands at almost every major league stadium sell sushi, and many colleges and universities offer it in their dining halls. But we're not just eating it out. The National Sushi Association reports that there are over 5,000 sushi bars in supermarkets, and that

(15) number is growing monthly. This incredible growth in availability and consumption points to the fact that Americans have decided that sushi isn't just good for them, or just convenient, but that this once-scorned food is truly delicious.

The origins of this food trend may be found in Asia, where it was developed as a way of preserving fish. Fresh, cleaned fish was pressed between rice and salt and weighted with a heavy stone over a period

(20) of several months. During this time, the rice fermented, producing lactic acid that pickled and preserved the fish. For many years, the fish was eaten and the rice was discarded. But about 500 years ago, that changed, and *hako-zushi* (boxed sushi) was created. In this type of sushi, the rice and fish are pressed together in a box and are consumed together.

In 1824, Yohei Hanaya of Edo (now called Tokyo) eliminated the fermentation process and began

(25) serving fresh slices of seafood on bases of vinegared rice. The vinegar was probably used to mimic the taste of fermented sushi. In fact, the word *sushi* actually refers to any vinegared rice dish, not to the fish, as many Americans believe (the fish is called *sashimi*). In Japanese, when sushi is combined with a modifier, it changes to the word *zushi*.

Chef Yohei's invention, called *nigiri zushi*, is still served today. It now refers to a slice of fish (cooked

(30) or uncooked) that is pressed by hand onto a serving of rice. Popular choices include *ama ebi* (raw shrimp), *shime saba* (marinated mackerel), and *maguro* (tuna). In addition to the vinegar flavor in the rice, *nigiri zushi* typically contains a taste of horseradish (*wasabi*), and is served with soy sauce for dipping.

Maki zushi contains strips of fish or vegetables rolled in rice and wrapped in thin sheets of *nori*, or dried seaweed. Popular ingredients include smoked salmon, fresh crab, shrimp, octopus, raw clams, and sea

(35) urchin. Americans have invented many of their own *maki zushi* combinations, including the California roll, which contains imitation crabmeat and avocado. They have also made innovations in the construction of

maki zushi. Some American sushi bars switch the placement of *nori* and rice, while others don't use *nori*, and instead roll the *maki zushi* in fish roe. These colorful, crunchy eggs add to the visual and taste appeal of the dish.

1. According to the passage, what other food also gained popularity in the 1970s?
a. salads
b. pepperoni pizza
c. fried chicken
d. fast-food burgers
e. fried rice

2. What was Yohei Hanaya's contribution to sushi?
a. He pressed the fish and rice together in a box.
b. He introduced the population of Edo to the dish.
c. He smoked the fish before putting it on vinegared rice.
d. He used *wasabi* to flavor it.
e. He used raw fish.

3. According to the passage, what does *shime* mean?
a. salmon
b. shrimp
c. marinated
d. roe
e. seaweed

4. All of the following can be explicitly answered by reading the passage EXCEPT
a. What is the definition of the word *sushi*?
b. Did Japan's economic status have a bearing on sushi's popularity?
c. Have Americans adapted sushi to make it more in keeping with their tastes?
d. Why do some Americans prefer *maki zushi* over *nigiri zushi*?
e. What happens to fish when it is layered together with rice and left for a period of months?

5. The passage describes Americans' sushi consumption as
a. more than it was in the late 1990s.
b. important when watching baseball.
c. taking place primarily in their homes.
d. a trend due to supermarket marketing.
e. beginning for many in college.

6. In line 2, *unpalatable* most nearly means
a. not visually appealing.
b. not good tasting.
c. bad smelling.
d. too expensive.
e. rough to the touch.

7. What happens when fish is pickled (line 20)?
a. It becomes crisp.
b. It turns green.
c. It dissolves into the rice.
d. It is preserved.
e. It gets dry.

8. What would be the best name for *maki zushi* that has the placement of the rice and *nori* switched?
a. rice ball
b. *maki maki*
c. *zushi* deluxe
d. inside-out
e. *wasabi sashimi*

Questions 9–15 are based on the following passage.

This passage details the life and illustrious career of Sir Isaac Newton, preeminent scientist and mathematician.

Line

Tradition has it that Newton was sitting under an apple tree when an apple fell on his head, and this made him understand that earthly and celestial gravitation are the same. A contemporary writer, William Stukeley, recorded in his *Memoirs of Sir Isaac Newton's Life* a conversation with Newton in Kensington on April 15, 1726, in which Newton recalled "when formerly, the notion of gravitation came into his mind.

(5)   It was occasioned by the fall of an apple, as he sat in contemplative mood. Why should that apple always descend perpendicularly to the ground, thought he to himself. Why should it not go sideways or upwards, but constantly to the earth's centre."

Sir Isaac Newton, English mathematician, philosopher, and physicist, was born in 1642 in Woolsthorpe-by-Colsterworth, a hamlet in the county of Lincolnshire. His father had died three months before Newton's

(10)   birth, and two years later, his mother went to live with her new husband, leaving her son in the care of his grandmother. Newton was educated at Grantham Grammar School. In 1661, he joined Trinity College, Cambridge, and continued there as Lucasian professor of mathematics from 1669 to 1701. At that time, the college's teachings were based on those of Aristotle, but Newton preferred to read the more advanced ideas of modern philosophers such as Descartes, Galileo, Copernicus, and Kepler. In 1665, he discovered the binomial theorem

(15)   and began to develop a mathematical theory that would later become calculus.

However, his most important discoveries were made during the two-year period from 1664 to 1666, when the university was closed because of the Great Plague. Newton retreated to his hometown and set to work on developing calculus, as well as advanced studies on optics and gravitation. It was at this time that he discovered the Law of Universal Gravitation and that white light is composed of all the colors of

(20)   the spectrum. These findings enabled him to make fundamental contributions to mathematics, astronomy, and theoretical and experimental physics.

Arguably, it is Newton's Laws of Motion for which he is most revered. These are the three basic laws that govern the motion of material objects. Together, they gave rise to a general view of nature known as the "clockwork universe." The laws are: (1) Every object moves in a straight line unless acted upon by a

(25)   force. (2) The acceleration of an object is directly proportional to the net force exerted and inversely proportional to the object's mass. (3) For every action, there is an equal and opposite reaction.

In 1687, Newton summarized his discoveries in terrestrial and celestial mechanics in his *Philosophiae naturalis principia mathematica* (Mathematical Principles of Natural Philosophy), one of the greatest milestones in the history of science. In this work, he showed how his principle of universal gravitation

(30)   provided an explanation both of falling bodies on the earth and of the motions of planets, comets, and other bodies in the heavens. The first part of the *Principia*, devoted to dynamics, includes Newton's three laws of motion; the second part to fluid motion and other topics; and the third part to the system of the world, in which, among other things, he provides an explanation of Kepler's laws of planetary motion.

This is not all of Newton's groundbreaking work. In 1704, his discoveries in optics were presented

(35)   in *Opticks*, in which he elaborated his theory that light is composed of corpuscles, or particles. Among his other accomplishments were his construction of a reflecting telescope (1668) and his anticipation of the

calculus of variations, founded by Gottfried Leibniz and the Bernoullis. In later years, Newton considered mathematics and physics a recreation and turned much of his energy toward alchemy, theology, and history, particularly problems of chronology.

(40)   Newton achieved many honors over his years of service to the advancement of science and mathematics, as well as for his role as warden, then master, of the mint. He represented Cambridge University in Parliament, and was president of the Royal Society from 1703 until his death in 1727. Sir Isaac Newton was knighted in 1705 by Queen Anne. Newton never married, nor had any recorded children. He died in London and was buried in Westminster Abbey.

9. Based on Newton's quote in lines 4–7 of the passage, what can best be surmised about the famous apple falling from the tree?
   a. There was no apple falling from a tree—it was entirely made up.
   b. Newton never sits beneath apple trees.
   c. Newton got distracted from his theory on gravity by a fallen apple.
   d. Newton used the apple anecdote as an easily understood illustration of the earth's gravitational pull.
   e. Newton invented a theory of geometry for the trajectory of apples falling perpendicularly, sideways, and up and down.

10. In what capacity was Newton employed?
    a. Physics Professor, Trinity College
    b. Trinity Professor of Optics
    c. Professor of Calculus at Trinity College
    d. Professor of Astronomy at Lucasian College
    e. Professor of Mathematics at Cambridge

11. In line 24, what does the term *clockwork universe* most nearly mean?
    a. eighteenth-century government
    b. the international dateline
    c. Newton's system of latitude
    d. Newton's system of longitude
    e. Newton's Laws of Motion

12. According to the passage, how did Newton affect Kepler's work?
    a. He discredited his theory at Cambridge, choosing to read Descartes instead.
    b. He provides an explanation of Kepler's laws of planetary motion.
    c. He convinced the dean to teach Kepler, Descartes, Galileo, and Copernicus instead of Aristotle.
    d. He showed how Copernicus was a superior astronomer to Kepler.
    e. He did not understand Kepler's laws, so he rewrote them in English.

13. Which of the following is NOT an accolade received by Newton?
a. Member of the Royal Society
b. Order of Knighthood
c. Master of the Royal Mint
d. Prime Minister of Parliament
e. Lucasian Professor of Mathematics

14. Of the following, which is last in chronology?
a. *Philosophiae naturalis principia mathematica*
b. *Memoirs of Sir Isaac Newton's Life*
c. Newton's Laws of Motion
d. *Optiks*
e. invention of a reflecting telescope

15. Which statement best summarizes the life of Sir Isaac Newton?
a. distinguished inventor, mathematician, physicist, and great thinker of the seventeenth century
b. eminent mathematician, physicist, and scholar of the Renaissance
c. noteworthy physicist, astronomer, mathematician, and British Lord
d. from master of the mint to master mathematician
e. founder of calculus and father of gravity

Questions 16–23 are based on the following passage.

In this passage, the author discusses the problem of maintaining privacy in our high-tech society.

Line

A recent *New York Times* "House and Home" article featured the story of a man who lives in a glass house. Every wall in his home is transparent; he has no walls to hide behind, not even in the bathroom. Of course, he lives in an isolated area, so he doesn't exactly have neighbors peering in and watching his every move. But he has chosen to live without any physical privacy in a home that allows every action to be seen. He
(5) has created his own panopticon of sorts, a place in which everything is in full view of others.

The term *panopticon* was coined by Jeremy Bentham in the late eighteenth century when he was describing an idea for how prisons should be designed. The prisoner's cells would be placed in a circle with a guard tower in the middle. All walls facing the center of the circle would be glass. In that way, every prisoner's cell would be in full view of the guards. The prisoners could do nothing unobserved, but the pris-
(10) oners would not be able to see the guard tower. They would know they were being watched—or rather, they would know that they could be being watched—but because they could not see the observer, they would never know when the guard was actually monitoring their actions.

It is common knowledge that people behave differently when they know they are being watched. We act differently when we know someone is looking; we act differently when we think someone else might
(15) be looking. In these situations, we are less likely to be ourselves; instead, we will act the way we think we should act when we are being observed by others.

In our wired society, many talk of the panopticon as a metaphor for the future. But in many ways, the panopticon is already here. Surveillance cameras are everywhere, and we often don't even know our actions are being recorded. In fact, the surveillance camera industry is enormous, and these cameras keep
(20) getting smaller and smaller to make surveillance easier and more ubiquitous. In addition, we leave a record of everything we do online; our cyber-whereabouts can be tracked and that information used for

various purposes. Every time we use a credit card, make a major purchase, answer a survey, apply for a loan, or join a mailing list, our actions are observed and recorded. And most of us have no idea just how much information about us has been recorded and how much data is available to various sources. The (25) scale of information gathering and the scale of exchange have both expanded so rapidly in the last decade that there are now millions of electronic profiles of individuals existing in cyberspace, profiles that are bought and sold, traded, and often used for important decisions, such as whether or not to grant someone a loan. However, that information is essentially beyond our control. We can do little to stop the information gathering and exchange and can only hope to be able to control the damage if something (30) goes wrong.

Something went wrong recently for me. Someone obtained my Social Security number, address, work number and address, and a few other vital pieces of data. That person then applied for a credit account in my name. The application was approved, and I soon received a bill for nearly $5,000 worth of computer-related purchases.

(35) Fraud, of course, is a different issue, but this kind of fraud couldn't happen—or at least, couldn't happen with such ease and frequency—in a world of paper-based records. With so much information floating about in cyberspace, and so much technology that can record and observe, our privacy has been deeply compromised.

I find it truly amazing that someone would want to live in a transparent house at any time, but espe-(40) cially in an age when individual privacy is becoming increasingly difficult to maintain and defend (against those who argue that information must be gathered for the social good). Or perhaps this man's house is an attempt to call our attention to the fact that the panopticon is already here, and that we are all just as exposed as he is.

16. According to the passage, a *panopticon* is
   a. a prison cell.
   b. a place in which everything can be seen by others.
   c. a tower that provides a panoramic view.
   d. a house that is transparent.
   e. a place in which surveillance cameras and other monitoring equipment are in use.

17. The description of how the panopticon would work in a prison (lines 6–12) implies that the panopticon
   a. can be an effective tool for social control.
   b. should be used regularly in public places.
   c. is not applicable outside of the prison dynamic.
   d. is an effective tool for sharing information.
   e. will redefine privacy for the twenty-first century.

18. In lines 17–30, the author suggests that the panopticon is a metaphor for our society because
   a. our privacy is transparent.
   b. we are all prisoners in our own homes.
   c. our actions are constantly observed and recorded.
   d. we are always afraid that someone might be watching us.
   e. there is rampant exchange of information in cyberspace.

19. According to the passage, a key difference between the prison panopticon and the modern technological panopticon is that
a. the prisoners can see their observers, but we can't.
b. today's prisons are too crowded for the panopticon to work.
c. prisoners are less informed about privacy issues than technology users.
d. the prisoners are aware that they may be being watched, but we often don't even know we are being monitored.
e. prisoners are more protected in their panopticon than we are in ours.

20. The passage suggests that all of the following contribute to the erosion of privacy EXCEPT
a. increased use of credit cards for purchases.
b. buying and selling of electronic profiles.
c. increasingly discreet surveillance equipment.
d. lack of controls over information exchange.
e. easy access to electronic information in cyberspace.

21. The author describes a personal experience with identity theft in order to
a. show how prevalent identity theft is.
b. show how angry he is about having his privacy invaded.
c. show an example of how private information can be taken and misused.
d. demonstrate a flaw in the panopticon.
e. demonstrate the vast scale of information exchange.

22. The word *compromised* in line 38 means
a. conceded.
b. agreed.
c. dishonored.
d. negotiated.
e. jeopardized.

23. Based on the passage, it can be inferred that the author would support which of the following?
a. widespread construction of glass houses
b. stricter sentencing for perpetrators of fraud
c. greater flexibility in loan approval criteria
d. stricter regulations for information gathering and exchange
e. modeling prisons after Bentham's panopticon

Questions 24–33 are based on the following passage.

In the following article, the author speculates about a connection between the low-fat, high-carbohydrate diet recommended by the medical establishment in the last 20 years and the increasing rate of obesity among Americans.

Line

American dietitians and members of the medical community have ridiculed low-carbohydrate diets as quackery for the past 30 years, while extolling a diet that cuts down on fat, limits meat consumption, and relies on carbohydrates as its staple. Many Americans are familiar with the food pyramid promoted by the U.S. government before 2005, with its foundation of carbohydrates such as breads, rice, and pasta, and its
(5)   apex allotted to fats, oils, and sweets. Adhering to the government's anti-fat, pro-carbohydrate gospel, food manufacturers have pumped out fat-free grain products that lure consumers with the promise of leaner days. Then, why are Americans getting so fat? Could the dietary recommendations of the last 20 years be wrong? And what's more, could the proponents of diets that push protein and fat be right?

(10) Fact: Obesity rates have soared throughout the country since the 1980s. The U.S. Centers of Disease Control report that the number of obese adults has doubled in the last 20 years. The number of obese children and teenagers has almost tripled, increasing 120% among African American and Latino children and 50% among white children. The risk for Type 2 diabetes, which is associated with obesity, has increased dramatically as well. Disturbingly, the disease now affects 25% to 30% of children, compared with 3% to 5% two decades ago.

(15) What is behind this trend? Supersized portions, cheap fast food, and soft drinks combined with a sedentary lifestyle of TV watching or Internet surfing have most likely contributed to the rapid rise of obesity. Yet, there might be more to it: Is it a coincidence that obesity rates increased in the last 20 years—the same time period in which the low-fat dietary doctrine has reigned? Before the 1980s, the conventional wisdom was that fat and protein created a feeling of satiation, so that overeating would be
(20) less likely. Carbohydrates, on the other hand, were regarded as a recipe for stoutness. This perception began to change after World War II when coronary heart disease reached near epidemic proportions among middle-aged men. A theory that dietary fat might increase cholesterol levels and, in turn, increase the risk of heart disease emerged in the 1950s and gained increasing acceptance by the late 1970s. In 1979, the focus of the food guidelines promoted by the U.S. Department of Agriculture (USDA) began
(25) to shift away from getting enough nutrients to avoiding excess fat, saturated fat, cholesterol, and sodium—the components believed to be linked to heart disease. The anti-fat credo was born.

To date, the studies that have tried to link dietary fat to increased risk of coronary heart disease have remained ambiguous. Studies have shown that cholesterol-lowering drugs help reduce the risk of heart disease, but whether a diet low in cholesterol can do the same is still questionable. While nutrition experts
(30) are debating whether a low-fat, carbohydrate-based diet is the healthiest diet for Americans, nearly all agree that the anti-fat message of the last 20 years has been oversimplified. For example, some fats and oils like those found in olive oil and nuts are beneficial to the heart and may deserve a larger proportion in the American diet than their place at the tip of the food pyramid indicates. Likewise, some carbohydrates that form the basis of the food pyramid, like the refined carbohydrates contained in white bread, pasta, and white
(35) rice, are metabolized in the body much the same way sweets are. According to one Harvard Medical School researcher, a breakfast of a bagel with low-fat cream cheese is "metabolically indistinguishable from a bowl of sugar."

So what about those high-fat, high-protein diets that restrict carbohydrates like the popular Atkins diet and others? A small group of nutrition experts within the medical establishment find it hard to ignore
(40) the anecdotal evidence that many lose weight successfully on these diets. They are arguing that those diets should not be dismissed out of hand, but researched and tested more closely. Still others fear that Americans, hungry to find a weight-loss regimen, may embrace a diet that has no long-term data about whether it works or is safe. What is clear is that Americans are awaiting answers, and in the meantime, we need to eat something.

24. The passage is primarily concerned with
   a. questioning the dietary advice of the past two decades.
   b. contrasting theories of good nutrition.
   c. displaying the variety of ways one can interpret scientific evidence.
   d. debunking the value of diets that restrict carbohydrates.
   e. isolating the cause of the rising rate of obesity.

25. The author's attitude toward the medical experts who ridiculed low-carbohydrate diets as quackery and praised low-fat diets is one of
   a. bemused agreement.
   b. seeming ambivalence.
   c. unconcerned apathy.
   d. implicit objection.
   e. shocked disbelief.

26. The term *gospel* (line 5) as it is used in the passage most nearly means
   a. one of the first four New Testament books.
   b. a proven principle.
   c. a message accepted as truth.
   d. American evangelical music.
   e. a singular interpretation.

27. The author uses the word *fact* (line 9) in order to
   a. draw a conclusion about the USDA's dietary recommendations.
   b. imply that statistical information can be misleading.
   c. hypothesize about the health effects of high-fat, high-protein diets.
   d. introduce a theory about the increased rate of obesity.
   e. emphasize a statistical reality regardless of its cause.

28. The passage suggests that the obesity trend in the United States is
   a. partly a result of inactive lifestyles.
   b. the predictable outcome of cutting down on saturated fat.
   c. a cyclical event that happens every 20 years.
   d. unrelated to a rise in diabetes cases.
   e. the unfortunate byproduct of the effort to reduce heart disease.

29. In lines 28–33, the author implies that the government's 1979 food guidelines
   a. relied more on folk wisdom than on scientific study.
   b. were based on the theoretical premise that eating less dietary fat reduces heart disease.
   c. were negligent in not responding to the increasing incidence of heart disease.
   d. no longer bothered to mention nutrient objectives.
   e. were successful in reducing heart disease rates.

30. The author characterizes the anti-fat message of the last 20 years as
   a. elusive.
   b. questionable.
   c. incoherent.
   d. beneficial.
   e. inventive.

31. The author cites the example of a breakfast of a bagel with low-fat cream cheese in order to
   a. show that getting a nutritional breakfast can be fast and convenient.
   b. demonstrate that carbohydrates are the ideal nutrient.
   c. overturn the notion that a carbohydrate-based breakfast is necessarily healthy.
   d. persuade readers that they should eat eggs and sausage for breakfast.
   e. argue that Americans should greatly restrict their carbohydrate intake.

32. The author of the passage would most likely agree with which statement?
a. The federal government knowingly gave the public misleading advice.
b. Soaring obesity rates are most certainly a result of low-fat diets.
c. Nutritionists should promote high-fat, high-protein diets like the Atkins diet.
d. Scientists should investigate every fad diet with equal scrutiny.
e. There is no definitive evidence connecting dietary fat to heart disease.

33. The tone of the last sentence of the passage (lines 43–44) is one of
a. optimism.
b. resolve.
c. indulgence.
d. irony.
e. revulsion.

Questions 34–42 are based on the following two passages.

Passage 1 describes the potlatch ceremony celebrated by native peoples of the Pacific Northwest. Passage 2 describes the kula *ring, a ceremonial trading circle practiced among Trobriand Islanders in Papua New Guinea.*

Lines

Passage 1

Among traditional societies of the Pacific Northwest—including the Haidas, Kwakiuls, Makahs, Nootkas, Tlingits, and Tsimshians—the gift-giving ceremony called *potlatch* was a central feature of social life. The word *potlatch*, meaning "to give," comes from a Chinook trading language that was used all along the Pacific Coast. Each nation, or tribe, had its own particular word for the ceremony and each had different pot-

(5)   latch traditions. However, the function and basic features of the ceremony were universal among the tribes.

Each nation held potlatches to celebrate important life passages, such as birth, coming of age, marriage, and death. Potlatches were also held to honor ancestors and to mark the passing of leadership. A potlatch, which could last four or more days, was usually held in the winter when the tribes were not engaged in gathering and storing food. Each potlatch included the formal display of the host family's crest

(10)   and masks. The hosts performed ritual dances and provided feasts for their guests. However, the most important ritual was the lavish distribution of gifts to the guests. Some hosts might give away most or all of their accumulated wealth in one potlatch. The more a host gave away, the more status was accorded him. In turn, the guests, who had to accept the proffered gifts, were then expected to host their own potlatches and give away gifts of equal value.

(15)   Prior to contact with Europeans, gifts might include food, slaves, copper plates, and goat's hair blankets. After contact, the potlatch was fundamentally transformed by the influx of manufactured goods. As tribes garnered wealth in the fur trade, gifts came to include guns, woolen blankets, and other Western goods. Although potlatches had always been a means for individuals to win prestige, potlatches involving manufactured goods became a way for nobles to validate tenuous claims to leadership, sometimes

(20)   through the destruction of property. It was this willful destruction of property that led Canadian authorities, and later the U.S. government, to ban potlatches in the late 1880s.

Despite the ban, the potlatch remained an important part of native Pacific Northwest culture. Giving wealth—not accumulating wealth, as is prized in Western culture—was a means of cementing leadership, affirming status, establishing and maintaining alliances, as well as ensuring the even distribution

(25) of food and goods. Agnes Alfred, an Indian from Alert Bay, explained the potlatch this way, "When one's heart is glad, he gives away gifts . . . The potlatch was given to us to be our way of expressing joy."

Passage 2

The inhabitants of the Trobriand Islands, an archipelago off the coast of Papua New Guinea in the South Pacific, are united by a ceremonial trading system called the *kula* ring. *Kula* traders sail to neighboring islands in large ocean-going canoes to offer either shell necklaces or shell armbands. The necklaces, made of red

(30) shells called *bagi*, travel around the trading ring clockwise, and the armbands, made of white shells called *mwali*, travel counterclockwise.

Each man in the *kula* ring has two *kula* trading partners—one partner to whom he gives a necklace for an armband of equal value, although the exchanges are made on separate occasions, and one partner with whom he makes the reverse exchange. Each partner has one other partner with whom he trades, thus

(35) linking all the men around the *kula* ring. For example, if A trades with B and C, B trades with A and D, and C trades with A and E, and so on. A man may have only met his own specific *kula* partners, but he will know by reputation all the men in his *kula* ring. It can take anywhere from two to ten years for a particular object to complete a journey around the ring. The more times an object has made the trip around the ring the more value it accrues. Particularly beautiful necklaces and armbands are also prized. Some

(40) famous *kula* objects are known by special names and through elaborate stories. Objects also gain fame through ownership by powerful men, and likewise, men can gain status by possessing particularly prized *kula* objects.

The exchange of these ceremonial items, which often accompanies trade in more mundane wares, is enacted with a host of ritual activities. The visitors, who travel to receive *kula* from their hosts, are seen as

(45) aggressors. They are met with ritual hostility and must charm their hosts in order to receive the necklaces or armbands. The visitors take care to make themselves beautiful, because beauty conveys strength and protects them from danger. The hosts, who are the "victims" of their visitors' charm and beauty, give the prized objects because they know that the next time it will be their turn to be the aggressor. Each man hopes that his charm and beauty will compel his trading partner to give him the most valuable *kula* object.

(50) The objects cannot be bought or sold. They have no value other than their ceremonial importance, and the voyages that the traders make to neighboring islands are hazardous, time-consuming, and expensive. Yet a man's standing in the *kula* ring is his primary concern. This ceremonial exchange has numerous tangible benefits. It establishes friendly relations through a far-flung chain of islands; it provides a means for the utilitarian exchange of necessary goods; and it reinforces the power of those individuals who win

(55) and maintain the most valuable *kula* items. Although the *kula* ring might mystify Western traders, this system, which has been in operation for hundreds of years, is a highly effective means of unifying these distant islanders and creating a common bond among peoples who might otherwise view one another as hostile outsiders.

34. According to Passage 1, potlatch is best defined as a
   a. ceremony with rigid protocol to which all Pacific Northwest tribes adhere.
   b. generic term for a gift-giving ceremony celebrated in the Pacific Northwest.
   c. socialist ritual of the Pacific Northwest.
   d. lavish feast celebrated in the Pacific Northwest.
   e. wasteful ritual that was banned in the 1880s.

35. According to Passage 1, the gift giving central to the potlatch can best be characterized as
   a. reciprocal.
   b. wasteful.
   c. selfless.
   d. spendthrift.
   e. commercialized.

36. In Passage 1, the author's attitude toward the potlatch can best be described as
   a. condescending.
   b. antagonistic.
   c. wistful.
   d. respectful.
   e. romantic.

37. According to Passage 2, the men in a *kula* ring are
   a. linked by mutual admiration.
   b. hostile aggressors.
   c. greedy.
   d. motivated by vanity.
   e. known to one another by reputation.

38. In Passage 2, line 47, the word *victims* is in quotation marks because the
   a. word might be unfamiliar to some readers.
   b. author is implying that the hosts are self-pitying.
   c. author is reinforcing the idea that the hosts are playing a prescribed role.
   d. author wants to stress the brutal nature of the exchange.
   e. author is taking care not to be condescending to the Trobriand culture.

39. According to Passage 2, necklaces and armbands gain value through all the following means EXCEPT being
   a. in circulation for a long time.
   b. especially attractive.
   c. owned by a powerful man.
   d. made of special shells.
   e. known by a special name.

40. Gift giving in the potlatch ceremony and the ritual exchange of the *kula* ring are both
   a. a ritualized means of maintaining community ties.
   b. dangerous and expensive endeavors.
   c. a means of ascending to a position of leadership.
   d. falling prey to Western culture.
   e. peculiar rituals of a bygone era.

41. Based on information presented in the two passages, both authors would be most likely to agree with which statement?
   a. Traditional societies are more generous than Western societies.
   b. The value of some endeavors cannot be measured in monetary terms.
   c. It is better to give than to receive.
   d. Westerners are only interested in money.
   e. Traditional societies could benefit from better business sense.

42. Which of the following titles would be most appropriate for both Passage 1 or Passage 2?
   a. A Gift-Giving Ceremony
   b. Ritual Exchange in Traditional Societies
   c. Ceremonial Giving and Receiving in a Traditional Society
   d. The Kindness of Strangers
   e. Giving and Receiving in a Faraway Land

Questions 43–52 are based on the following passage.

This passage describes the public's growing interest in alternative medicine practices in twenty-first century United States.

Line

Once people wore garlic around their necks to ward off disease. Today, most Americans would scoff at the idea of wearing a necklace of garlic cloves to enhance their well-being. However, you might find a number of Americans willing to ingest capsules of pulverized garlic or other herbal supplements in the name of health.

(5)   Complementary and alternative medicine (CAM), which includes a range of practices outside of conventional medicine such as herbs, homeopathy, massage, yoga, and acupuncture, holds increasing appeal for Americans. In fact, according to one estimate, 62% of Americans have used alternative therapies. A Harvard Medical School survey found that young adults (those born between 1965 and 1979) are the most likely to use alternative treatments, whereas people born before 1945 are the least likely to use these ther-

(10)   apies. Nonetheless, in all age groups, the use of unconventional healthcare practices has steadily increased since the 1950s, and the trend is likely to continue.

CAM has become a big business as Americans dip into their wallets to pay for alternative treatments. A 1997 American Medical Association study estimated that the public spent $36 billion to $47 billion for alternative medicine therapies in that year, and between $12 billion and $20 billion was spent on "out-

(15)   of-pocket" expenditures, meaning they were not covered by health insurance. Indeed, Americans made more out-of-pocket expenditures for alternative services than they did for out-of-pocket payments for hospital stays in 1997. In addition, the number of total visits to alternative medicine providers (about 629 million) exceeded the tally of visits to primary care physicians (386 million) in that year.

However, the public has not abandoned conventional medicine for alternative healthcare. Most Amer-

(20)   icans seek out alternative therapies as a complement to their conventional healthcare, whereas only a small percentage of Americans rely primarily on alternative care. Why have so many patients turned to alternative therapies? Frustrated by the time constraints of managed care and alienated by conventional medicine's focus on technology, some feel that a holistic approach to healthcare better reflects their beliefs and values. Others seek therapies that will relieve symptoms associated with chronic disease, symptoms that main-

(25)   stream medicine cannot treat.

Some alternative therapies have crossed the line into mainstream medicine as scientific investigation has confirmed their safety and efficacy. For example, today physicians may prescribe acupuncture for pain management or to control the nausea associated with chemotherapy. Most U.S. medical schools teach courses in alternative therapies and many health insurance companies offer some alternative medicine ben-

(30)   efits. Yet, despite their gaining acceptance, the majority of alternative therapies have not been researched in controlled studies. New research efforts aim at testing alternative methods and providing the public with information about which are safe and effective and which are a waste of money, or possibly dangerous.

So what about those who swear by the health benefits of the "smelly rose," garlic?

Observational studies that track disease incidence in different populations suggest that garlic use in

(35)   the diet may act as a cancer-fighting agent, particularly for prostate and stomach cancer. However, these findings have not been confirmed in clinical studies. And yes, reported side effects include garlic odor.

43. The author's primary purpose in the passage is to
  a. confirm the safety and effectiveness of alternative medicine approaches.
  b. convey the excitement of crossing new medical frontiers.
  c. describe the recent increase in the use of alternative therapies.
  d. explore the variety of practices that fall into the category of alternative medicine.
  e. criticize the use of alternative therapies that have not been scientifically tested.

44. The author describes wearing garlic (line 1) as an example of
  a. an arcane practice considered odd and superstitious today.
  b. the ludicrous nature of complementary and alternative medicine.
  c. a scientifically tested medical practice.
  d. a socially unacceptable style of jewelry.
  e. a safe and reliable means to prevent some forms of cancer.

45. The word *conventional* as it is used in lines 5–6 most nearly means
  a. appropriate.
  b. established.
  c. formal.
  d. moralistic.
  e. reactionary.

46. The author most likely uses the Harvard survey results (lines 7–10) to imply that
  a. as people age they always become more conservative.
  b. people born before 1945 view alternative therapies with disdain.
  c. the survey did not question baby boomers (those born between 1945 and 1965) on the topic.
  d. many young adults are open-minded to alternative therapies.
  e. the use of alternative therapies will decline as those born between 1965 and 1979 age.

47. The statistic comparing total visits to alternative medicine practitioners with those to primary care physicians (lines 17–18) is used to illustrate the
  a. popularity of alternative medicine.
  b. public's distrust of conventional healthcare.
  c. accessibility of alternative medicine.
  d. affordability of alternative therapies.
  e. ineffectiveness of most primary care physicians.

48. In line 20, *complement* most nearly means
  a. tribute.
  b. commendation.
  c. replacement.
  d. substitute.
  e. addition.

49. The information in lines 22–25 indicates that Americans believe that conventional healthcare

a. offers the best relief from the effects of chronic diseases.

b. should not use technology in treating illness.

c. combines caring for the body with caring for the spirit.

d. falls short of their expectations in some aspects.

e. needs a complete overhaul to become an effective system.

50. The author suggests that crossing the line into mainstream medicine (lines 26–27) involves

a. performing stringently controlled research on alternative therapies.

b. accepting the spiritual dimension of preventing and treating illness.

c. approving of any treatments that a patient is interested in trying.

d. recognizing the popularity of alternative therapies.

e. notifying your physician about herbs or alternative therapies you are using.

51. In lines 33–36, the author refers to garlic use again in order to

a. cite an example of the fraudulent claims of herbal supplements.

b. suggest that claims about some herbs may be legitimate.

c. mock people who take garlic capsules.

d. reason that some Americans are drawn to alternative health methods.

e. argue that observational studies provide enough evidence.

52. Which of the following best describes the approach of the passage?

a. matter-of-fact narration

b. historical analysis

c. sarcastic criticism

d. playful reporting

e. impassioned argument

Questions 53–59 are based on the following passage.

This passage explores the theory that the first three years of life are critical in the development of a child's character and suggests a parenting model that strengthens moral behavior.

Line

Does a baby have a moral conscience? While a baby is not faced with many serious ethical dilemmas, his or her moral character is formed from the earliest stages of infancy. Recent research has shown that the type of parenting an infant receives has a dramatic impact on the child's moral development and, consequently, success later in life. The renowned childcare expert T. Berry Brazelton claims that he can observe a child

(5) of eight months and tell if that child will succeed or fail in life. This may be a harsh sentence for an eight-month-old baby, but it underscores the importance of educating parents in good child-rearing techniques and of intervening early in cases of child endangerment. But what are good parenting techniques?

The cornerstone of good parenting is love, and the building blocks are trust, acceptance, and discipline. The concept of "attachment parenting" has come to dominate early childhood research. It is the

(10) relatively simple idea that an infant who is firmly attached to his or her "primary caregiver"—often, but not always, the mother—develops into a secure and confident child. Caregivers who respond promptly and affectionately to their infants' needs—to eat, to play, to be held, to sleep, and to be left alone—form

secure attachments with their children. A study conducted with rhesus monkeys showed that infant monkeys preferred mothers who gave comfort and contact but no food to mothers who gave food but (15) no comfort and contact. This study indicates that among primates love and nurturing are even more important than food.

Fortunately, loving their infants comes naturally to most parents, and the first requisite for good parenting is one that is easily met. The second component—setting limits and teaching self-discipline—can be more complicated. Many parents struggle to find a balance between responding promptly to their (20) babies' needs and "spoiling" their child. Norton Garfinkle, chair of the Executive Committee of the Lamaze Institute for Family Education, has identified four parenting styles: warm and restrictive, warm and permissive, cold and restrictive, and cold and permissive. A warm parent is one who exhibits love and affection; a cold parent withholds love. A restrictive parent sets limits on her child's behavior. A permissive parent does not restrict her child. Garfinkle finds that the children of warm-restrictive parents (25) exhibit self-confidence and self-control; the children of warm-permissive parents are self-assured but have difficulty following rules; children of cold-restrictive parents tend to be angry and sullenly compliant, and the most troubled children are those of cold-permissive parents. These children are hostile and defiant.

The warm-restrictive style of parenting helps develop the two key dimensions of moral character: (30) empathy and self-discipline. A warm attachment with his or her parent helps the child develop empathetic feelings about other human beings, while parental limit-setting teaches the child self-discipline and the ability to defer gratification. The ability to defer gratification is an essential skill for negotiating the adult world. A study conducted by Daniel Goleman, author of *Emotional Intelligence*, tested a group of four-year-olds' ability to defer gratification. Each child in the study was offered a marshmallow. The child could (35) choose to eat the marshmallow right away or wait 15 minutes to eat the marshmallow and receive another marshmallow as a reward for waiting. Researchers followed the children and found that by high school those children who ate their marshmallow right away were more likely to be lonely, more prone to stress, and more easily frustrated. Conversely, the children who demonstrated self-control were outgoing, confident, and dependable.

(40) This research seems to answer the old adage "You can't spoil a baby." It seems that a baby who is fed at the first sign of hunger and picked up on demand can perhaps be "spoiled." Most parents, however, tend to balance their baby's needs with their own. Many parents will teach their baby to sleep through the night by not picking up the baby when she awakes in the middle of the night. Although it can be heart wrenching for these parents to ignore their baby's cries, they are teaching their baby to fall asleep on her own and (45) getting the benefit of a full night's sleep.

While many parents will come to good parenting techniques instinctually and through various community supports, others parents are not equipped for the trials of raising a baby. Are these babies doomed to lives of frustration, poor impulse control, and anti-social behavior? Certainly not. Remedial actions—such as providing enrichment programs at day-care centers and educating parents—can be taken to reverse (50) the effects of bad parenting. However, the research indicates that the sooner these remedies are put into action the better.

53. The primary purpose of the passage is to
   a. advocate for the ability to defer gratification.
   b. educate readers about moral development in infants.
   c. chastise parents for spoiling their children.
   d. inform readers of remedies for bad parenting.
   e. demonstrate the importance of love in child rearing.

54. In line 5, the word *sentence* most nearly means
   a. statement.
   b. pronouncement.
   c. declaration.
   d. judgment.
   e. punishment.

55. The author presents the study about rhesus monkeys (lines 13–16) to
   a. prove that humans and monkeys have a lot in common.
   b. suggest that food is used as a substitute for love.
   c. support her assertion that love is the most important aspect of good parenting.
   d. disprove the idea that you can't spoil a baby.
   e. broaden the scope of her argument to include all primates.

56. According to the third paragraph of the passage, a cold-restrictive parent can best be characterized as
   a. an aloof disciplinarian.
   b. an angry autocrat.
   c. a frustrated teacher.
   d. a sullen despot.
   e. an unhappy dictator.

57. Based on the information in the fourth paragraph, one can infer that children who are unable to defer gratification are most unlikely to succeed because
   a. they are unpopular.
   b. they lack empathy.
   c. their parents neglected them.
   d. they are unable to follow directions.
   e. they lack self-discipline.

58. Which of the following techniques is used in lines 46–51?
   a. explanation of terms
   b. comparison of different arguments
   c. contrast of opposing views
   d. generalized statement
   e. illustration by example

59. The author of this passage would be most likely to agree with which statement?
   a. Babies of cold-permissive parents are doomed to lives of failure.
   b. Good parenting is the product of education.
   c. Instincts are a good guide for most parents.
   d. Conventional wisdom is usually wrong.
   e. Parents should strive to raise self-sufficient babies.

Questions 60–67 are based on the following passage.

In this excerpt from John Steinbeck's 1936 novel In Dubious Battle, *Mac and Doc Burton discuss "the cause" that leads hundreds of migratory farm workers to unite and strike against landowners.*

Lines

Mac spoke softly, for the night seemed to be listening. "You're a mystery to me, too, Doc."

"Me? A mystery?"

"Yes, you. You're not a Party man, but you work with us all the time; you never get anything for it. I don't know whether you believe in what we're doing or not, you never say, you just work. I've been out
(5)   with you before, and I'm not sure you believe in the cause at all."

Dr. Burton laughed softly. "It would be hard to say. I could tell you some of the things I think; you might not like them. I'm pretty sure you won't like them."

"Well, let's hear them anyway."

"Well, you say I don't believe in the cause. That's not like not believing in the moon. There've been
(10) communes before, and there will be again. But you people have an idea that if you can establish the thing, the job'll be done. Nothing stops, Mac. If you were able to put an idea into effect tomorrow, it would start changing right away. Establish a commune, and the same gradual flux will continue."

"Then you don't think the cause is good?"

Burton sighed. "You see? We're going to pile up on that old rock again. That's why I don't like to talk
(15) very often. Listen to me, Mac. My senses aren't above reproach, but they're all I have. I want to see the whole picture—as nearly as I can. I don't want to put on the blinders of 'good' and 'bad,' and limit my vision. If I used the term 'good' on a thing I'd lose my license to inspect it, because there might be bad in it. Don't you see? I want to be able to look at the whole thing."

Mac broke in heatedly, "How about social injustice? The profit system? You have to say they're bad."
(20) Dr. Burton threw back his head and looked at the sky. "Mac," he said. "Look at the physiological injustice, the injustice of tetanus [. . .], the gangster methods of amoebic dysentery—that's my field."

"Revolution and communism will cure social injustice."

"Yes, and disinfection and prophylaxis will prevent others."

"It's different, though; men are doing one, and germs are doing the other."
(25) "I can't see much difference, Mac."

[. . .] "Why do you hang around with us if you aren't for us?"

"I want to see," Burton said. "When you cut your finger, and streptococci get in the wound, there's a swelling and a soreness. That swelling is the fight your body puts up, the pain is the battle. You can't tell which one is going to win, but the wound is the first battleground. If the cells lose the first fight the strep-
(30) tococci invade, and the fight goes on up the arm. Mac, these little strikes are like the infection. Something has got into the men; a little fever has started and the lymphatic glands are shooting in the reinforcements. I want to see, so I go to the seat of the wound."

"You figure the strike is a wound?"

"Yes. Group-men are always getting some kind of infection. This seems to be a bad one. I want to
(35) see, Mac. I want to watch these group-men, for they seem to me to be a new individual, not at all like

single men. A man in a group isn't himself at all, he's a cell in an organism that isn't like him any more than the cells in your body are like you. I want to watch the group, and see what it's like. People have said, 'mobs are crazy, you can't tell what they'll do.' Why don't people look at mobs not as men, but as mobs? A mob nearly always seems to act reasonably, for a mob."

(40)   "Well, what's this got to do with the cause?"

      "It might be like this, Mac: When group-man wants to move, he makes a standard. 'God wills that we recapture the Holy Land'; or he says, 'We fight to make the world safe for democracy'; or he says, 'We will wipe out social injustice with communism.' But the group doesn't care about the Holy Land, or Democracy, or Communism. Maybe the group simply wants to move, to fight, and uses these words simply to reassure

(45)   the brains of individual men. I say it might be like that, Mac."

      "Not with the cause, it isn't," Mac cried.

60. In lines 9–12, Doc Burton argues that
  a. even if the cause succeeds, it won't change anything.
  b. the cause is unstoppable.
  c. the supporters of the cause should establish a commune.
  d. the cause itself is always changing.
  e. change can only come about gradually.

61. The cause the men refer to throughout the passage is
  a. democracy.
  b. communism.
  c. capitalism.
  d. insurgency.
  e. freedom.

62. Doc Burton is best described as
  a. an objective observer.
  b. a representative of the government.
  c. a staunch supporter of the cause.
  d. a visionary leader.
  e. a reluctant participant.

63. According to Doc Burton, the strikes are like the infection (line 30) because
  a. the strikes are life-threatening.
  b. many of the strikers are ill.
  c. the size of the group has swollen.
  d. the strikes are a reaction to an injury.
  e. the strikes are taking place on a battleground.

64. By comparing group-men to a living organism (lines 34–37), Doc Burton
  a. reinforces his idea that individuals are lost in the larger whole.
  b. shows that group-men are constantly changing and growing.
  c. supports his assertion that the strikers are like an infection.
  d. explains why he is with the strikers.
  e. reflects his opinion that the strikes' success depends upon unity within the group.

65. According to Doc Burton, the main difference between group-men and the individual is that
  a. individuals can be controlled but groups cannot.
  b. individuals do not want to fight but groups do.
  c. individuals may believe in a cause but groups do not.
  d. groups are often crazy but individuals are not.
  e. people in groups can reassure one another.

66. It can be inferred from this passage that Doc Burton believes the cause
- **a.** is just an excuse for fighting.
- **b.** is reasonable.
- **c.** will fail.
- **d.** will correct social injustice.
- **e.** will make America a more democratic place.

67. Doc Burton repeats the word *might* in lines 41 and 45 because
- **a.** he doesn't believe Mac is sincere about the cause.
- **b.** he really wants Mac to consider the possibility that the group is blind to the cause.
- **c.** he is asking a rhetorical question.
- **d.** he doesn't want Mac to know the truth about the cause.
- **e.** he wants Mac to see that he isn't really serious in his criticism of the cause.

Questions 68–76 are based on the following passage.

The following passage is an excerpt from Jack London's The Cruise of the Snark. *In this selection, London discusses his experience of learning to surf in Waikiki in the early 1900s.*

Line

A wave is a communicated agitation. The water that composes the body of a wave does not move. If it did, when a stone is thrown into a pond and the ripples spread away in an ever-widening circle, there would appear at the center an ever-increasing hole. No, the water that composes the body of a wave is stationary. Thus, you may watch a particular portion of the ocean's surface and you will see the same water rise

(5) and fall a thousand times to the agitation communicated by a thousand successive waves. Now imagine this communicated agitation moving shoreward. As the bottom shoals, the lower portion of the wave strikes land first and is stopped. But water is fluid, and the upper portion has not struck anything, wherefore it keeps on communicating its agitation, keeps on going. And when the top of the wave keeps on going, while the bottom of it lags behind, something is bound to happen. The bottom of the wave drops out from under

(10) and the top of the wave falls over, forward, and down, curling and cresting and roaring as it does so. It is the bottom of a wave striking against the top of the land that is the cause of all surfs.

But the transformation from a smooth undulation to a breaker is not abrupt except where the bottom shoals abruptly. Say the bottom shoals gradually from a quarter of a mile to a mile, then an equal distance will be occupied by the transformation. Such a bottom is that off the beach of Waikiki, and it produces

(15) a splendid, surf-riding surf. One leaps upon the back of a breaker just as it begins to break, and stays on it as it continues to break all the way in to shore.

And now to the particular physics of surf-riding. Get out on a flat board, six feet long, two feet wide, and roughly oval in shape. Lie down upon it like a small boy on a coaster and paddle with your hands out to deep water, where the waves begin to crest. Lie out there quietly on the board. Sea after sea breaks before,

(20) behind, and under and over you, and rushes in to shore, leaving you behind. When a wave crests, it gets steeper. Imagine yourself, on your board, on the face of that steep slope. If it stood still, you would slide down just as a boy slides down a hill on his coaster. "But," you object, "the wave doesn't stand still." Very true, but the water composing the wave stands still, and there you have the secret. If ever you start sliding down the face of that wave, you'll keep on sliding and you'll never reach the bottom. Please don't laugh.

(25)   The face of that wave may be only six feet, yet you can slide down it a quarter of a mile, or half a mile, and not reach the bottom. For, see, since a wave is only a communicated agitation or impetus, and since the water that composes a wave is changing every instant, new water is rising into the wave as fast as the wave travels. You slide down this new water, and yet remain in your old position on the wave, sliding down the still newer water that is rising and forming the wave. You slide precisely as fast as the wave travels. If it trav-

(30)   els 15 miles an hour, you slide 15 miles an hour. Between you and shore stretches a quarter of mile of water. As the wave travels, this water obligingly heaps itself into the wave, gravity does the rest, and down you go, sliding the whole length of it. If you still cherish the notion, while sliding, that the water is moving with you, thrust your arms into it and attempt to paddle; you will find that you have to be remarkably quick to get a stroke, for that water is dropping astern just as fast as you are rushing ahead.

68. The author compares surfing to
   a. an ever-increasing hole forming in the water.
   b. a chemistry experiment gone wrong.
   c. a boy sledding down a hill on a coaster.
   d. a transformation of time and space.
   e. flying through the air like a bird.

69. All of the following are true based on information from the passage EXCEPT
   a. When a wave crests, it gets steeper.
   b. If a wave is moving at eight miles per hour, so is the surfer on that wave.
   c. A wave is constantly recomposing itself with new water.
   d. A flat board is the most popular type of surfboard.
   e. The conditions at Waikiki are excellent for surfing.

70. According to the author, why is Waikiki ideal for surfing?
   a. The weather is great and the water is warm.
   b. The waves break abruptly as they approach the shore.
   c. The waves at Waikiki are a communicated agitation.
   d. Waikiki has some of the biggest waves in the world.
   e. The waves break gradually as they approach the shore.

71. The word *shoals* in line 6 refers to
   a. the sand kicked up as the waves break upon the beach.
   b. water becoming shallower as it approaches the shore.
   c. the steep cresting of a wave.
   d. the salty smell of the sea.
   e. water becoming deeper as you move away from the shore.

72. What part of a wave is responsible for the form-ing of surf?
   a. the upper portion of the wave
   b. the lower portion of the wave
   c. the strongest part of the wave
   d. the trailing portion of the wave
   e. the roaring part of the wave.

73. The word *impetus* in line 26 most nearly means
   a. a moving force.
   b. a serious obstacle.
   c. a slight annoyance.
   d. a slight hindrance.
   e. an area of very warm water.

74. The author's description of the transformation of a smooth undulating wave to a breaking wave (lines 8–11) indicates that
   a. the distance of a wave's break is dependent upon the bottom of the approaching the shoreline.
   b. it is rare for a wave to break gradually.
   c. it is common for a wave to break abruptly.
   d. the size of a wave has to do with its speed through the water.
   e. a wave travels only through deep water.

75. The sentence *A wave is a communicated agitation* (line 1) is best defined by which statement?
   a. The roar of a wave sounds angry when it breaks upon the shore.
   b. Waves are a display of the ocean's fury.
   c. A wave is a surging movement that travels through the water.
   d. The size of a wave can vary.
   e. The ocean has baffled sailors for centuries.

76. What is the secret referred to in line 23?
   a. Why a good wave for surfing must to be at least six feet tall
   b. A six-foot wave is between a quarter mile and a half mile in length.
   c. how a surfer can slide down a six-foot wave for a quarter of mile
   d. The smarter surfers paddle out to the deep water to catch the best waves.
   e. The water that composes a wave remains with the wave until it reaches the shore.

Questions 77–85 are based on the following passages.

In Passage 1, the author describes the life and influence of blues guitarist Robert Johnson. In Passage 2, the author provides a brief history of the blues.

Line

Passage 1
There is little information available about the legendary blues guitarist Robert Johnson, and the information that is available is as much rumor as fact. What is undisputable, however, is Johnson's impact on the world of rock and roll. Some consider Johnson to be the father of modern rock; his influence extends to artists from Muddy Waters to Led Zeppelin, from the Rolling Stones to the Allman Brothers Band. Eric Clapton,
(5)   arguably the greatest living rock guitarist, has said that "Robert Johnson to me is the most important blues musician who ever lived. [. . .] I have never found anything more deeply soulful than Robert Johnson."

While the impact of Johnson's music is evident, the genesis of his remarkable talent remains shrouded in mystery.

(10) For Johnson, born in 1911 in Hazelhurst, Mississippi, music was a means of escape from working in the cotton fields. As a boy he worked on the farm that belonged to Noel Johnson—the man rumored to be his father. He married young, at age 17, and lost his wife a year later in childbirth. That's when Johnson began traveling and playing the blues.

Initially, Johnson played the harmonica. Later, he began playing the guitar, but apparently, he was not very good. He wanted to learn, however, so he spent his time in blues bars watching the local blues
(15) legends Son House and Willie Brown. During their breaks, Johnson would go up on stage and play. House reportedly thought Johnson was so bad that he repeatedly told Johnson to get lost. Finally, one day, he did. For six months, Johnson mysteriously disappeared. No one knew what happened to him.

When Johnson returned half a year later, he was suddenly a first-rate guitarist. He began drawing crowds everywhere he played. Johnson never revealed where he had been and what he had done in those
(20) six months that he was gone. People had difficulty understanding how he had become so good in such a short time. Was it genius? Magic? Soon, rumors began circulating that he had made a deal with the devil. Legend has it that Johnson met the devil at midnight at a crossroads and sold his soul to the devil so he could play guitar.

Johnson recorded only 29 songs before his death in 1938, purportedly at the hands of a jealous hus-
(25) band. He was only 27 years old, yet he left an indelible mark on the music world. There are countless versions of "Walkin' Blues," and his song "Cross Road Blues" (later retitled "Crossroads") has been recorded by dozens of artists, with Cream's 1969 version of "Crossroads" being perhaps the best-known Johnson remake. Again and again, contemporary artists return to Johnson, whose songs capture the very essence of the blues, transforming our pain and suffering with the healing magic of his guitar.

Passage 2
(30) There are more than 50 types of blues music, from the famous Chicago and Memphis blues to the less familiar Juke Joint and Acoustic Country blues. This rich variety comes as no surprise to those who recognize the blues as a fundamental American art form. Indeed, in its resolution to name 2003 the Year of the Blues, Congress declared that the blues is "the most influential form of American roots music." In fact, the two most popular American musical forms—rock and roll and jazz—owe their genesis in large part (some
(35) would argue entirely) to the blues.

The blues—a neologism attributed to the American writer Washington Irving (author of "The Legend of Sleepy Hollow") in 1807—evolved from black American folk music. Its beginnings can be traced to songs sung in the fields and around slave quarters on southern plantations, songs of pain and suffering, of injustice, of longing for a better life. A fundamental principle of the blues, however, is that the music
(40) be cathartic. Listening to the blues will drive the blues away; it is music that has the power to overcome sadness. Thus, "the blues" is something of a misnomer, for the music is moving but not melancholy; it is, in fact, music born of hope, not despair.

The blues began to take shape as a musical movement in the years after emancipation, around the turn of the century when blacks were technically free but still suffered from social and economic discrim-
(45) ination. Its poetic and musical forms were popularized by W.C. Handy just after the turn of the century.

Handy, a classical guitarist who reportedly heard the blues for the first time in a Mississippi train station, was the first to compose and distribute "blues" music officially throughout the United States, although its popularity was chiefly among blacks in the South. The movement coalesced in the late 1920s and indeed became a national craze with records by blues singers such as Bessie Smith selling millions.

(50)   The 1930s and 1940s saw a continued growth in the popularity of the blues as many blacks migrated north and as the blues and jazz forms continued to develop, diversify, and influence each other. It was at this time that Son House, Willie Brown, and Robert Johnson played, while the next decade saw the emergence of the blues greats Muddy Waters, Willie Dixon, and Johnny Lee Hooker.

After rock and roll exploded on the music scene in the 1950s, many rock artists began covering blues
(55)   songs, thus bringing the blues to a young white audience and giving it true national and international exposure. In the early 1960s, the Rolling Stones, Yardbirds, Cream, and others remade blues songs such as Robert Johnson's "Crossroads" and Big Joe Williams' "Baby Please Don't Go" to wide popularity. People all across America—black and white, young and old, listened to songs with lyrics that were intensely honest and personal, songs that told about any number of things that give us the blues: loneliness, betrayal, unrequited
(60)   love, a run of bad luck, being out of work or away from home or broke or broken-hearted. It was a music perfectly suited for a nation on the brink of the Civil Rights movement—a kind of music that had the power to cross boundaries, to heal wounds, and to offer hope to a new generation of Americans.

77. In Passage 1, the author's main goal is to
  a. solve the mystery of the genesis of Johnson's talent.
  b. provide a detailed description of Johnson's music and style.
  c. provide a brief overview of Johnson's life and influence.
  d. prove that Johnson should be recognized as the greatest blues musician who ever lived.
  e. explain how Johnson's music impacted the world of rock and roll.

78. The information provided in the passage suggests that Johnson
  a. really did make a deal with the devil.
  b. was determined to become a great guitarist, whatever the cost.
  c. wasn't as talented as we have been led to believe.
  d. disappeared because he had a breakdown.
  e. owed his success to Son House and Willie Brown.

79. The word *neologism* in Passage 2, line 36 means
  a. a new word or use of a word.
  b. a grassroots musical form.
  c. a fictional character or fictitious setting.
  d. the origin or source of something.
  e. the evolution of a person, place, or thing.

80. In Passage 2, the sentence *People all across America—black and white, young and old, listened to songs with lyrics that were intensely honest and personal, songs that told about any number of things that give us the blues: loneliness, betrayal, unrequited love, a run of bad luck, being out of work or away from home or broke or broken-hearted* (lines 57–60), the author is
  a. defining blues music.
  b. identifying the origin of the blues.
  c. describing the lyrics of a famous blues song.
  d. explaining why blues remakes were so popular.
  e. making a connection between the blues and the Civil Rights movement.

81. In the last paragraph of Passage 2 (lines 54–62), the author suggests that
   a. the blues should be recognized as a more important and complex musical form than rock and roll.
   b. the golden age of rock and roll owes much to the popularity of blues cover songs.
   c. music has always been a means for people to deal with intense emotions and difficulties.
   d. a shared interest in the blues may have helped blacks and whites better understand each other and ease racial tensions.
   e. the rock and roll versions of blues songs were better than the originals.

82. Both authors would agree on all of the following points EXCEPT
   a. listening to the blues is cathartic.
   b. Robert Johnson is the best blues guitarist from the 1930s and 1940s.
   c. the blues are an important part of American history.
   d. "Crossroads" is one of the most well-known blues songs.
   e. blues music is deeply emotional.

83. The passages differ in tone and style in that
   a. Passage 1 is intended for a general audience while Passage 2 is intended for readers with a musical background.
   b. Passage 1 is far more argumentative than Passage 2.
   c. Passage 1 is often speculative while Passage 2 is factual and assertive.
   d. Passage 1 is more formal than Passage 2, which is quite casual.
   e. Passage 1 is straight-forward while Passage 2 often digresses from the main point.

84. Which of the following best describes the relationship between these two passages?
   a. specific : general
   b. argument : support
   c. fiction : nonfiction
   d. first : second
   e. cause : effect

85. Which of the following sentences from Passage 2 could most effectively be added to Passage 1?
   a. *In fact, the two most popular American musical forms—rock and roll and jazz—owe their genesis in large part (some would argue entirely) to the blues.* (lines 33–35)
   b. *A fundamental principle of the blues, however, is that the music be cathartic.* (lines 39–40)
   c. *Thus, "the blues" is something of a misnomer, for the music is moving but not melancholy; it is, in fact, music born of hope, not despair.* (lines 41–42)
   d. *It was at this time that Son House, Willie Brown, and Robert Johnson played, while the next decade saw the emergence of the blues greats Muddy Waters, Willie Dixon, and Johnny Lee Hooker.* (lines 51–53)
   e. *After rock and roll exploded on the music scene in the 1950s, many rock artists began covering blues songs, thus bringing the blues to a young white audience and giving it true national and international exposure.* (lines 54–56)

Questions 86–93 are based on the following passage.

The following passage explores the role of Chinese Americans in the nineteenth-century westward expansion of the United States, specifically their influence on the development of California.

Line

While the Chinese, in particular those working as sailors, knew the west coast of North America before the Gold Rush, our story begins in 1850, as the documentation from the Gold Rush provides the starting point with which to build a more substantial narrative. Most Chinese immigrants entered California through the port of San Francisco. From San Francisco and other ports, many sought their fortunes in other parts of Cal-

(5)   ifornia. The Chinese comprised a part of the diverse gathering of peoples from throughout the world who contributed to the economic and population explosion that characterized the early history of the state of California. The Chinese who emigrated to the United States at this time were part of a larger exodus from southeast China searching for better economic opportunities and fleeing a situation of political corruption and decline. Most immigrants came from the Pearl River Delta in Guangdong (Canton) Province.

(10)   Chinese immigrants proved to be productive and resourceful contributors to a multitude of industries and businesses. The initial group of Chinese argonauts sought their livelihood in the gold mines, calling California Gam Saan, Gold Mountain. For the mining industry, they built many of the flumes and roads, allowing for easier access and processing of the minerals being extracted. Chinese immigrants faced discrimination immediately upon arrival in California. In mining, they were forced to work older claims

(15)   or to work for others. In the 1850s, the U.S. Constitution reserved the right of naturalization for white immigrants to this country. Thus, Chinese immigrants lived at the whim of local governments with some allowed to become naturalized citizens, but most not. Without this right, it was difficult to pursue livelihoods. For example, Chinese immigrants were unable to own land or file mining claims. Also in the 1850s, the California legislature passed a law taxing all foreign miners. Although stated in general terms, it was

(20)   enforced chiefly against the Mexicans and the Chinese through 1870. This discrimination occurred in spite of the fact that the Chinese often contributed the crucial labor necessary to the mining enterprise.

Discriminatory legislation forced many Chinese out of the gold fields and into low-paying, menial, and often arduous jobs. In many cases, they took on the most dangerous and least desirable components of work available. They worked on reclaiming marshes in the Central Valley so that the land could

(25)   become agriculturally productive. They built the stone bridges and fences, constructed roads, and excavated storage areas for the wine industry in Napa and Sonoma counties. The most impressive construction feat of Chinese Americans was their work on the western section of the transcontinental railroad. Chinese American workers laid much of the tracks for the Central Pacific Railroad through the foothills and over the high Sierra Nevada, much of which involved hazardous work with explosives to tunnel

(30)   through the hills. Their speed, dexterity, and outright perseverance, often in brutally cold temperatures and heavy snow through two record breaking winters, is a testimony to their outstanding achievements and contributions to opening up the West.

86. The first paragraph (lines 1–9) of the passage serves what function in the development of the passage?
 a. provides an expert's opinion to support the author's thesis
 b. introduces the topic by describing general patterns
 c. compares common myths with historical facts
 d. draws a conclusion about the impact of Chinese immigration on the state of California
 e. condemns outdated concepts

87. Which of the following best describes the approach of the passage?
 a. theoretical analysis
 b. historical overview
 c. dramatic narrative
 d. personal assessment
 e. description through metaphor

88. Lines 10–13 portray Chinese immigrants as
 a. fortuitous.
 b. prideful.
 c. vigorous.
 d. effusive.
 e. revolutionary.

89. The author cites the U.S. Constitution (lines 15–16) in order to
 a. praise the liberties afforded by the Bill of Rights.
 b. show that the government valued the contributions of its immigrants.
 c. imply that all American citizens are equal under the law.
 d. emphasize the importance of a system of checks and balances.
 e. suggest that it did not protect Chinese immigrants from discrimination.

90. The word *enterprise* as it is used in line 21 most nearly means
 a. organization.
 b. corporation.
 c. industry.
 d. partnership.
 e. occupation.

91. According to the passage, which of the following is NOT a contribution made by Chinese immigrants?
 a. worked the land so that it would yield more crops
 b. performed dangerous work with explosives
 c. built roads and bridges
 d. purchased older mining claims and mined them
 e. dug storage areas for California wine

92. In line 24, *reclaiming* most nearly means
 a. redeeming.
 b. protesting.
 c. objecting.
 d. approving.
 e. extolling.

93. The last sentence (lines 30–32) in the passage provides
 a. an example supporting the thesis of the passage.
 b. a comparison with other historical viewpoints.
 c. a theory explaining historical events.
 d. a summary of the passage.
 e. an argument refuting the position taken earlier in the passage.

Questions 94–101 are based on the following passage.

Written by John Henry Newman in 1852, the following passage presents Newman's idea of the purpose and benefits of a university education.

Line

I have said that all branches of knowledge are connected together, because the subject-matter of knowledge is intimately united in itself [. . .]. Hence it is that the Sciences, into which our knowledge may be said to be cast, have multiple bearings on one another, and an internal sympathy, and admit, or rather demand, comparison and adjustment. They complete, correct, and balance each other. This consideration,

(5) if well-founded, must be taken into account, not only as regards the attainment of truth, which is their common end, but as regards the influence which they excise upon those whose education consists in the study of them. I have already said, that to give undue prominence to one is to be unjust to another; to neglect or supersede these is to divert those from their proper object. It is to unsettle the boundary lines between science and science, to disturb their action, to destroy the harmony which binds them together. Such a pro-

(10) ceeding will have a corresponding effect when introduced into a place of education. There is no science but tells a different tale, when viewed as a portion of a whole, from what it is likely to suggest when taken by itself, without the safeguard, as I may call it, of others.

Let me make use of an illustration. In the combination of colors, very different effects are produced by a difference in their selection and juxtaposition; red, green, and white, change their shades, according

(15) to the contrast to which they are submitted. And, in like manner, the drift and meaning of a branch of knowledge varies with the company in which it is introduced to the student. If his reading is confined simply to one subject, however such division of labor may favor the advancement of a particular pursuit, a point into which I do not here enter, certainly it has a tendency to contract his mind. If it is incorporated with others, it depends on those others as to the kind of influence that it exerts upon him. Thus the Classics, which

(20) in England are the means of refining the taste, have in France subserved the spread of revolutionary and deistical doctrines. [. . .] In a like manner, I suppose, Arcesilas would not have handled logic as Aristotle, nor Aristotle have criticized poets as Plato; yet reasoning and poetry are subject to scientific rules.

It is a great point then to enlarge the range of studies which a University professes, even for the sake of the students; and, though they cannot pursue every subject which is open to them, they will be the gain-

(25) ers by living among those and under those who represent the whole circle. This I conceive to be the advantage of a seat of universal learning, considered as a place of education. An assemblage of learned men, zealous for their own sciences, and rivals of each other, are brought, by familiar intercourse and for the sake of intellectual peace, to adjust together the claims and relations of their respective subjects of investigation. They learn to respect, to consult, to aid each other. Thus is created a pure and clear atmosphere of thought, which

(30) the student also breathes, though in his own case he only pursues a few sciences out of the multitude. He profits by an intellectual tradition, which is independent of particular teachers, which guides him in his choice of subjects, and duly interprets for him those which he chooses. He apprehends the great outlines of knowledge, the principles on which it rests, the scale of its parts, its lights and its shades, its great points and its little, as he otherwise cannot apprehend them. Hence it is that his education is called "Liberal." A

(35) habit of mind is formed which lasts through life, of which the attributes are, freedom, equitableness,

calmness, moderation, and wisdom; or what in a former discourse I have ventured to call a philosophical habit. This then I would assign as the special fruit of the education furnished at a University, as contrasted with other places of teaching or modes of teaching. This is the main purpose of a University in its treatment of its students.

94. The main idea of the first paragraph (lines 1–12) is that
   a. each science should be studied independently.
   b. the sciences are interrelated.
   c. the boundary lines between each of the sciences should be clearer.
   d. some sciences are unduly given more emphasis than others at the university level.
   e. it is difficult to attain a proper balance among the sciences.

95. By the word *Sciences* (line 2), the author means
   a. the physical sciences only.
   b. the social sciences only.
   c. the physical and social sciences.
   d. all branches of knowledge, including the physical and social sciences and the humanities.
   e. educational methodologies.

96. The word *excise* in line 6 most nearly means
   a. remove.
   b. cut.
   c. impose.
   d. arrange.
   e. compete.

97. By using the word *safeguard* in line 12, the author suggests that
   a. it is dangerous to limit one's education to one field or area of specialization.
   b. it is not safe to study the sciences.
   c. the more one knows, the safer one will feel.
   d. one should choose a second area of specialization as a backup in case the first does not work out.
   e. each science has its own specific safety guidelines.

98. The purpose of the second paragraph (lines 13–22) is to
   a. introduce a new idea.
   b. develop the idea presented in the previous paragraph.
   c. state the main idea of the passage.
   d. present an alternative point of view.
   e. compare and contrast different branches of knowledge.

99. The word *apprehends* as used in lines 32 and 34 means
   a. understands.
   b. captures.
   c. fears.
   d. believes.
   e. contains.

100. Which of the following best describes the author's idea of a liberal education?
  a. in-depth specialization in one area
  b. free education for all
  c. a broad scope of knowledge in several disciplines
  d. training for a scientific career
  e. an emphasis on the arts rather than the sciences

101. The author believes that a university should
  I. have faculty representing a wide range of subjects and philosophies
  II. teach students how to see the relationships among ideas
  III. teach students to understand and respect other points of view
  IV. teach students liberal rather than conservative ideals
  a. I and II only
  b. I, II, and III
  c. I and IV
  d. IV only
  e. all of the above

Questions 102–108 are based on the following passage.

The following passage discusses the unique musical traditions that developed along the Rio Grande in colonial New Mexico.

Line

From 1598 to 1821, the area along the Rio Grande that is now the state of New Mexico formed the northernmost border of the Spanish colonies in the New World. The colonists lived on a geographic frontier surrounded by deserts and mountains. This remote colony with its harsh climate was far removed from the cultural centers of the Spanish Empire in the New World, and music was a necessary part of social life.
(5) The isolated nature of the region and needs of the community gave rise to a unique, rich musical tradition that included colorful ballads, popular dances, and some of the most extraordinary ceremonial music in the Hispanic world.

The popular music along the Rio Grande, especially the heroic and romantic ballads, reflected the stark and rough nature of the region. Unlike the refined music found in Mexico, the music of the Rio Grande
(10) had a rough-cut "frontier" quality. The music also reflected the mixing of cultures that characterized the border colony. The close military and cultural ties between the Spanish and the native Pueblos of the region led to a uniquely New Mexican fusion of traditions. Much of the music borrowed from both European and native cultures. This mixing of traditions was especially evident in the dances.

The *bailes*, or village dances—instrumental music played on violin and guitar—were a lively focus
(15) of frontier life. Some *bailes* were derived from traditional European waltzes, but then adapted to the singular style of the region. The *bailes* had an unusual melodic structure, and the players had unique methods of bowing and tuning their instruments. Other *bailes*, such as *indita* (little Indian girl) and *vaquero* (cowboy), were found only in New Mexico. The rhythms and melodies of the *indita* had definite Puebloan influences. Its themes, which ranged from love to tragedy, almost always featured dramatic

(20)   interactions between Spanish and Native Americans. Similarly, the *Matachines* dance drama was an alle-
gorical representation of the meeting of European and Native American cultures. Its European melodies,
played on violin and guitar, were coupled with the use of insistent repetition, which came from the Native
American tradition.

(25)   In addition to the *bailes*, waltzes—the Waltz of the Days and the Waltz of the Immanuels—were also
performed to celebrate New Year's Eve and New Year's Day. Groups of revelers went singing from house
to house throughout the night to bring in the New Year. In New Mexico, January 1 is the Feast of
Immanuel, so the singers visited the houses of people named Manuel or Manuela. Many songs were sung
on these visits but especially popular were the *coplas*, or improvised couplets, composed on the spot to
honor or poke fun of the person being visited.

(30)   Like in the New Year's celebration, music was central to many social rituals in colonial New Mexico.
In the Rio Grande region, weddings were performed in song in a folk ceremony called "The Delivery of
the Newlyweds." The community would gather to sanction the new couple and "deliver" them in song to
each other and to their respective families. The verses of the song, played to a lively waltz, were improvised
but followed a familiar pattern. The first verses spoke about marriage in general. These were followed by
(35)   serious and humorous verses offering practical advice to the couple. Then all the guests filed past to bless
the couple, and concluding verses were sung to honor specific individuals such as the best man. At the wedding dance, *la marcha* was performed. In this triumphal march, couples formed into single files of men
and women. After dancing in concentric circles, the men and women lined up opposite one another with
their hands joined overhead to form a tunnel of love from which the new couple was the last to emerge.

(40)   By the turn of the twentieth century, styles were evolving and musical forms popular in previous eras
were giving way to new tastes. The ancient romance ballads were replaced by newer forms that featured
more local and contemporary events. The extraordinary *indita* was no longer performed, and the *canción*,
or popular song, had begun its rise. However, many of the wedding traditions of the colonial era are still
in practice today. The music that was so central to life in the remote colony of New Mexico has much to
(45)   teach us about the unique and vibrant culture that once flourished there.

102. The primary purpose of the first paragraph is to
   a. describe the geography of New Mexico.
   b. instruct readers about the history of the
       Spanish colonies along the Rio Grande.
   c. introduce readers to the unique culture and
       musical traditions along the Rio Grande.
   d. list the types of music that were prevalent in
       colonial New Mexico.
   e. explain the unique musical traditions of the
       New Mexican colonies.

103. In lines 15–16, the word *singular* most nearly
   means
   a. strange.
   b. monotone.
   c. separate.
   d. unusual.
   e. superior.

104. According to the passage, the musical tradition found in New Mexico was the result of all the following EXCEPT
   a. distance from cultural centers.
   b. the blending of cultures.
   c. the geography of the region.
   d. the imposition of European culture on native traditions.
   e. unique ways of playing instruments.

105. The New Year's celebration and wedding ceremony described in the passage share in common
   a. offering of practical advice.
   b. use of a lively march.
   c. use of improvised verses.
   d. visiting of houses.
   e. singing and dancing.

106. According to the passage, the main purpose of "The Delivery of the Newlyweds" was to
   a. sanction and bless the new couple.
   b. form a tunnel of love.
   c. marry couples who did not want a church wedding.
   d. offer advice to the new couple.
   e. sing improvised songs to newlyweds.

107. Which of the titles provided below is most appropriate for this passage?
   a. Wedding Marches and New Year's Waltzes of the Rio Grande
   b. The Fading Era of Colonial Music in New Mexico
   c. Cowboy Songs of the Past
   d. Between Deserts and Mountains New Mexico Sings a Unique Song
   e. The Extraordinary Popular and Ceremonial Music of the Rio Grande

108. The author's attitude toward the music of colonial New Mexico can best be described as
   a. bemusement.
   b. admiration.
   c. alienation.
   d. condescension.
   e. awe.

Questions 109–118 are based on the following passage.

In 1804, President Thomas Jefferson sent Army Officers Meriwether Lewis and William Clark on an expedition to explore the territory of the Louisiana Purchase and beyond and to look for a waterway that would connect the Atlantic and Pacific oceans. This passage describes the collision of cultures that occurred between Native Americans and the representatives of the U.S. government.

Line

When Thomas Jefferson sent Lewis and Clark into the West, he patterned their mission on the methods of Enlightenment science: to observe, collect, document, and classify. Such strategies were already in place for the epic voyages made by explorers like Cook and Vancouver. Like their contemporaries, Lewis and Clark were more than representatives of European rationalism. They also represented a rising American
(5)   empire, one built on aggressive territorial expansion and commercial gain.

But there was another view of the West: that of the native inhabitants of the land. Their understandings of landscapes, peoples, and resources formed both a contrast and counterpoint to those of Jefferson's travelers. One of Lewis and Clark's missions was to open diplomatic relations between the United States and the Native American nations of the West. As Jefferson told Lewis, "It will now be proper you should inform

(10) those through whose country you will pass . . . that henceforth we become their fathers and friends." When Euro-Americans and Native Americans met, they used ancient diplomatic protocols that included formal language, ceremonial gifts, and displays of military power. But behind these symbols and rituals, there were often very different ways of understanding power and authority. Such differences sometimes made communication across the cultural divide difficult and open to confusion and misunderstanding.

(15) An important organizing principle in Euro-American society was hierarchy. Both soldiers and civilians had complex gradations of rank to define who gave orders and who obeyed. While kinship was important in the Euro-American world, it was even more fundamental in tribal societies. Everyone's power and place depended on a complex network of real and symbolic relationships. When the two groups met—whether for trade or diplomacy—each tried to reshape the other in their own image. Lewis and Clark

(20) sought to impose their own notions of hierarchy on Native Americans by "making chiefs" with medals, printed certificates, and gifts. Native people tried to impose the obligations of kinship on the visitors by means of adoption ceremonies, shared names, and ritual gifts.

The American republic began to issue peace medals during the first Washington administration, continuing a tradition established by the European nations. Lewis and Clark brought at least 89 medals in five

(25) sizes in order to designate five "ranks" of chief. In the eyes of Americans, Native Americans who accepted such medals were also acknowledging American sovereignty as "children" of a new "great father." And in a moment of imperial bravado, Lewis hung a peace medal around the neck of a Piegan Blackfeet warrior killed by the expedition in late July 1806. As Lewis later explained, he used a peace medal as a way to let the Blackfeet know "who we were."

(30) In tribal society, kinship was like a legal system—people depended on relatives to protect them from crime, war, and misfortune. People with no kin were outside of society and its rules. To adopt Lewis and Clark into tribal society, the Plains Indians used a pipe ceremony. The ritual of smoking and sharing the pipe was at the heart of much Native American diplomacy. With the pipe the captains accepted sacred obligations to share wealth, aid in war, and revenge injustice. At the end of the ceremony, the pipe was pre-

(35) sented to them so they would never forget their obligations.

Gift giving was an essential part of diplomacy. To Native Americans, gifts proved the giver's sincerity and honored the tribe. To Lewis and Clark, some gifts advertised the technological superiority and others encouraged the Native Americans to adopt an agrarian lifestyle. Like salesmen handing out free samples, Lewis and Clark packed bales of manufactured goods to open diplomatic relations with Native

(40) American tribes. Jefferson advised Lewis to give out corn mills to introduce the Native Americans to mechanized agriculture as part of his plan to "civilize and instruct" them. Clark believed the mills were "verry Thankfully recived [sic]," but by the next year, the Mandan people had demolished theirs to use the metal for weapons.

109. The goals of the Lewis and Clark expedition include all of the following purposes EXCEPT to
   a. expand scientific knowledge.
   b. strengthen American claims to Western territory.
   c. overcome Native American resistance with military force.
   d. introduce native inhabitants to the ways of Euro-American culture.
   e. make peaceful contact with native inhabitants.

110. According to the passage, the U.S. government primarily viewed its role in relation to Native Americans as one of
   a. creator.
   b. master.
   c. admirer.
   d. collaborator.
   e. agitator.

111. The word *protocols* as it is used in line 11 most nearly means
   a. beliefs.
   b. tenets.
   c. codes.
   d. tactics.
   e. endeavors.

112. According to the passage, the distribution of peace medals exemplifies
   a. the American republic's attempt to forge a relationship of equals with native people.
   b. a cultural bridge connecting the Euro-Americans with Native American tribes.
   c. the explorers' respect for Native American sovereignty.
   d. the imposition of societal hierarchy on Native Americans.
   e. the acknowledgment of the power and authority of Native American chiefs.

113. The description of Lewis's actions in lines 26–29 is used to
   a. depict the expedition in a patriotic light.
   b. contradict commonly held views of imperialism.
   c. make an ironic statement about the meaning of the peace medals.
   d. give an explanation for the killing of a Piegan Blackfeet warrior.
   e. provide a balanced report of two opposing points of view.

114. The description of the pipe ceremony in lines 26–29 is used to illustrate
   a. the naiveté of the Plains Native Americans.
   b. cultural confusion.
   c. the superiority of the native inhabitants.
   d. how Plains Native Americans honored low-ranking members of society.
   e. the addictive properties of tobacco.

115. In line 38, *adopt* most nearly means
   a. advocate.
   b. nurture.
   c. promote.
   d. foster.
   e. practice.

116. The author uses the image of salesmen handing out free samples (lines 38–40) in order to
   a. depict Lewis and Clark as entrepreneurs.
   b. illustrate the generosity Lewis and Clark showed the tribal people they met.
   c. suggest that Lewis and Clark hoped to personally profit from their travels.
   d. imply that everyone likes to get something for free.
   e. show the promotional intent behind the explorers' gift giving.

117. The passage is developed primarily through
   a. the contrast of different abstract principles.
   b. quotations from one specific text.
   c. the analysis of one extended example.
   d. first-person narratives.
   e. recurring symbols.

118. The author's primary purpose in the passage is to
   a. describe Lewis and Clark's expedition into the West.
   b. show the clashing views of the Indian nations versus those of the American republic.
   c. explore the tribal system of kinship.
   d. make an argument supporting Jefferson's quest for scientific knowledge.
   e. criticize Lewis and Clark's use of peace medals to designate the rank of a chief.

Questions 119–129 are based on the following passages.

The following passages detail two very different perspectives of life aboard a ship in the age of sailing. The first passage describes an English pleasure yacht in the early 1800s. The second passage recounts a young boy's impressions of the first time he set sail in a merchant vessel.

Line

Passage 1

Reader, have you ever been at Plymouth? If you have, your eye must have dwelt with ecstasy upon the beautiful property of the Earl of Mount Edgcumbe: If you have not been at Plymouth, the sooner that you go there the better. You will see ships building and ships in ordinary; and ships repairing and ships fitting; and hulks and convict ships, and the guard-ship; ships ready to sail and ships under sail; besides lighters,

(5)   men-of-war's boats, dockyard-boats, bum-boats, and shore-boats. In short, there is a great deal to see at Plymouth besides the sea itself: but what I particularly wish now is, that you will stand at the battery of Mount Edgcumbe and look into Barn Pool below you, and there you will see, lying at single anchor, a cutter; and you may also see, by her pendant and ensign, that she is a yacht.

     You observe that this yacht is cutter-rigged, and that she sits gracefully on the smooth water. She is

(10) just heaving up her anchor; her foresail is loose, all ready to cast her—in a few minutes, she will be under way. You see that there are ladies sitting at the taffrail; and there are five haunches of venison hanging over the stern. Of all amusements, give me yachting. But we must go on board. The deck, you observe, is of narrow deal planks as white as snow; the guns are of polished brass; the bitts and binnacles of mahogany: she is painted with taste; and all the moldings are gilded. There is nothing wanting; and yet how clear and unen-

(15) cumbered are her decks! Let us go below.

     There is the ladies' cabin: Can anything be more tasteful or elegant? Is it not luxurious? And, although so small, does not its very confined space astonish you, when you view so many comforts so beautifully arranged? This is the dining-room, and where the gentlemen repair. And just peep into their staterooms and bed-places. Here is the steward's room and the buffet: The steward is squeezing lemons for the

(20) punch, and there is the champagne in ice; and by the side of the pail the long-corks are ranged up, all ready. Now, let us go forwards: here are the men's berths, not confined as in a man-of-war. No! Luxury starts from

abaft, and is not wholly lost, even at the fore-peak. This is the kitchen; is it not admirably arranged? And how delightful are the fumes of the turtle-soup! At sea we do meet with rough weather at times; but, for roughing it out, give me a yacht.

Passage 2

(25) My very first sea voyage was in a small merchant vessel out of New York called the *Alba*. I was only 12 years old at the time and full of dreams of boundless adventure upon the high seas. I was to serve as the ship's boy. I was given the post by my Uncle Joseph, the weathered old captain of the *Alba* who uttered few words, choosing to speak more with his menacing gaze than with his mouth. The moment I stepped upon the bustling deck my Uncle Joseph set me straight about shipboard life. There were to be no special priv-
(30) ileges afforded to me because of our relations. I was to live and mess in the 'tween decks with the other seamen, and because I was his nephew, I would probably have to work twice as hard as the others to prove my worth. From that point on I was to refer to my uncle as "Sir" or "Captain," and speak to him only when he addressed me. He then told me a bit about the *Alba*. I learned that she was a cutter, and all cutters were fore-and-aft rigged, and possessed only a single mast. After my brief lesson, he then sent me below deck
(35) to get myself situated.

What I found when I dismounted the ladder below was an entirely different world than the orderly brightness of the top deck. Here was a stuffy and dimly lit space barely tall enough for me to stand up straight in. It was the middle of July, and the heat was oppressive. There seemed to be no air at all—there certainly were no windows, and the stench that rose up from the bilge was so pungent, it made me gag.
(40) From the shadows, a pair of eyes materialized. They belonged to a grimy boy no older than me.

"Hello, mate, you must be the new lubber just shipped aboard. I'm Nigel. Follow me, we're just in time for dinner."

My new friend led me into the tiny dining room where the crew messed. The men ate shoulder to shoulder on wooden tables bolted to the deck. The horrific smell of so many men crammed together was
(45) overpowering. We received our food from the ship's cook, a portly man in a filthy apron who, with the dirt-iest hands I'd ever seen, ladled us out a sort of stew. We found two open spots at a mess table and sat down to eat. The stew was lukewarm, and the mysterious meat in it was so tough, I could barely chew it. I man-aged to swallow a few spoonfuls and pushed my dish aside.

With a smile that was a graveyard of yellow sincerity, Nigel pushed the dish back to me and said, "I'd
(50) get used to the grub, mate. It ain't so bad. Besides, this is the freshest it'll be on the voyage."

After dinner, Nigel showed me our berth. It was a tiny lightless cubbyhole near the bow of the boat that was barely six feet long and only five feet high. There was a small area where I could stow my clothes, and at night we would string up our hammocks side by side with two other boys, both of whom were on duty at the moment.
(55) That night when we were under way, the boat ran into a vicious Atlantic storm. The waves tossed the *Alba* around like it was a tiny raft. The ship made such noises; I was afraid it would simply break apart at any moment. The seawater that crashed upon the deck leaked through the planks and dripped upon my head. It would have bothered me if I were not already horribly seasick. As I lay there miserably rocking back and forth in my damp hammock, I asked myself, "What have I gotten myself into?"

119. According to both passages, it is not uncommon for ships to
  a. meet rough seas.
  b. run out of fresh drinking water.
  c. not return home for quite a while.
  d. leak in heavy weather.
  e. have children onboard.

120. In the last sentence of Passage 2, the narrator suggests that he
  a. may never recover from the seasickness.
  b. does not like Nigel.
  c. made a mistake taking the voyage aboard the *Alba*.
  d. should have eaten the stew.
  e. should have stayed in school.

121. Which statement best summarizes the narrator's description of Plymouth in lines 1–15?
  a. The port at Plymouth is full of rowdy sailors.
  b. Plymouth is a dreary and overcrowded place.
  c. Plymouth is a deserted and over-industrialized area.
  d. There are many interesting sights to behold at Plymouth.
  e. The British Royal Navy anchors at Plymouth.

122. What do the yacht in Passage 1 and the *Alba* in Passage 2 have in common?
  a. They were both built in England.
  b. They both have only a single mast.
  c. They are both made of iron.
  d. They both have lifeboats.
  e. They are both fast.

123. How do the yacht in Passage 1 and the *Alba* in Passage 2 differ?
  a. The yacht does not carry cargo.
  b. The yacht is much bigger than the *Alba*.
  c. There are no passengers aboard the *Alba*, only crew.
  d. The yacht is much more luxurious than the *Alba*.
  e. The yacht is much faster than the *Alba*.

124. Why does the captain in Passage 2 (lines 30–33) demand that his nephew call him Sir or Captain?
  a. The captain wanted his nephew to understand who was in charge.
  b. The captain did not want any member of the crew to know the narrator was his nephew.
  c. The captain was afraid that if he showed affection to his nephew, he would lose his authority over the crew.
  d. The captain was not really the narrator's uncle.
  e. It was important that the crew understood that the boy was no more privileged than anyone else aboard.

125. In Passage 1, line 18, the use of the word *repair* most nearly means
  a. go.
  b. fix things.
  c. sit in pairs.
  d. get dressed.
  e. exercise.

126. The narrator of Passage 1 most probably
   a. is a seasoned sea captain.
   b. is very wealthy.
   c. is an experienced yachtsman.
   d. suffers from seasickness.
   e. was in the Royal Navy.

127. In Passage 2, line 49, the narrator describes Nigel's smile as *a graveyard of yellow sincerity.* What figure of speech is the narrator employing?
   a. onomatopoeia
   b. simile
   c. personification
   d. alliteration
   e. metaphor

128. Together, these two passages illustrate the idea that
   a. the reality of two seemingly similar situations can often be extremely different.
   b. boating is a very dangerous pastime.
   c. dreams sometimes fall very short of reality.
   d. Plymouth is much nicer than New York.
   e. hard work pays off in the end.

129. The word *berth*, found in Passage 1, line 21 and Passage 2, line 51, most nearly means
   a. a sailor's hometown.
   b. the sleeping quarters aboard a boat.
   c. the kitchen aboard a boat.
   d. the bathroom aboard a boat.
   e. the lower deck of a boat.

Questions 130–138 are based on the following passage.

In the following passage, the author tells of public art and its functions.

Line

In Manhattan's Eighth Avenue–14th Street subway station, a grinning bronze alligator with human hands pops out of a manhole cover to grab a bronze "baby" whose head is the shape of a moneybag. In the Bronx General Post Office, a giant 13-panel painting called Resources of America celebrates the hard work and industrialism of America in the first half of the twentieth century. And in Brooklyn's MetroTech Center
(5) just over the Brooklyn Bridge, several installations of art are on view at any given time—from an iron lasso resembling a giant charm bracelet to a series of wagons that play recordings of great American poems to a life-sized seeing eye dog that looks so real people are constantly stopping to pet it.

There exists in every city a symbiotic relationship between the city and its art. When we hear the term *art*, we tend to think of private art—the kind displayed in private spaces such as museums, concert halls,
(10) and galleries. But there is a growing interest in, and respect for, public art: the kind of art created for and displayed in public spaces such as parks, building lobbies, and sidewalks.

Although all art is inherently public—created in order to convey an idea or emotion to others— "public art," as opposed to art that is sequestered in museums and galleries, is art specifically designed for a public arena where the art will be encountered by people in their normal day-to-day activities. Pub-
(15) lic art can be purely ornamental or highly functional; it can be as subtle as a decorative door knob or as conspicuous as the Chicago Picasso. It is also an essential element of effective urban design.

The more obvious forms of public art include monuments, sculptures, fountains, murals, and gardens. But public art also takes the form of ornamental benches or street lights, decorative manhole covers, and mosaics on trash bins. Many city dwellers would be surprised to discover just how much public art is

(20) really around them and how much art they have passed by without noticing, and how much impact public art has on their day-to-day lives.

Public art fulfills several functions essential to the health of a city and its citizens. It educates about history and culture—of the artist, the neighborhood, the city, the nation. Public art is also a "place-making device" that instantly creates memorable, experiential landmarks, fashioning a unique identity for

(25) a public place, personalizing it and giving it a specific character. It stimulates the public, challenging viewers to interpret the art and arousing their emotions, and it promotes community by stimulating interaction among viewers. In serving these multiple and important functions, public art beautifies the area and regenerates both the place and the viewer.

One question often debated in public art forums is whether public art should be created with or

(30) by the public rather than for the public. Increasingly, cities and artists are recognizing the importance of creating works with meaning for the intended audience, and this generally requires direct input from the community or from an artist entrenched in that community. At the same time, however, art created for the community by an "outsider" often adds fresh perspective. Thus, cities and their citizens are best served by a combination of public art created by members of the community, art created with input from

(35) members of the community, and art created by others for the community.

130. The primary purpose of the opening paragraph is to
a. show how entertaining public art can be.
b. introduce readers to the idea of public art.
c. define public art.
d. get readers to pay more attention to public art.
e. show the prevalence and diversity of public art.

131. The word *inherently* in line 12 most nearly means
a. essentially.
b. complicated.
c. wealthy.
d. snobby.
e. mysteriously.

132. According to lines 8–11, public art is differentiated from private art mainly by
a. the kind of ideas or emotions it aims to convey to its audience.
b. its accessibility.
c. its perceived value.
d. its importance to the city.
e. the recognition that artists receive for their work.

133. The use of the word *sequestered* in line 13 suggests that the author feels
a. private art is better than public art.
b. private art is too isolated from the public.
c. the admission fees for public art arenas prevent many people from experiencing the art.
d. private art is more difficult to understand than public art.
e. private art is often controversial in nature.

134. According to lines 22–28, public art serves all of the following functions EXCEPT
a. beautification.
b. creation of landmarks.
c. the fostering of community.
d. the promotion of good citizenship.
e. education.

135. Which sentence best sums up the main idea of the passage?
- **a.** Public art serves several important functions in the city.
- **b.** Public art is often in direct competition with private art.
- **c.** Public art should be created both by and for members of the community.
- **d.** In general, public art is more interesting than private art.
- **e.** Few people are aware of how much public art is around them.

136. The author's goals in this passage include all of the following EXCEPT
- **a.** to make readers more aware of public art works.
- **b.** to explain the difference between public art and private art.
- **c.** to explain how public art impacts the city.
- **d.** to inspire readers to become public artists.
- **e.** to argue that public art should be created by artists from both inside and outside the community.

137. Which of the following does the author NOT provide in this passage?
- **a.** an explanation of how the city affects art
- **b.** specific examples of urban art
- **c.** a reason that outsiders should create public art
- **d.** a clear distinction between public and private art
- **e.** an explanation of how public art regenerates the community

138. Given the author's main purpose, which of the following would most strengthen the passage?
- **a.** a more detailed discussion of the differences between public and private art
- **b.** specific examples of art that fulfills each of the functions discussed in paragraph 5
- **c.** interviews with public artists about how public art should be created
- **d.** a specific example of public art created by a community member versus one created by an outsider, to expand paragraph 6
- **e.** a brief lesson in how to interpret art

Questions 139–146 are based on the following passage.

In this excerpt from Susan Glaspell's one-act play Trifles, *Mrs. Hale and Mrs. Peters make an important discovery in Mrs. Wright's home as their husbands try to determine who strangled Mr. Wright.*

Line

MRS. PETERS: Well, I must get these things wrapped up. They may be through sooner than we think. [Putting apron and other things together.] I wonder where I can find a piece of paper, and string.

MRS. HALE: In that cupboard, maybe.

MRS. PETERS [looking in cupboard]: Why, here's a birdcage. [Holds it up.] Did she have a bird,
(5)   Mrs. Hale?

MRS. HALE: Why, I don't know whether she did or not—I've not been here for so long. There was a man around last year selling canaries cheap, but I don't know as she took one; maybe she did. She used to sing real pretty herself.

MRS. PETERS [glancing around]: Seems funny to think of a bird here. But she must have had one, or
(10)   why would she have a cage? I wonder what happened to it.

MRS. HALE: I s'pose maybe the cat got it.

MRS. PETERS: No, she didn't have a cat. She's got that feeling some people have about cats—being afraid of them. My cat got in her room and she was real upset and asked me to take it out.

MRS. HALE: My sister Bessie was like that. Queer, ain't it?

(15) MRS. PETERS [examining the cage]: Why, look at this door. It's broke. One hinge is pulled apart.

MRS. HALE [looking too]: Looks as if someone must have been rough with it.

MRS. PETERS: Why, yes.

[She brings the cage forward and puts it on the table.]

MRS. HALE: I wish if they're going to find any evidence they'd be about it. I don't like this place.

(20) MRS. PETERS: But I'm awful glad you came with me, Mrs. Hale. It would be lonesome for me sitting here alone.

MRS. HALE: It would, wouldn't it? [Dropping her sewing.] But I tell you what I do wish, Mrs. Peters. I wish I had come over sometimes when she was here. I—[looking around the room]—wish I had.

MRS. PETERS: But of course you were awful busy, Mrs. Hale—your house and your children.

(25) MRS. HALE: I could've come. I stayed away because it weren't cheerful—and that's why I ought to have come. I—I've never liked this place. Maybe because it's down in a hollow and you don't see the road. I dunno what it is but it's a lonesome place and always was. I wish I had come over to see Minnie Foster sometimes. I can see now—

[Shakes her head.]

(30) MRS. PETERS: Well, you mustn't reproach yourself, Mrs. Hale. Somehow we just don't see how it is with other folks until—something comes up.

MRS. HALE: Not having children makes less work—but it makes a quiet house, and Wright out to work all day, and no company when he did come in. Did you know John Wright, Mrs. Peters?

MRS. PETERS: Not to know him; I've seen him in town. They say he was a good man.

(35) MRS. HALE: Yes—good; he didn't drink, and kept his word as well as most, I guess, and paid his debts. But he was a hard man, Mrs. Peters. Just to pass the time of day with him—[shivers]. Like a raw wind that gets to the bone. [Pauses, her eyes falling on the cage.] I should think she would'a wanted a bird. But what do you suppose went with it?

MRS. PETERS: I don't know, unless it got sick and died.

(40) [She reaches over and swings the broken door, swings it again. Both women watch it.]

MRS. HALE: You weren't raised round here, were you? [MRS. PETERS shakes her head.] You didn't know—her?

MRS. PETERS: Not till they brought her yesterday.

MRS. HALE: She—come to think of it, she was kind of like a bird herself—real sweet and pretty, but

(45) kind of timid and—fluttery. How—she—did—change. [Silence; then as if struck by a happy thought and relieved to get back to every day things.] Tell you what, Mrs. Peters, why don't you take the quilt in with you? It might take up her mind.

MRS. PETERS: Why, I think that's a real nice idea, Mrs. Hale. There couldn't possibly be any objection to it, could there? Now, just what would I take? I wonder if her patches are in here—and her things.

(50) [They look in the sewing basket.]

MRS. HALE: Here's some red. I expect this has got sewing things in it. [Brings out a fancy box.] What a pretty box. Looks like something somebody would give you. Maybe her scissors are in here. [Opens box. Suddenly puts her hand to her nose.] Why—[MRS. PETERS bends nearer, then turns her face away.] There's something wrapped in this piece of silk.

(55) MRS. PETERS [lifting the silk]: Why this isn't her scissors.

MRS. HALE [lifting the silk]: Oh, Mrs. Peters—it's—

[MRS. PETERS bends closer.]

MRS. PETERS: It's the bird.

MRS. HALE [jumping up]: But, Mrs. Peters—look at it! Its neck! Look at its neck! It's all—to the

(60) other side.

MRS. PETERS: Somebody—wrung—its—neck.

[Their eyes meet. A look of growing comprehension, of horror. Steps are heard outside. MRS. HALE slips box under quilt pieces, and sinks into her chair. Enter SHERIFF and COUNTY ATTORNEY HALE. MRS. PETERS rises.]

139. Based on the passage, the reader can conclude that
  a. Mrs. Peters and Mrs. Hale are old friends.
  b. Mrs. Peters and Mrs. Hale both know Mrs. Wright very well.
  c. Mrs. Peters and Mrs. Hale don't know each other very well.
  d. Neither Mrs. Peters nor Mrs. Hale like Mrs. Wright.
  e. Neither Mrs. Peters nor Mrs. Hale have children.

140. Mrs. Hale says she wishes she had come to Mrs. Wright's house (lines 22–23 and 25–28) because
  a. she realizes that Mrs. Wright must have been lonely.
  b. she enjoyed Mr. Wright's company.
  c. she always felt at home in the Wright's house.
  d. she realizes how important it is to keep good relationships with one's neighbors.
  e. she had a lot in common with Mrs. Wright.

141. According to Mrs. Hale, what sort of man was Mr. Wright?
  a. gentle and loving
  b. violent and abusive
  c. honest and dependable
  d. quiet and cold
  e. a strict disciplinarian

142. In lines 44–45, Mrs. Hale suggests that Mrs. Wright
  a. had become even more like a bird than before.
  b. had grown bitter and unhappy over the years.
  c. was too shy to maintain an intimate friendship.
  d. must have taken excellent care of her bird.
  e. was always singing and flitting about.

143. The phrase *take up her mind* in line 47 means
   a. worry her.
   b. make her angry.
   c. refresh her memory.
   d. keep her busy.
   e. make her think.

144. It can be inferred that Mrs. Wright
   a. got the bird as a present for her husband.
   b. was forced into marrying Mr. Wright.
   c. loved the bird because it reminded her of how she used to be.
   d. had a pet bird as a little girl.
   e. fought often with Mr. Wright.

145. When the women share *a look of growing comprehension, of horror* (line 62), they realize that
   a. Mrs. Wright killed the bird.
   b. Mr. Wright killed the bird, and Mrs. Wright killed him.
   c. they would get in trouble if the sheriff found out they were looking around in the kitchen.
   d. there's a secret message hidden in the quilt.
   e. they might be Mrs. Wright's next victims.

146. The stage directions in lines 62–64 suggest that
   a. the women are mistaken in their conclusion.
   b. the women will tell the men what they found.
   c. the women will confront Mrs. Wright.
   d. the women will keep their discovery a secret.
   e. the men had been eavesdropping on the women.

Questions 147–154 are based on the following passage.

The following passage is an excerpt from a recent introduction to the momentous 1964 Report on Smoking and Health issued by the U.S. Surgeon General. It discusses the inspiration behind the report and the report's effect on public attitudes toward smoking.

Line

No single issue has preoccupied the Surgeons General of the past four decades more than smoking. The reports of the Surgeons General have alerted the nation to the health risk of smoking, and have transformed the issue from one of individual and consumer choice, to one of epidemiology, public health, and risk for smokers and non-smokers alike.

(5)   Debate over the hazards and benefits of smoking has divided physicians, scientists, governments, smokers, and non-smokers since *Tobacco nicotiana* was first imported to Europe from its native soil in the Americas in the sixteenth century. A dramatic increase in cigarette smoking in the United States in the twentieth century called forth anti-smoking movements. Reformers, hygienists, and public health officials argued that smoking brought about general malaise, physiological malfunction, and a decline in mental

(10)   and physical efficiency. Evidence of the ill effects of smoking accumulated during the 1930s, 1940s, and 1950s.

Epidemiologists used statistics and large-scale, long-term, case-control surveys to link the increase in lung cancer mortality to smoking. Pathologists and laboratory scientists confirmed the statistical relationship of smoking to lung cancer as well as to other serious diseases, such as bronchitis, emphysema, and coronary heart disease. Smoking, these studies suggested, and not air pollution, asbestos contamination,

(15)   or radioactive materials, was the chief cause of the epidemic rise of lung cancer in the twentieth century.

On June 12, 1957, Surgeon General Leroy E. Burney declared it the official position of the U.S. Public Health Service that the evidence pointed to a causal relationship between smoking and lung cancer.

The impulse for an official report on smoking and health, however, came from an alliance of prominent private health organizations. In June 1961, the American Cancer Society, the American Heart Asso-
(20) ciation, the National Tuberculosis Association, and the American Public Health Association addressed a letter to President John F. Kennedy, in which they called for a national commission on smoking, dedicated to "seeking a solution to this health problem that would interfere least with the freedom of industry or the happiness of individuals." The Kennedy administration responded the following year, after prompting from a widely circulated critical study on cigarette smoking by the Royal College of Physicians of London. On
(25) June 7, 1962, recently appointed Surgeon General Luther L. Terry announced that he would convene a committee of experts to conduct a comprehensive review of the scientific literature on the smoking question.

Meeting at the National Library of Medicine on the campus of the National Institutes of Health in Bethesda, Maryland, from November 1962 through January 1964, the committee reviewed more than 7,000 scientific articles with the help of over 150 consultants. Terry issued the commission's report on January
(30) 11, 1964, choosing a Saturday to minimize the effect on the stock market and to maximize coverage in the Sunday papers. As Terry remembered the event, two decades later, the report "hit the country like a bombshell. It was front page news and a lead story on every radio and television station in the United States and many abroad."

The report highlighted the deleterious health consequences of tobacco use. *Smoking and Health:*
(35) *Report of the Advisory Committee to the Surgeon General* held cigarette smoking responsible for a 70% increase in the mortality rate of smokers over non-smokers. The report estimated that average smokers had a nine- to ten-fold risk of developing lung cancer compared to non-smokers: Heavy smokers had at least a 20-fold risk. The risk rose with the duration of smoking and diminished with the cessation of smoking. The report also named smoking as the most important cause of chronic bronchitis and pointed to a
(40) correlation between smoking and emphysema, and smoking and coronary heart disease. It noted that smoking during pregnancy reduced the average weight of newborns. On one issue the committee hedged: nicotine addiction. It insisted that the "tobacco habit should be characterized as an habituation rather than an addiction," in part because the addictive properties of nicotine were not yet fully understood, and in part because of differences over the meaning of addiction.

(45) The 1964 report on smoking and health had an impact on public attitudes and policy. A Gallup survey conducted in 1958 found that only 44% of Americans believed smoking caused cancer, while 78% believed so by 1968. In the course of a decade, it had become common knowledge that smoking damaged health, and mounting evidence of health risks gave Terry's 1964 report public resonance. Yet, while the report proclaimed that "cigarette smoking is a health hazard of sufficient importance in the United States
(50) to warrant appropriate remedial action," it remained silent on concrete remedies. That challenge fell to politicians. In 1965, Congress required all cigarette packages distributed in the United States to carry a health warning, and since 1970 this warning is made in the name of the Surgeon General. In 1969, cigarette advertising on television and radio was banned, effective September 1970.

147. The primary purpose of the passage is to
 a. show the mounting evidence of the deleterious health consequences of smoking.
 b. explain why the Kennedy administration called for a national commission on smoking.
 c. describe the government's role in protecting public health.
 d. show the significance of the 1964 Surgeon General's report.
 e. account for the emergence of anti-smoking movements in twentieth-century United States.

148. In line 1, *preoccupied* most nearly means
 a. distressed.
 b. beset.
 c. absorbed.
 d. inconvenienced.
 e. fomented.

149. The first sentence of the second paragraph (lines 5–7) is intended to express the
 a. long-standing controversy about the effects of smoking.
 b. current consensus of the medical community regarding smoking.
 c. government's interest in improving public health.
 d. ongoing colloquy between physicians, scientists, and governments.
 e. causal relationship between smoking and lung disease.

150. In line 18, the author implies that the *impulse* to create a government report on smoking
 a. was an overdue response to public demand.
 b. would not have been pursued if John F. Kennedy was not president.
 c. came from within the U.S. Public Health Service.
 d. would meet with significant opposition from smokers around the country.
 e. was the result of pressure from forces outside of the government.

151. The quotation by Surgeon General Luther L. Terry (lines 31–33) is used to illustrate the
 a. outrage of consumers wanting to protect their right to smoke.
 b. disproportionate media coverage of the smoking report.
 c. overreaction of a hysterical public.
 d. explosive response to the revelation of smoking's damaging effects.
 e. positive role government can play in people's lives.

152. In line 42, *hedged* most nearly means
 a. exaggerated.
 b. evaded.
 c. deceived.
 d. speculated.
 e. hindered.

153. The statement that the 1964 Surgeon General's report remained *silent on concrete remedies* (line 50) implies that it
  a. served primarily as a manifesto that declared the views of the Surgeon General.
  b. could have recommended banning cigarette advertising but it did not.
  c. was ignorant of possible remedial actions.
  d. maintained its objectivity by abstaining from making policy recommendations.
  e. did not deem it necessary to recommend specific actions that would confront the health problem of smoking.

154. In the last paragraph of the passage, the attitude of the author toward the legacy of the 1964 Surgeon General's report is one of
  a. unqualified praise.
  b. appreciation.
  c. wonderment.
  d. cynicism.
  e. disillusionment.

Questions 155–161 are based on the following passage.

The following selection is adapted from a news story about a bill recently introduced in Congress.

Line

In the past 30 years, Americans' consumption of restaurant and take-out food has doubled. The result, according to many health watchdog groups, is an increase in overweight and obesity. Approximately 60 million Americans are obese, costing about $100 billion each year in healthcare and related costs. Members of Congress have decided they need to do something about the obesity epidemic. In 2006, Repre-
(5)   sentative Rosa DeLauro plans to introduce a bill that would require restaurants with 20 or more locations to list the nutritional content of their food on their menus. Senator Tom Harkin will also introduce a menu-labeling bill, although he already introduced a nutrition bill last year that included menu-labeling language.

Our legislators point to the trend of restaurants' marketing larger meals at attractive prices. People order these meals believing that they are getting a great value, but what they are also getting could be, in
(10)   one meal, more than the daily recommended allowances of calories, fat, and sodium. The question is, would people stop "supersizing," or make other, healthier choices if they knew the nutritional content of the food they're ordering? Lawmakers think they would, and the gravity of the obesity problem has caused them to act to change menus.

A menu-labeling bill might require menus that look like the nutrition facts panels found on food in
(15)   supermarkets. Those panels are required by the 1990 Nutrition Labeling and Education Act, which exempted restaurants. The new restaurant menus would list calories, fat, and sodium on printed menus, and calories on menu boards, for all items that are offered on a regular basis (daily specials don't apply). But isn't this simply asking restaurants to state the obvious? Who isn't aware that an order of supersize fries isn't health food? Does anyone order a double cheeseburger thinking they're being virtuous?
(20)   Studies have shown that it's not that simple. In one study, registered dieticians couldn't come up with accurate estimates of the calories found in certain fast foods. Who would have guessed that a milk

shake, which sounds pretty healthy (it does contain milk, after all) has more calories than three McDonald's cheeseburgers? Or that one chain's chicken breast sandwich, another better-sounding alternative to a burger, contains more than half a day's calories and twice the recommended daily amount of sodium?
(25)   Even a fast-food coffee drink, without a doughnut to go with it, has almost half the calories needed in a day.

The restaurant industry isn't happy about the new bill. Arguments against it include the fact that diet alone is not the reason for America's obesity epidemic. A lack of adequate exercise is also to blame. In addition, many fast-food chains already post nutritional information on their websites or on posters located
(30)   in their restaurants.

Those who favor menu-labeling and similar legislation say in response that we must do all we can to help people maintain a healthy weight. While the importance of exercise is undeniable, the quantity and quality of what we eat must be changed. They believe that if we want consumers to make better choices when they eat out, nutritional information must be provided where they are selecting their food. Restau-
(35)   rant patrons are not likely to have memorized the calorie counts they may have looked up on the Internet, nor are they going to leave their tables, or a line, to check out a poster that might be on the opposite side of the restaurant.

155. The purpose of the passage is to
  a. argue the restaurant industry's side of the debate.
  b. explain why dieticians have trouble estimating the nutritional content of fast food.
  c. help consumers make better choices when dining out.
  d. explain one way legislators propose to deal with the obesity epidemic.
  e. argue for the right of consumers to understand what they are ordering in fast food restaurants.

156. According to the passage, the larger meals now being offered in restaurants
  a. cost less than smaller meals.
  b. add an extra side dish not offered with smaller meals.
  c. include a larger drink.
  d. save consumers money.
  e. contain too many calories, fat, and sodium.

157. In line 12, the word *gravity* most nearly means
  a. the force of attraction toward earth.
  b. a cemetery plot.
  c. seriousness.
  d. jealousy.
  e. presumption of wrongdoing.

158. According to the passage, why is the restaurant industry against the proposed congressional bill?
  a. They don't want any healthy items on their menus.
  b. Lack of adequate exercise is also responsible for the obesity epidemic.
  c. They don't want to be sued if they incorrectly calculate the calories in their menu items.
  d. They feel their industry is already over-regulated.
  e. People would stop coming to their establishments if they knew what was in the food.

159. Why is the chicken breast sandwich mentioned in paragraph 4?

    a. It is an example of a menu item that contains more fat than one would assume.

    b. It is the only healthy choice on some restaurants' menus.

    c. It has twice as much salt as the recommended daily allowance.

    d. It has as many calories as three McDonald's hamburgers.

    e. It is a typical selection in a Value Meal.

160. The passage explains that those in favor of menu-labeling want nutritional information placed

    a. anywhere the consumer can make a menu selection.

    b. in print advertisements.

    c. on websites.

    d. on toll-free hotlines.

    e. on posters with print large enough to read from any position in the restaurant.

161. If a menu-labeling bill is passed, consumers would see

    a. menus that tell them how to select the healthiest complete meal.

    b. menus that look like nutritional labels on packaged food.

    c. restaurants with more extensive information on their websites.

    d. less television advertising of fast food restaurants.

    e. restaurants that serve healthier food choices.

Questions 162–172 are based on the following passages.

These passages concern themselves with the nineteenth-century arguments made for and against women's right to vote in the United States. Passage 1 is an excerpt from an address by Isabella Beecher Hooker before the International Council of Women in 1888. Passage 2 is an excerpt from an 1878 report from the Senate's Committee on Privileges and Elections in response to a proposed constitutional amendment that would give women the right to vote.

Line

Passage 1

First let me speak of the constitution of the United States, and assert that there is not a line in it, nor a word, forbidding women to vote; but, properly interpreted, that is, interpreted by the Declaration of Independence, and by the assertions of the Fathers, it actually guarantees to women the right to vote in all elections, both state and national. Listen to the preamble to the constitution, and the preamble you know, is

(5)   the key to what follows; it is the concrete, general statement of the great principles which subsequent articles express in detail. The preamble says: "We, The People of the United States, in order to form a more perfect union, establish justice, insure domestic tranquility, provide for the common defense, promote the general welfare, and secure the blessings of liberty to ourselves and our posterity, do ordain and establish this Constitution for the United States of America."

(10)   Commit this to memory, friends; learn it by heart as well as by head, and I should have no need to argue the question before you of my right to vote. For women are "people" surely, and desire, as much as men, to say the least, to establish justice and to insure domestic tranquility; and, brothers, you will never insure domestic tranquility in the days to come unless you allow women to vote, who pay taxes and bear equally with yourselves all the burdens of society; for they do not mean any longer to submit patiently and

(15) quietly to such injustice, and the sooner men understand this and graciously submit to become the political equals of their mothers, wives, and daughters—aye, of their grandmothers, for that is my category, instead of their political masters, as they now are, the sooner will this precious domestic tranquility be insured. Women are surely "people," I said, and were when these words were written, and were as anxious as men to establish justice and promote the general welfare, and no one will have the hardihood to deny

(20) that our foremothers (have we not talked about our forefathers alone long enough?) did their full share in the work of establishing justice, providing for the common defense, and promoting the general welfare in all those early days.

        The truth is, friends, that when liberties had to be gained by the sword and protected by the sword, men necessarily came to the front and seemed to be the only creators and defenders of these liberties; hence

(25) all the way down women have been content to do their patriotic work silently and through men, who are the fighters by nature rather than themselves, until the present day; but now at last, when it is established that ballots instead of bullets are to rule the world . . . now, it is high time that women ceased to attempt to establish justice and promote the general welfare, and secure the blessings of liberty to themselves and their posterity, through the votes of men . . .

Passage 2

(30) This proposed amendment forbids the United States or any State to deny or abridge the right to vote on account of sex. If adopted, it will make several millions of female voters, totally inexperienced in political affairs, quite generally dependent upon the other sex, all incapable of performing military duty and without the power to enforce the laws which their numerical strength may enable them to make, and comparatively very few of whom wish to assume the irksome and responsible political duties which this measure

(35) thrusts upon them.

        An experiment so novel, a change so great, should only be made slowly and in response to a general public demand, of the existence of which there is no evidence before your committee. Petitions from various parts of the country, containing by estimate about 30,000 names, have been presented to Congress asking for this legislation. They were procured through the efforts of woman-suffrage societies, thoroughly

(40) organized, with active and zealous managers. The ease with which signatures may be procured to any petition is well known. The small number of petitioners, when compared with that of the intelligent women in the country, is striking evidence that there exists among them no general desire to take up the heavy burden of governing, which so many men seek to evade. It would be unjust, unwise, and impolitic to impose that burden on the great mass of women throughout the country who do not wish for it, to gratify the com-

(45) paratively few who do.

        It has been strongly urged that without the right of suffrage women are and will be subjected to great oppression and injustice. But every one who has examined the subject at all knows that without female suffrage, legislation for years has improved and is still improving the condition of women. The disabilities imposed upon her by the common law have, one by one, been swept away until in most of the States

(50)   she has the full right to her property and all, or nearly all the rights which can be granted without impairing or destroying the marriage relation. These changes have been wrought by the spirit of the age, and are not, generally at least, the result of any agitation by women in their own behalf.

Nor can women justly complain of any partiality in the administration of justice. They have the sympathy of judges and particularly of juries to an extent which would warrant loud complaint on the part
(55)   of their adversaries of the sterner sex. Their appeals to legislatures against injustice are never unheeded, and there is no doubt that when any considerable part of the women of any State really wish for the right to vote it will be granted without the intervention of Congress.

Any State may grant the right of suffrage to women. Some of them have done so to a limited extent, and perhaps with good results. It is evident that in some States public opinion is much more strongly
(60)   in favor of it than it is in others. Your committee regards it as unwise and inexpedient to enable three-fourths in number of the States, through an amendment to the National Constitution, to force woman suffrage upon the other fourth in which the public opinion of both sexes may be strongly adverse to such a change.

For these reasons, your committee reports back said resolution with a recommendation that it be
(65)   indefinitely postponed.

162. The author of Passage 1 supports her argument by
  a. providing information about the educational levels achieved by women.
  b. sharing anecdotes about women who fought in the American Revolution.
  c. referring to principles already accepted by her audience.
  d. describing her personal experience as a citizen of the United States.
  e. listing the states in the union that had granted women voting rights.

163. The phrase *learn it by heart as well as by head* in Passage 1, line 10, suggests
  a. an emotional and intellectual response.
  b. rote memorization.
  c. learning from experience rather than books.
  d. accepting an argument on faith.
  e. presupposition of an outcome.

164. In line 18 of Passage 1, *anxious* most nearly means
  a. irritable.
  b. neurotic.
  c. apprehensive.
  d. hasty.
  e. eager.

165. Lines 18–22 of Passage 1 portray American women as
   a. rebellious.
   b. ambitious.
   c. patriotic.
   d. uneducated.
   e. vulnerable.

166. Which of the following best describes the author's strategy in Passage 2?
   a. summarizing public perceptions of the issue
   b. anticipating opposing viewpoints and then refuting them
   c. relating an incident and describing its significance
   d. persuading his audience through emotional appeal
   e. providing evidence that supports both sides of the issue

167. As used in Passage 2, line 36, *novel* most nearly means
   a. rare.
   b. original.
   c. untried.
   d. brilliant.
   e. intellectual.

168. In the third paragraph of Passage 2 (lines 46–52), the author characterizes the activists of the women's suffrage movement as
   a. ardent.
   b. courageous.
   c. conformist.
   d. modest.
   e. genteel.

169. The author of Passage 2 cites the example of a woman's right to her property (lines 48–51) in order to
   a. show that women are well represented by the legislature even if they cannot vote.
   b. demonstrate that if women can be responsible for property, they can be responsible voters.
   c. prove that unjust laws affect the condition of women.
   d. support the belief that political change should happen quickly.
   e. argue that political equality strengthens marriages.

170. Which aspect of the topic of women's voting rights is emphasized in Passage 2, but not in Passage 1?
   a. the interpretation of the Constitution
   b. the contributions of American women
   c. the tax-paying status of women
   d. how the judiciary treats women
   e. how ready the country is to allow women the right to vote

171. The two authors would most likely agree with which statement?
   a. Most women do not desire the right to vote.
   b. Women are not meant to be soldiers.
   c. Voting is more of a burden than a privilege.
   d. American society is ready for female voters.
   e. Men and women should be political equals.

172. The approaches of the two passages to the topic differ in that only Passage 1
   a. describes an incident from the author's personal experience.
   b. gives a point and argues its counterpoint.
   c. cites several specific examples of laws that benefit women.
   d. addresses its audience in the second person.
   e. recommends an action to be taken.

Questions 173–180 are based on the following passage.

The following passage offers the author's perspective on the need for healthcare providers with specialized training to care for a rapidly expanding population of older Americans.

Line

The U.S. population is going gray. A rising demographic tide of aging baby boomers—those born between 1946 and 1964—and increased longevity have made adults age 65 and older the fastest growing segment of today's population. In 30 years, this segment of the population will be nearly twice as large as it is today. By then, an estimated 70 million people will be over age 65. The number of "oldest old"—those age 85 and

(5)   older—is 34 times greater than in 1900 and likely to expand five-fold by 2050.

This unprecedented "elder boom" will have a profound effect on American society, particularly the field of healthcare. Is the U.S. health system equipped to deal with the demands of an aging population? Although we have adequate physicians and nurses, many of them are not trained to handle the multiple needs of older patients. Today we have about 9,000 geriatricians (physicians who are experts in aging-related

(10)   issues). Some studies estimate a need for 36,000 geriatricians by 2030.

Many doctors today treat a patient of 75 the same way they would treat a 40-year-old patient. However, although seniors are healthier than ever, physical challenges often increase with age. By age 75, adults often have two to three medical conditions. Diagnosing multiple health problems and knowing how they interact is crucial for effectively treating older patients. Healthcare professionals— often pressed for time

(15)   in hectic daily practices—must be diligent about asking questions and collecting "evidence" from their elderly patients. Finding out about a patient's over-the-counter medications or living conditions could reveal an underlying problem.

Lack of training in geriatric issues can result in healthcare providers overlooking illnesses or conditions that may lead to illness. Inadequate nutrition is a common, but often unrecognized, problem among

(20)   frail seniors. An elderly patient who has difficulty preparing meals at home may become vulnerable to malnutrition or another medical condition. Healthcare providers with training in aging issues may be able to address this problem without the costly solution of admitting a patient to a nursing home.

Depression, a treatable condition that affects nearly five million seniors, also goes undetected by some healthcare providers. Some healthcare professionals view depression as "just part of getting old." Untreated,

(25)   this illness can have serious, even fatal consequences. According to the National Institute of Mental Health, older Americans account for a disproportionate share of suicide deaths, making up 18% of suicide deaths in 2000. Healthcare providers could play a vital role in preventing this outcome—several studies have shown that up to 75% of seniors who die by suicide visited a primary care physician within a month of their death.

(30)   Healthcare providers face additional challenges to providing high-quality care to the aging population. Because the numbers of ethnic minority elders are growing faster than the aging population as a whole, providers must train to care for a more racially and ethnically diverse population of elderly. Respect and understanding of diverse cultural beliefs is necessary to provide the most effective healthcare to all patients. Providers must also be able to communicate complicated medical conditions or treatments to

(35)   older patients who may have a visual, hearing, or cognitive impairment.

As older adults make up an increasing proportion of the healthcare caseload, the demand for aging specialists must expand as well. Healthcare providers who work with the elderly must understand and address not only the physical but mental, emotional, and social changes of the aging process. They need to be able to distinguish between "normal" characteristics associated with aging and illness. Most crucially, they should look beyond symptoms and consider ways that will help a senior maintain and improve his or her quality of life.

(40)

173. The author uses the phrase *going gray* (line 1) in order to
   a. maintain that everyone's hair loses its color eventually.
   b. suggest the social phenomenon of an aging population.
   c. depict older Americans in a positive light.
   d. demonstrate the normal changes of aging.
   e. highlight the tendency of American culture to emphasize youth.

174. The tone of the passage is primarily one of
   a. bemused inquiry.
   b. detached reporting.
   c. informed argument.
   d. hysterical plea.
   e. playful speculation.

175. The author implies that doctors who treat an elderly patient the same as they would a 40-year-old patient (lines 11–12)
   a. provide equitable, high-quality care.
   b. avoid detrimental stereotypes about older patients.
   c. encourage middle-age adults to think about the long-term effects of their habits.
   d. do not offer the most effective care to their older patients.
   e. willfully ignore the needs of the elderly.

176. In line 22, the word *address* most nearly means
   a. manage.
   b. identify.
   c. neutralize.
   d. analyze.
   e. dissect.

177. The author cites the example of untreated depression in elderly people (lines 23–29) in order to
   a. prove that mental illness can affect people of all ages.
   b. undermine the perception that mental illness affects only young people.
   c. support the claim that healthcare providers need age-related training.
   d. show how mental illness is a natural consequence of growing old.
   e. illustrate how unrecognized illnesses increase the cost of healthcare.

178. According to the passage, which of the following is NOT a possible benefit of geriatric training for healthcare providers?
   a. improved ability to explain a medical treatment to a person with a cognitive problem
   b. knowledge of how heart disease and diabetes may act upon each other in an elderly patient
   c. improved ability to attribute disease symptoms to the natural changes of aging
   d. more consideration for ways to improve the quality of life for seniors
   e. increased recognition of and treatment for depression in elders

179. The author implies that a healthcare system that routinely looks beyond symptoms (lines 39–41) is one that
   a. intrudes on the private lives of individuals.
   b. considers more than just the physical aspects of a person.
   c. rivals the social welfare system.
   d. misdiagnoses diseases that are common in the elderly.
   e. promotes the use of cutting-edge technology in medical care.

180. In the last paragraph of the passage (lines 36–41), the author's tone is one of
   a. unmitigated pessimism.
   b. personal reticence.
   c. hypocritical indifference.
   d. urgent recommendation.
   e. frenzied panic.

Questions 181–188 are based on the following passage.

Beginning in the 1880s, southern states and municipalities established statutes called Jim Crow laws that legalized segregation between blacks and whites. The following passage is concerned with the fight against racial discrimination and segregation and the struggle for justice for African Americans in post–World War II United States.

Line

The post–World War II era marked a period of unprecedented energy against the second-class citizenship accorded to African Americans in many parts of the nation. Resistance to racial segregation and discrimination with strategies like those described above—civil disobedience, non-violent resistance, marches, protests, boycotts, "freedom rides," and rallies—received national attention as newspaper, radio, and tel-
(5)   evision reporters and cameramen documented the struggle to end racial inequality.

When Rosa Parks refused to give up her seat to a white person in Montgomery, Alabama, and was arrested in December 1955, she set off a train of events that generated a momentum the Civil Rights movement had never before experienced. Local civil rights leaders were hoping for such an opportunity to test the city's segregation laws. Deciding to boycott the buses, the African American community soon formed
(10)   a new organization to supervise the boycott, the Montgomery Improvement Association (MIA). The young pastor of the Dexter Avenue Baptist Church, Reverend Martin Luther King, Jr., was chosen as the first MIA leader. The boycott, more successful than anyone hoped, led to a 1956 Supreme Court decision banning segregated buses.

(15)   In 1960, four black freshmen from North Carolina Agricultural and Technical College in Greensboro strolled into the F.W. Woolworth store and quietly sat down at the lunch counter. They were not served, but they stayed until closing time. The next morning, they came with 25 more students. Two weeks later, similar demonstrations had spread to several cities, within a year similar peaceful demonstrations took place in over a hundred northern and southern cities. At Shaw University in Raleigh, North Carolina, the students formed their own organization, the Student Non-Violent Coordinating Committee (SNCC, pro-

(20) nounced "Snick"). The students' bravery in the face of verbal and physical abuse led to integration in many stores even before the passage of the Civil Rights Act of 1964.

     The August 28, 1963, March on Washington riveted the nation's attention. Rather than the antic-ipated hundred thousand marchers, more than twice that number appeared, astonishing even its organ-izers. Blacks and whites, side by side, called on President John F. Kennedy and Congress to provide equal

(25) access to public facilities, quality education, adequate employment, and decent housing for African Americans. During the assembly at the Lincoln Memorial, the young preacher who had led the successful Montgomery, Alabama, bus boycott, Reverend Dr. Martin Luther King, Jr., delivered a stirring message with the refrain, "I Have a Dream."

     There were also continuing efforts to challenge segregation legally through the courts. Success crowned

(30) these efforts: the Brown decision in 1954, the Civil Rights Act of 1964, and the Voting Rights Act in 1965 helped bring about the demise of the entangling web of legislation that bound blacks to second-class citizenship. One hundred years after the Civil War, blacks and their white allies still pursued the battle for equal rights in every area of American life. Although there is more to achieve in ending discrimination, major mile-stones in civil rights laws are on the books for the purpose of regulating equal access to public accommo-

(35) dations, equal justice before the law, and equal employment, education, and housing opportunities. African Americans have had unprecedented openings in many fields of learning and in the arts. The black struggle for civil rights also inspired other liberation and rights movements, including those of Native Americans, Latinos, and women, and African Americans have lent their support to liberation struggles in Africa.

181. The passage is primarily concerned with
  a. enumerating the injustices that African Americans faced.
  b. describing the strategies used in the struggle for civil rights.
  c. showing how effective sit-down strikes can be in creating change.
  d. describing the nature of discrimination and second-class citizenship.
  e. recounting the legal successes of the Civil Rights movement.

182. The author cites the example of Rosa Parks (lines 6–8) refusing to relinquish her bus seat in order to
  a. demonstrate the accidental nature of political change.
  b. show a conventional response to a common situation.
  c. describe a seminal event that influenced a larger movement.
  d. portray an outcome instead of a cause.
  e. give a detailed account of what life was like in Montgomery, Alabama, in 1955.

183. In line 8, the word *test* most nearly means
   a. analyze.
   b. determine.
   c. prove.
   d. quiz.
   e. challenge.

184. The passage suggests that the college students in Greensboro, North Carolina (lines 14–18)
   a. were regulars at the Woolworth lunch counter.
   b. wanted to provoke a violent reaction.
   c. were part of an ongoing national movement of lunch-counter demonstrations.
   d. inspired other students to protest peacefully against segregation.
   e. did not plan to create a stir.

185. The passage implies that the 1963 March on Washington
   a. resulted in immediate legislation prohibiting segregation in public accommodations.
   b. was a successful demonstration that drew attention to its causes.
   c. was overshadowed by the rousing speech by Reverend Dr. Martin Luther King, Jr.
   d. represented only the attitudes of a fringe group.
   e. reflected unanimous public opinion that segregation laws must end.

186. The term *refrain* as it is used in line 28 most nearly means
   a. song lyric.
   b. allegory.
   c. recurring phrase.
   d. poem stanza.
   e. aria.

187. The term *second-class citizenship* (line 31) most nearly refers to
   a. native or naturalized people who do not owe allegiance to a government.
   b. foreign-born people who wish to become a citizen of a new country.
   c. those who deny the rights and privileges of a free person.
   d. having inferior status and rights in comparison to other citizens.
   e. having inferior status and rights under a personal sovereign.

188. All of the following questions can be explicitly answered on the basis of the passage EXCEPT
   a. What are some of the barriers African Americans faced in postwar America?
   b. What tangible achievements did the Civil Rights movement attain?
   c. What judicial rulings are considered milestones in the struggle for civil rights?
   d. What strategies did civil rights protesters use to provoke political change?
   e. What hurtles remain today for ending racial discrimination in the United States?

Questions 189–197 are based on the following passage.

The following passage chronicles the 1919 "Black Sox" baseball scandal.

Line

Professional baseball suffered during the two years the United States was involved in World War I. Many Americans who were preoccupied with the seriousness of the war raging overseas had little concern for the trivialities of a baseball game. After the war ended in 1919, many Americans wanted to put those dark years behind them and get back to the normal activities of a peaceful life. One of those activities was watch-

(5)   ing baseball. In the summer of 1919, ballparks that just one year earlier had been practically empty were now filled daily with the sights and sounds of America's favorite pastime. That year, both the Cleveland Indians and New York Yankees were two of the strongest teams in baseball's American League, but one team stood head and shoulders above the rest: the Chicago White Sox.

The Chicago White Sox, called the White Stockings until 1902, were owned by an ex-ballplayer named

(10)   Charles Comiskey. Between the years of 1900 and 1915 the White Sox had won the World Series only once, and Comiskey was determined to change that. In 1915, he purchased the contracts of three of the most promising stars in the league: outfielders "Shoeless" Joe Jackson and "Happy" Oscar Felsch, and second baseman Eddie Collins. Comiskey had only to wait two years for his plan to come to fruition; the 1917 White Sox, playing in a park named for their owner, won the World Series. Two years later, they had the

(15)   best record in all of baseball and were again on their way to the Series.

Baseball players' salaries in that era were much different than the exorbitant paychecks of today's professional athletes. Often, ballplayers would have second careers in the off-season because of the mediocrity of their pay. To make matters worse, war-torn 1918 was such a horrible year for baseball attendance that many owners cut player salaries for the following season. However, it is said in all of baseball, there was no owner

(20)   as parsimonious as Charles Comiskey. In 1917, he reportedly promised every player on the White Sox a bonus if they won the American League Championship. After winning the championship, they returned to the clubhouse to receive their bonus—a bottle of inexpensive champagne. Unlike other owners, Comiskey also required the players to pay for the cleaning of their uniforms. The Sox had the best record in baseball, but they were the least paid, were the most discontented, and wore the dirtiest uniforms.

(25)   Comiskey's frugality did not sit well with the players. They were most upset with the fact that he did not raise salaries back to their 1918 levels, even though the ballpark attendance figures for 1919 were higher than any previous year. One player, Eddie Ciccotte, felt especially ill-treated by Comiskey. The owner promised the pitcher a bonus of $10,000 if he won 30 games, but after Ciccotte won his 29th game, he was benched by Comiskey for the rest of the season.

(30)   Gamblers were such a common sight around the Chicago ballpark that Charles Comiskey had signs proclaiming "No Betting Allowed in This Park" posted conspicuously in the stands. The money with which these gamblers tempted the players was hard to refuse, and it was rumored that to supplement their income some of the lower-paid athletes would offer inside tips to the bettors. But gamblers' mingling with ballplayers wasn't solely confined to the White Sox. In 1920, allegations involving gambling among

(35)   Chicago Cubs players brought to light a scandal that would shock Chicago and the rest of America: Eight members of the White Sox had thrown the 1919 World Series.

The exact facts regarding the scandal will never be known, but the most accepted theory is that just prior to the World Series, White Sox player Chick Gandil had approached a gambler by the name of Joseph Sullivan with a proposal that for $100,000 Gandil would make sure the Sox lost the Series. Gandil needed
(40) to recruit other players for the plan to work. It was not hard for him to do—there were many underpaid players on the White Sox who were dissatisfied with the way Comiskey operated the team. Ultimately, the seven other players that were allegedly involved in the scheme were Eddie Cicotte, Happy Felsch, Joe Jackson, Fred McMullin, Charles "Swede" Risberg, Buck Weaver, and Claude Williams.

They were successful. The Chicago White Sox, heavily favored to beat an inferior Cincinnati Reds
(45) team, lost the nine-game World Series in eight games, due in most part to the inferior play of the eight conspiring players. When the scandal made headlines the following year, the press began to refer to them as the Black Sox, and the ignominious label would be used to describe them forever.

When the eight players stood before an Illinois grand jury, it was determined that that there was not enough substantial evidence for any convictions, and the players were all eventually acquitted of any crim-
(50) inal wrongdoing. Interestingly enough, Charles Comiskey paid for the players' high-priced defense lawyers. Unfortunately for Comiskey, there was to be no similar reprieve from major league baseball: Every single one of the accused players was banned from the game for life. Comiskey's once mighty team was decimated by the loss of its most talented players, and the 1921 White Sox finished the season in seventh place.

189. According to the passage, who was the supposed ringleader of the Black Sox scandal?
   a. Charles Comiskey
   b. "Shoeless" Joe Jackson
   c. Eddie Ciccotte
   d. Eddie Collins
   e. Chick Gandil

190. In line 20, the word *parsimonious* most nearly means
   a. generous.
   b. stingy.
   c. powerful.
   d. friendly.
   e. jovial.

191. According to facts from the passage, what was the name of the White Sox's ballpark?
   a. Chicago Park
   b. Comiskey Park
   c. Sullivan Stadium
   d. White Sox Park
   e. Sox Field

192. In line 36, the word *thrown* refers to
   a. losing intentionally.
   b. pitching a baseball.
   c. projecting upon.
   d. dashing upon.
   e. abandoning something.

193. According to the passage, how many World Series did the White Sox win between 1900 and 1919?
   a. none
   b. one
   c. two
   d. three
   e. four

194. All of the following questions can be answered based on information from the passage EXCEPT
   a. Who was the second baseman for the 1915 White Sox?
   b. Did the White Sox play in the American League or the National League?
   c. What was the White Sox's original name?
   d. How many games did Eddie Ciccotte pitch in 1918?
   e. Why did many baseball owners lower player salaries for the 1919 season?

195. In line 47, word *ignominious* most nearly means
   a. uneducated.
   b. dishonorable.
   c. exalted.
   d. worthy.
   e. unentertaining.

196. The last paragraph of the passage suggests that Charles Comiskey
   a. thought the team was better off without the eight players.
   b. hoped all eight players would be convicted and sent to jail.
   c. wanted the players involved in the scandal to return to the team.
   d. was contemplating retirement.
   e. had a plan to get the White Sox back to the World Series.

197. The passage as a whole suggests that
   a. the White Sox probably fixed the 1917 World Series, too.
   b. Charles Comiskey may have been in part to blame for his players' actions.
   c. ballplayers betting on games was a highly unusual occurrence.
   d. baseball never recovered after World War I.
   e. Charles Comiskey often bet against his own team.

Questions 198–205 are based on the following passage.

In this excerpt from Charlotte Bronte's novel Jane Eyre, *the narrator decides to leave Lowood, the boarding school where she has lived for eight years.*

Line

Miss Temple, through all changes, had thus far continued superintendent of the seminary; to her instruction I owed the best part of my acquirements; her friendship and society had been my continual solace: she had stood me in the stead of mother, governess, and, latterly, companion. At this period she married, removed with her husband (a clergyman, an excellent man, almost worthy of such a wife) to a distant
(5)   county, and consequently was lost to me.

From the day she left I was no longer the same: with her was gone every settled feeling, every association that had made Lowood in some degree a home to me. I had imbibed from her something of her

nature and much of her habits: more harmonious thoughts: what seemed better-regulated feelings had become inmates of my mind. I had given in allegiance to duty and order; I was quiet; I believed I was con-
(10)   tent: to the eyes of others, usually even to my own, I appeared a disciplined and subdued character.

But destiny, in the shape of the Rev. Mr. Nasmyth, came between me and Miss Temple: I saw her in her traveling dress step into a post-chaise, shortly after the marriage ceremony; I watched the chaise mount the hill and disappear beyond its brow; and then retired to my own room, and there spent in solitude the greatest part of the half-holiday granted in honor of the occasion.

(15)   I walked about the chamber most of the time. I imagined myself only to be regretting my loss, and thinking how to repair it; but when my reflections concluded, and I looked up and found that the afternoon was gone, and evening far advanced, another discovery dawned on me, namely, that in the interval I had undergone a transforming process; that my mind had put off all it had borrowed of Miss Temple—or rather that she had taken with her the serene atmosphere I had been breathing in her vicinity—and that
(20)   now I was left in my natural element, and beginning to feel the stirring of old emotions. It did not seem as if a prop were withdrawn, but rather as if a motive were gone; it was not the power to be tranquil which had failed me, but the reason for tranquility was no more. My world had for some years been in Lowood: my experience had been of its rules and systems; now I remembered that the real world was wide, and that a varied field of hopes and fears, of sensations and excitements, awaited those who had courage to go forth
(25)   into its expanse, to seek real knowledge of life amidst its perils.

I went to my window, opened it, and looked out. There were the two wings of the building; there was the garden; there were the skirts of Lowood; there was the hilly horizon. My eye passed all other objects to rest on those most remote, the blue peaks: it was those I longed to surmount; all within their boundary of rock and heath seemed prison-ground, exile limits. I traced the white road winding round the base
(30)   of one mountain, and vanishing in a gorge between two: how I longed to follow it further! I recalled the time when I had traveled that very road in a coach; I remembered descending that hill at twilight: an age seemed to have elapsed since the day which brought me first to Lowood, and I had never quitted it since. My vacations had all been spent at school: Mrs. Reed had never sent for me to Gateshead; neither she nor any of her family had ever been to visit me. I had had no communication by letter or message with the
(35)   outer world: school-rules, school-duties, school-habits and notions, and voices, and faces, and phrases, and costumes, and preferences, and antipathies: such was what I knew of existence. And now I felt that it was not enough: I tired of the routine of eight years in one afternoon. I desired liberty; for liberty I gasped; for liberty I uttered a prayer; it seemed scattered on the wind then faintly blowing. I abandoned it and framed a humbler supplication; for change, stimulus: that petition, too, seemed swept off into vague space:
(40)   "Then," I cried, half desperate, "grant me at least a new servitude!"

198. Miss Temple was the narrator's
      I. teacher.
      II. friend.
      III. mother.
  a. I only
  b. II only
  c. III only
  d. I and II
  e. all of the above

199. While Miss Temple was at Lowood, the narrator
  a. was calm and content.
  b. was often alone.
  c. had frequent disciplinary problems.
  d. longed to leave Lowood.
  e. felt as if she were in a prison.

200. The word *inmates* in line 9 means
  a. captives.
  b. patients.
  c. prisoners.
  d. residents.
  e. convalescents.

201. Mrs. Reed (line 33) is most likely
  a. the narrator's mother.
  b. the headmistress of Lowood.
  c. the narrator's former guardian.
  d. the narrator's friend.
  e. a fellow student at Lowood.

202. It can be inferred from the passage that life at Lowood was
  a. very unconventional and modern.
  b. very structured and isolated.
  c. harsh and demeaning.
  d. liberal and carefree.
  e. urban and sophisticated.

203. After Miss Temple's wedding, the narrator
  a. realizes she wants to experience the world.
  b. decides that she must get married.
  c. realizes she can never leave Lowood.
  d. decides to return to her family at Gateshead.
  e. determines to follow Miss Temple.

204. The passage suggests that the narrator
  a. will soon return to Lowood.
  b. was sent to Lowood by mistake.
  c. is entirely dependent upon Miss Temple.
  d. has run away from Lowood before.
  e. is naturally curious and rebellious.

205. In lines 37–40, the narrator reduces her petition to simply a new servitude because she
  a. doesn't believe in prayer.
  b. is not in a free country.
  c. has been offered a position as a servant.
  d. knows so little of the real world.
  e. has been treated like a slave at Lowood.

Questions 206–213 are based on the following passages.

Both of these passages were adapted from high school newspaper editorials concerning reality television.

Line

Passage 1

There comes a time in every boy's life when he becomes a man. On this fateful day, he will be swept up and put on an island to compete for one million dollars. Then, this man will realize that money can't buy happiness. He will find his soul mate, as we all do, on national TV, picking a woman out of a line of 20. By then it will be time for him to settle down, move to the suburbs, make friends with the neighbors, and
(5)   then refurbish the neighbors' house.

Welcome to real life. That is, real life as the television networks see it.

Reality TV is flawed in many ways, but the most obvious is in its name. It purports to portray reality, but no "reality" show has succeeded in this endeavor. Instead, reality TV is an extension of fiction, and there are no writers who need to be paid. Television executives love it because it is so much cheaper to pro-
(10)   duce than any other type of programming, and it's popular. But the truth is that there is little or no reality in reality TV.

Do you sing in the shower while dreaming of getting your own record deal? There are a couple of shows made just for you. Audition and make the cut, so some British guy who has never sung a note can rip you to pieces on live television. Or maybe you're lonely and fiscally challenged and dream of walking
(15)   down the aisle with a millionaire? Real marriage doesn't involve contestants who know each other for a couple of days. The people on these shows seem to be more interested in how they look on camera than in the character of the person they might spend the rest of their life with. Let's hope that isn't reality.

There are also about a dozen decorating shows. In one case, two couples trade rooms and redecorate for each other. The catch is, interior designers help them. This is where the problem starts. Would either
(20)   couple hire someone who thinks it's a great idea to swathe a room in hundreds of yards of muslin, or to adhere 5,000 plastic flowers as a mural in a bathroom? The crimes committed against defenseless walls are outrageous. When you add the fact that the couples are in front of cameras as well as the designers, and thus unable to react honestly to what is going on, you get a new level of "unreality."

Then there is the show that made the genre mainstream—*Survivor*. The show that pits men and
(25)   women from all walks of life against each other for a million dollar prize in the most successful of all the reality TV programs. What are record numbers of viewers tuning in to see? People who haven't showered or done their laundry in weeks are shown scavenging for food and competing in ridiculous physical challenges. Where's the reality? From the looks of it, the contestants spend most of their time, when not on a reality TV show, driving to the Burger Barn and getting exercise only when the remote goes missing.
(30)   So the television networks have used reality TV to replace the dramas and comedies that once filled their schedules, earning millions in advertising revenue. The lack of creativity, of producing something worth watching, is appalling. We are served up hundreds of hours of reality TV each week, so we can watch real people in very unreal situations, acting as little like themselves as possible. What's real about that?

Passage 2

Why does reality TV get such a bad rap? Editorials on the subject blame its popularity on everything from
(35) the degenerate morals of today's youth to our ever-decreasing attention spans. The truth is that reality-
based programs have been around for decades. *Candid Camera* first aired in 1948, a *Cops*-like show called
Wanted was on CBS's lineup in the mid-1950s, and PBS aired a controversial 12-hour documentary
filmed inside a family's home in 1973. But it was *Survivor*, which debuted on American TV in the summer of 2000, which spawned the immense popularity of the "reality" genre. There are now more than 40
(40) reality shows on the air, and, hinting that they are here to stay, the Academy of Television Arts and Sciences added "Best Reality Show" as an Emmy category in 2002.

Why are these shows so popular today? Are they really a sign that our morals, and our minds, are on
a decline? People have been tuning in to reality TV for generations, so what makes today's shows any worse
than their predecessors? Let's look at a number of current, popular shows to see what the fuss is about.
(45) MTV's *The Real World* has been on the air for over ten years. It places seven strangers in one house and
tapes them as they live together for a few months. The show has been a ratings homerun for MTV, and
tens of thousands of hopefuls audition each time they announce they are producing another show. Those
who make the cut are attractive young singles not only looking for a good time, but also looking for fame,
too. It's not uncommon for them to hire a show business agent before the taping starts.
(50) Other reality shows take fame-seekers to the next level by having them compete against one
another. *American Idol*, *Star Search*, and *Fame* showcase singers, actors, dancers, and model hopefuls, and
offer them a chance at professional success. Even those who don't win the big prize get national television
exposure and have a better chance than they did before the show of becoming famous. *Survivor* offers
another twist: You not only can become an instant celebrity, but also you have a chance to win a million
(55) dollars. The combination of fame and money has helped to make *Survivor* the most popular reality TV
program of all time. But it's not alone in the format. *Big Brother* combines the "group living together in
a beautiful setting" concept of *The Real World* with a $500,000 prize, and *Fear Factor* pays $50,000 to the
contestant who completes the most terrifying stunts.

Given television's long history of reality-based programming, why is there a problem now? Most real-
(60) ity TV centers on two common motivators: fame and money. The shows have pulled waitresses, hair styl-
ists, investment bankers, and counselors, to name a few, from obscurity to being household names. These
lucky few successfully parlayed their 15 minutes of fame into celebrity. Even if you are not interested in
fame, you can probably understand the desire for lots of money. Watching people eat large insects, jump
off cliffs, and be filmed 24 hours a day for a huge financial reward makes for interesting viewing. What's
(65) wrong with people wanting to be rich and famous? Not much, and, if you don't like it, you can always
change the channel.

206. The author's tone in Passage 1, lines 1–5, may best be described as
   a. satire concerning a man's journey through life.
   b. cynicism about the reasons people go on reality TV shows.
   c. humor regarding the content of reality TV.
   d. irony about the maturation process.
   e. sarcasm toward the television networks.

207. Based on the passages, which statement would both authors agree with?
   a. reality TV has had a long history.
   b. *Big Brother* is about the desire for fame and money.
   c. The popularity of reality TV is an indication of a decline in morals.
   d. *Survivor* is the most successful reality TV show.
   e. There is nothing wrong with reality TV.

208. The primary purpose of Passage 2 is to
   a. refute an argument.
   b. explore possible outcomes.
   c. give a brief history.
   d. explain how to get famous.
   e. show the need for change.

209. The two passages differ in that the author of Passage 1
   a. defends reality TV, while the author of Passage 2 does not.
   b. explains what he or she thinks is wrong with reality TV, while the author of Passage 2 does not.
   c. believes reality TV has many faults, while the author of Passage 2 thinks no one has a problem with it.
   d. blames reality TV for the lack of variety in programming, while the author of Passage 2 thinks it has improved variety.
   e. says reality TV is cheap to produce, while the author of Passage 2 disagrees.

210. In Passage 2, line 46, the phrase *ratings home-run* means that
   a. a lot of people watch *The Real World*.
   b. *The Real World* beats baseball games in TV ratings.
   c. there are baseball players on *The Real World*.
   d. the Nielsen company likes *The Real World*.
   e. *The Real World* contestants play softball on the show.

211. Both passages illustrate the idea that
   a. people on reality TV shows become famous.
   b. reality TV is all about getting rich.
   c. reality TV is a good alternative to traditional programming.
   d. the producers of reality TV are getting rich.
   e. reality TV is controversial.

212. *Swathe* in Passage 1, line 20 most nearly means
   a. to stitch.
   b. a combination of pleating and stapling.
   c. to cover.
   d. a way of making curtains.
   e. to cover the floor.

213. What does the author of Passage 1 find most troublesome about reality TV?
   a. It isn't original.
   b. It doesn't need writers to come up with scripts.
   c. It invades people's privacy.
   d. It doesn't accurately show reality.
   e. It shows how shallow people are.

Questions 214–217 are based on the following passage.

The following passage describes the composition and nature of ivory.

Line

Ivory skin, ivory teeth, Ivory Soap, Ivory Snow—we hear "ivory" used all the time to describe something fair, white, and pure. But where does ivory come from, and what exactly is it? Is it natural or man-made? Is it a modifier, meaning something pure and white, or is it a specialized and discrete substance?

(5) Historically, the word *ivory* has been applied to the tusks of elephants. However, the chemical structure of the teeth and tusks of mammals is the same regardless of the species of origin, and the trade in certain teeth and tusks other than elephant is well established and widespread. Therefore, ivory can correctly be used to describe any mammalian tooth or tusk of commercial interest that is large enough to be carved or scrimshawed. Teeth and tusks have the same origins. Teeth are specialized structures adapted for food mastication. Tusks, which are extremely large teeth projecting beyond the lips, have evolved from teeth

(10) and give certain species an evolutionary advantage that goes beyond chewing and breaking down food in digestible pieces. Furthermore, the tusk can be used to secure food through hunting, killing, and then breaking up large chunks of food into manageable bits.

The teeth of most mammals consist of a root as well as the tusk proper. Teeth and tusks have the same physical structures: pulp cavity, dentine, cementum, and enamel. The innermost area is the pulp cavity.

(15) The pulp cavity is an empty space within the tooth that conforms to the shape of the pulp. Odontoblastic cells line the pulp cavity and are responsible for the production of dentine. Dentine, which is the main component of carved ivory objects, forms a layer of consistent thickness around the pulp cavity and comprises the bulk of the tooth and tusk. Dentine is a mineralized connective tissue with an organic matrix of collagenous proteins. The inorganic component of dentine consists of dahllite. Dentine contains a micro-

(20) scopic structure called dentinal tubules which are micro-canals that radiate outward through the dentine from the pulp cavity to the exterior cementum border. These canals have different configurations in different ivories and their diameter ranges between 0.8 and 2.2 microns. Their length is dictated by the radius of the tusk. The three-dimensional configuration of the dentinal tubules is under genetic control and is, therefore, a characteristic unique to the order of the mammal.

(25) Exterior to the dentine lies the cementum layer. Cementum forms a layer surrounding the dentine of tooth and tusk roots. Its main function is to adhere the tooth and tusk root to the mandibular and maxillary jaw bones. Incremental lines are commonly seen in cementum.

Enamel, the hardest animal tissue, covers the surface of the tooth or tusk which receives the most wear, such as the tip or crown. Ameloblasts are responsible for the formation of enamel and are lost after the

(30) enamel process is complete. Enamel exhibits a prismatic structure with prisms that run perpendicular to the crown or tip. Enamel prism patterns can have both taxonomic and evolutionary significance.

Tooth and tusk ivory can be carved into an almost infinite variety of shapes and objects. A small example of carved ivory objects are small statuary, netsukes, jewelry, flatware handles, furniture inlays,

and piano keys. Additionally, warthog tusks and teeth from sperm whales, killer whales, and hippos
(35) can also be scrimshawed or superficially carved, thus retaining their original shapes as morphologically
recognizable objects.

The identification of ivory and ivory substitutes is based on the physical and chemical class characteristics of these materials. A common approach to identification is to use the macroscopic and microscopic physical characteristics of ivory in combination with a simple chemical test using ultraviolet light.

214. In line 3, what does the term *discrete* most
nearly mean?
a. tactful
b. distinct
c. careful
d. prudent
e. judicious

215. Which of the following titles is most appropriate for this passage?
a. Ivory: An Endangered Species
b. Elephants, Ivory, and Widespread Hunting in Africa
c. Ivory: Is It Organic or Inorganic?
d. Uncovering the Aspects of Natural Ivory
e. Scrimshaw: A Study of the Art of Ivory Carving

216. The word *scrimshawed* in line 8 and line 35
most nearly means
a. floated.
b. waxed.
c. carved.
d. sunk.
e. buoyed.

217. Which of the following choices is NOT part of
the physical structure of teeth?
a. pulp cavity
b. dentine
c. cementum
d. tusk
e. enamel

▶ Answers

1. a. Salad is the best choice, because at the time, Americans were beginning to eat healthier foods, such as vegetables.

2. e. Lines 24 and 25 explain that he skipped the fermentation process, which means that the fish was fresh, or raw. If you answered choice **b**, check the passage. There is no reason to believe that sushi with fermented rice was not being consumed in Edo before Yohei's innovation. If you answered choice **d**, note that the passage does not indicate when, or with whom, *wasabi* began being used as a condiment with *nigiri zushi*.

3. c. It states in line 31 that *ama ebi* is raw shrimp, and *shime saba* is marinated mackerel. You can infer that *ebi* means shrimp, because "raw" is not one of your choices. You can also infer that *shime* means marinated, because mackerel is not one of your choices. Therefore, *shime ebi* means marinated shrimp.

4. d. Nowhere in the passage does the author mention a preference for either type of sushi. The answer to choice **a** may be found in lines 6–7. Choice **b** is found in lines 7–9, choice **c** is answered by lines 35–38, and choice **e** is answered by lines 20–21.

5. a. It is noted in line 11 that sushi consumption in America is 40% higher than it was in the late 1990s. Although the other answers might be true, they are not described in the passage.

6. b. *Unpalatable* may be defined as "not agreeable to taste"; from the Latin *palatum*, which refers to the roof of the mouth. You know the word palate as the roof of the mouth, so unpalatable most likely has to do with the sense of taste. The biggest clue to the definition comes in lines 16–17, which states that Americans have decided, *this once-scorned food is truly delicious.*

7. d. It is mentioned in lines 18–19 that sushi was developed for the purpose of preserving fish. Lines 20–21 clearly state that pickling, which takes place at the end of the sushi-making process, is a means of preserving.

8. d. The *nori* is typically on the outside of the roll, surrounding the rice. If the rice is wrapped around the seaweed, the inside (rice) is now on the outside. In addition, you could use the process of elimination, as none of the other choices make sense.

9. d. The anecdote contrasts with the ensuing quote in paragraph 1 and depicts a plausible reason for the apple story—Newton wanted to make his theory understood to the general public. Speaking in physics terminology is abstract, but using an illustration that regular people have witnessed again and again would aid in understanding. The quote gives credence to the anecdote, ruling out choice **a**. Choices **b** and **e** are never mentioned, and choice **c** is not backed up by the passage.

10. e. The passage clearly states that Newton became Professor of Mathematics at Trinity College, Cambridge.

11. e. In paragraph 4, Newton's Laws of Motion are said to govern the motion of objects and are the basis for the concept of the clockwork universe. Nowhere in the passage is it stated that Newton or his laws are responsible for

the international dateline (choice **b**), latitude (choice **c**), or longitude (choice **d**). Choice **a** plays on the word *govern* and is misleading.

12. b. The passage specifically states that Newton provided an explanation of Kepler's laws.

13. d. All of the other titles were bestowed on Newton during his lifetime.

14. b. William Stukeley published *Memoirs of Sir Isaac Newton's Life* in 1726, after Newton's death. The other choices are all accomplishments of Newton in his lifetime.

15. a. Choice **a** is correct because it lists the proper accolades and the proper time frame in which he lived. Choice **b** is incorrect because he did not live in the Renaissance; choices **c** and **d** are incorrect because he was not a lord, but a knight; and choice **e** is incorrect because it is not the best summary of his vast accomplishments.

16. b. The passage defines *panopticon*: a place in which everything is in the full view of others. The second paragraph repeats this definition: Every prisoner's cell would be in full view of the guards.

17. a. In the third paragraph, the author states that people behave differently when they know they are being watched—and that when we are being watched, or even think we are being watched, we will act the way we think we should act when we are being observed by others. Thus, the panopticon would be a useful tool for social control. If prisoners know they may be being watched by guards, it is logical to conclude that they are less likely to commit any wrongdoings; thus, the panopticon helps maintain order.

18. c. The author states that the panopticon is already here and then states that surveillance cameras are everywhere and we often don't even know our actions are being recorded. The rest of the paragraph provides additional examples of how our cyber-whereabouts are observed and recorded.

19. d. In Bentham's panopticon, the prisoners would know they were being watched—or rather, they would know that they could be being watched. However, in our modern panopticon, the author states, we often don't even know our actions are being recorded.

20. a. Although information from our credit card purchases is often recorded and exchanged, the author makes no mention of an increased use of credit card purchases contributing to the erosion of privacy. All of the other options, however, are listed in the fourth and sixth paragraphs.

21. c. The paragraph describing the author's experience with identity theft immediately follows the sentence: *We can do little to stop the information gathering and exchange and can only hope to be able to control the damage if something goes wrong.* This serves as an example of something going wrong—the misuse of private information.

22. e. The example of identity theft makes it clear that in cyberspace, with so much information floating about and so much technology that can record and observe, our privacy is in jeopardy—it is constantly at risk of being exploited.

23. d. Because of the author's personal experience with identity theft, and because the author finds it truly amazing that someone would want to live in a transparent house, it can be inferred that the author greatly values privacy. The passage also expresses great concern for the lack of control over information in cyberspace (paragraph 4), stating that we can only hope to be able to control the damage if something goes wrong. Thus, the author would likely support stricter regulations for information gathering and exchange, especially on the Internet.

24. a. The article raises the question: Could the dietary recommendations of the last 20 years be wrong?

25. d. The author expresses her objection by depicting the medical experts as extreme, ridiculing one diet while extolling another.

26. c. Choices **a** and **d** are alternate definitions that do not apply to the passage. The author uses *gospel*, with its religious implications, as an ironic statement, implying that scientists accepted a premise based on faith instead of on evidence.

27. e. The author begins with *Fact* to introduce and highlight statistical information. She does not speculate about the meaning of the statistics until the next paragraph.

28. a. The author names a *sedentary lifestyle of TV watching or Internet surfing* as a contributing factor to the rise in obesity rates.

29. b. The passage suggests that the 1979 dietary guidelines responded to a theory that dietary fat increases heart disease.

30. b. The passage describes the anti-fat message as oversimplified and goes on to cite the importance of certain beneficial types of fat found in olive oil and nuts.

31. c. This example supports the claim that the body uses refined carbohydrates in much the same way that it does sweets.

32. e. Lines 28–29 support this statement.

33. d. The last sentence is ironic—it expresses an incongruity between conflicting dietary advice that targets different types of food as unhealthy and the reality that humans need to eat.

34. b. The passage clearly states that potlatch is a gift-giving ceremony. The author explains that *potlatch* is a generic word for the ceremony that comes from a shared trading language, while each nation has its own specific word for potlatch.

35. a. The passage states that guests were expected to give a potlatch with gifts of equal value to what they received. This arrangement can best be described as reciprocal. The other choices are not supported by the passage.

36. d. The author describes the ceremony in mostly neutral terms but in the last paragraph emphasizes the positive aspects of the tradition, which indicates a degree of respect.

37. e. The passage explicitly states that a man will know by reputation all the men in his *kula* ring. None of the other choices is explicitly stated in the passage.

38. c. The passage states that the visitors are seen as aggressors and are met with ritual hostility. This indicates that the visitors and hosts are playing the roles of aggressor and victims. The author uses quotes to indicate that the hosts are not really victims, but might call themselves the victims in the exchange.

39. d. The passage states the ways in which a *kula* object gains value; special shells are not mentioned.

40. a. The final paragraph of each passage explicitly states the ways in which these ceremonies, or rituals, maintain community ties. None of the other choices is true for both passages.

41. b. Both authors specifically discuss the non-monetary value of each ceremony. In Passage 1, the author states, *Giving wealth—not accumulating wealth, as is prized in Western culture— was a means of cementing leadership, affirming status* . . . In Passage 2, the author states the objects have no value, and yet, this ceremonial exchange has numerous tangible benefits. None of the other choices is supported by the texts.

42. c. Both potlatches and the *kula* ring involve giving and receiving, and both of the societies that participate in these rituals can be described as traditional. The tone of the title in choice **e** is more whimsical than the serious tone of each passage. Choice **b** is incorrect because neither article draws conclusions about traditional societies in general.

43. c. Choice **d** is true but too specific to be the author's primary purpose. Choice **e** can be eliminated because it is too negative and choices **a** and **b** are too positive.

44. a. The author contrasts the public's dismissal of the arcane practice of wearing garlic with its increasing acceptance of herbal remedies.

45. b. In this context, *conventional* refers to the established system of Western medicine or biomedicine.

46. d. Choice **a** is overly general, and choice **b** is too negative to be inferred from the survey's findings. Choice **c** is incorrect—the author does not mention the "baby boom" age group, but that does not imply that the survey does not include it. The survey does not support the prediction in choice **e**.

47. a. The statistic illustrates the popularity of alternative therapies without giving any specific information as to why.

48. e. The author states that Americans are not replacing conventional healthcare but are adding to or supplementing it with alternative care.

49. d. The shortcomings of conventional healthcare mentioned are the time constraints of managed care, the focus on technology, and the inability to relieve symptoms associated with chronic disease.

50. a. The author states that once scientific investigation has confirmed their safety and efficacy, alternative therapies may be accepted by the medical establishment.

51. b. The author gives evidence of observational studies to show that garlic may be beneficial. Choice **d** is incorrect, however, because the author emphasizes that these findings have not been confirmed in clinical studies.

52. d. The passage does not offer a criticism or argument about alternative healthcare, but rather reports on the phenomenon with some playfulness.

53. b. The primary purpose of the passage is to educate readers about the importance of good parenting in developing moral character in children. Choices **a**, **d**, and **e** are too narrow. Choice **c** is not supported by the passage.

54. d. The author is using *sentence* in the sense of a conclusion reached by a judge in a criminal trial. She is asserting that to conclude that an eight-month-old baby is already destined for success or failure is a harsh judgment on such a small child. Note that choice **e**, is incorrect because punishment is the result of a sentence and does not make sense in this context.

55. c. The author opens the paragraph with the assertion that love is the cornerstone (foundation) of good parenting. The monkey study, which indicates that the need for love supersedes the need for food, is used to support that assertion.

56. a. The passage clearly defines cold parents as withholding love. *Aloof* means reserved or removed in feeling. Restrictive parenting is defined in the passage as setting limits. A disciplinarian is one who enforces order.

57. e. This paragraph links the ability to defer gratification with self-discipline and self-control. Hence, children who are unable to defer gratification are unlikely to succeed because they lack self-discipline.

58. e. The subject of this paragraph is parents balancing their needs with those of their child. Teaching a child to sleep through the night is an example of parents balancing their needs (for a full night's sleep) with the needs of their baby (to be picked up in the middle of the night).

59. c. The passage clearly states that many parents will come to good parenting techniques instinctually, which indicates that instincts are a good guide for parents. Also, the passage states that loving an infant comes naturally to most parents—something that comes naturally is instinctual. None of the other choices is supported by the passage.

60. d. Doc Burton emphasizes change. He tells Mac that nothing stops and that as soon as an idea (such as the cause) is put into effect, it (the idea) would start changing right away. Then he specifically states that once a commune is established, the same gradual flux will continue. Thus, the cause itself is in flux and is always changing.

61. b. The several references to communes suggest that the cause is communism, and this is made clear when Mac says revolution and communism will cure social injustice.

62. a. Doc Burton describes his desire to see the whole picture, to look at the whole thing. He tells Mac he doesn't want to judge the cause as good or bad so that he doesn't limit his vision. Thus, he is best described as an objective observer.

63. d. In the first part of his analogy, Doc Burton says that infections are a reaction to a wound—the wound is the first battleground. Without a wound, there is no place for the infection to fester. The strikes, then, are like the infection in that they are a reaction to a wound (social injustice).

64. a. By comparing an individual in a group to a cell within the body, Doc Burton emphasizes the idea that the individual is really not an individual at all but rather part of a whole.

65. c. Doc Burton argues that the group doesn't care about the standard or cause it has created because the group simply wants to move, to fight. Individuals such as Mac, however, believe in a cause (or at least think they do).

66. a. Doc Burton seems to feel quite strongly that group-man simply wants to move, to fight, without needing a real cause—in fact, he states that the group uses the cause simply to reassure the brains of individual men.

67. b. Doc Burton knows how deeply Mac believes in the cause and knows that if he outright says the group doesn't really believe in the cause that Mac would not listen. Thus, he says "It might be like this," emphasizing the possibility. Still Mac reacts hotly.

68. c. The author states a surfer should lie upon a surfboard like a small boy on a coaster, and then goes on to say that the surfer slides down a wave just as a boy slides down a hill on his coaster.

69. d. The question asks for the statement that cannot be answered based on information given in the passage. The author describes the shape and dimensions of a flat board and tells the reader how to paddle and lie upon it. But nowhere in the passage does the author state that a flat board is the most popular type of surfboard.

70. e. The author states that the bottom shoals gradually from a quarter of a mile to a mile toward the beach at Waikiki, producing a splendid surf-riding surf.

71. b. When the word *shoal* is used as a verb, it usually means to become shallow (as in water) or to come to a shallow or less deep part. As the wave approaches the shore, the lower portion of the wave strikes land first and is stopped. If the sea bottom is rising, the water will, therefore, be not as deep, in other words—it will be shallower.

72. b. It is the bottom of a wave striking against the top of the land that is the cause of all surfs.

73. a. As it is used in the passage, *impetus* most nearly means a moving force. In this case, a wave is a moving force through the water. If you did not know the correct definition, the best way to answer this question would be to replace *impetus* in the sentence with each of the given answer choices to see which one makes the most sense in context.

74. a. The best approach to this question is to reread the passage for each answer choice to see which choice is directly supported by the given text. For this question, you would not have to go far to find the answer: choice **a** quickly summarizes the text of those lines. All the other answer choices are unsupported or contradicted by the given text.

75. c. Context clues are your best aid in answering this question, and an important context clue is given in lines 1, 2, and 3. The author goes on to state that the water that composes the body of a wave is stationary, and gives the example of the thrown stone causing ripples in the water. The rock that is thrown is the cause of the agitation of the water. The ripples (or the waves) that surge away from that agitation are the communication of that agitation moving through the water. Therefore, choice **c** is the correct answer.

76. c. The author compares surfing to sliding down a hill. But unlike a six-foot-tall hill, a surfer can slide down a six-foot-tall wave for more than a quarter of a mile without ever reaching the bottom. The author explains that this is possible because the water that composes the wave is, like a hill, standing still and new water is rising into the wave as fast as the wave travels, preventing the surfer from reaching the bottom. So while it looks like a surfer is sliding along moving water, he or she is actually stationary on a wave as it moves through the water. That's the secret.

77. c. In Passage 1, the author provides a limited chronology of Johnson's life (paragraphs 2, 3, and 4) and briefly describes his influence on blues and rock and roll (paragraphs 1 and 5).

78. b. In paragraph 3 of Passage 1, the author describes how Johnson was not very good at playing the guitar but that he wanted to learn, so he spent his time in blues bars watching the local blues legends. Then he disappeared for some time and returned as a first-rate guitarist, which also suggests Johnson's determination.

79. a. In Passage 2, the author describes how the blues came to be called the blues—thus, *neologism* means a new word or new meaning or use of a word.

80. d. This sentence states that the blues remakes were enjoyed by all kinds of people—black and white, young and old—and suggests why the songs were so popular by describing how the lyrics touched a common emotional chord in listeners, all of whom have had the blues from one or more of the sources listed in the sentence.

81. d. The author states that the blues was a music perfectly suited for a nation on the brink of the Civil Rights movement because it was music that had the power to cross boundaries, to heal wounds, and to offer hope to a new generation of Americans. The previous sentence states that the music was popular with both the black and white, young and old. Thus, the author suggests that this shared musical experience helped promote understanding across racial boundaries and thereby eased racial tensions.

82. b. Neither author explicitly states that Robert Johnson is the best blues guitarist of his era, although this is implied by the author of Passage 1, who states that Johnson's impact on the world of rock and roll is indisputable and quotes Eric Clapton as saying Johnson is the most important blues musician who ever lived. However, the author of Passage 2 simply lists Johnson in the same sentence as his mentors Son House and Willie Brown, without suggesting that any one of these artists was better than the other.

83. c. Passage 1 states from the beginning that there is little information about Johnson and that the information that is available is as much rumor as fact. There is also no definitive answer regarding how Johnson acquired his talent (paragraph 4), and the author uses the word *purportedly* to emphasize further the speculative nature of the narrative. Passage 2, on the other hand, provides many specific facts in the form of names and dates to present a text that is factual and assertive.

84. a. Passage 1 describes the life and influence of one specific blues artist, while Passage 2 provides a general overview of the history of the blues.

85. c. At the end of Passage 1, the author describes the reason so many artists record Johnson's songs: His music *captures the very essence of the blues, transforming our pain and suffering with the healing magic of his guitar*. This sentence "proves" the idea stated in Passage 2 that "the blues" is something of a misnomer. This is the only sentence from Passage 2 that fits the focus of Passage 1; the others concern the development or defining characteristics of the blues.

86. b. The first paragraph introduces the passage's thesis and gives an overview about who emigrated to California and why they came.

87. b. The passage provides a historical overview supported by facts and interpreted by the author. The author's opinion is evidenced in the last sentence of the passage: a testimony to their outstanding achievements and contributions.

88. c. The passage states that the Chinese immigrants proved to be productive and resourceful. The passage praises their speed, dexterity, and outright perseverance.

89. e. The passage states that at the time, the U.S. Constitution reserved the right of naturalization for white immigrants, excluding Chinese immigrants. Chinese immigrants could become citizens, depending on the whim of local governments.

90. c. *Enterprise* means an undertaking that is especially risky. It could also mean a unit of economic organization. In this instance, industry fits best within the context.

91. d. Chinese immigrants faced discriminatory laws that made them unable to own land or file mining claims.

92. a. One meaning of *reclaim* is to reform or protest improper conduct. Other meanings are to rescue from an undesirable state, or to make something available for human use—this definition applies to the context.

93. a. The last sentence provides an example (Chinese immigrants performing hazardous railroad work in brutal conditions) that supports the general thesis of the passage—that Chinese immigrants made major contributions to opening up the West.

94. b. In the first sentence, the author states that the subject-matter of knowledge is intimately united, while in the second sentence, he adds the "Sciences [. . .] have multiple bearings on one another." Then, he states that the sciences complete, correct, balance each other.

95. d. In the first sentence, the author states that all branches of knowledge are connected together. Then, in the second sentence, he writes *Hence it is that the Sciences, into which our knowledge may be said to be cast. . . . Thus,* Newman is using the term *the Sciences* to refer to all branches of knowledge.

96. c. The word *excise* here is used in an unusual way to mean impose or put upon. The main context clue is the word *influence*, which suggests a giving to rather than a taking away.

97. a. Throughout the first paragraph, the author emphasizes the interdependence of the branches of knowledge and warns against focusing on one branch at the neglect of others. He states that to give *undue prominence to one* [area of study] *is to be unjust to another; to neglect or supersede these is to divert those from their proper object.* More important, he states that this action would serve *to unsettle the boundary lines between science and science,* to destroy the harmony which binds them together. Thus, the knowledge received would be skewed; it would tell a different tale when it is not viewed as a portion of a whole.

98. b. The first sentence of the second paragraph shows that its purpose is to develop the idea in the first further by way of example. Newman writes, *Let me make use of an illustration*—an illustration that further demonstrates how one's understanding of an idea changes in relation to the other ideas around it.

99. a. Here, *apprehends* is used to mean "understands." In this paragraph, the author describes what it is the university student would learn from his or her professors.

100. c. Throughout the passage, Newman argues that the branches of knowledge are interrelated and should be studied in combination and in relation to each other. He argues against focusing on one science or discipline, and he states that the university student apprehends the great outlines of knowledge, suggesting that he understands the broad issues in many subject areas.

101. b. At the beginning of the third paragraph, Newman states that it is a great point then to enlarge the range of studies that a university professes and that students would be best served by living among those and under those who represent the whole circle of knowledge. He argues that students will learn from the atmosphere created by their professors who adjust together the claims and relations of their respective subjects and who learn to respect, to consult, and to aid each other.

102. c. The first paragraph introduces the topic of the passage, the musical traditions of colonial New Mexico. Choices **a** and **d** are too narrow, and choice **b** is too broad. Choice **e** is the purpose of the entire passage, not the first paragraph alone.

103. d. *Singular* means of or relating to a single instance, or something considered by itself. Although *strange* and *superior* can be synonyms for singular, the author emphasizes throughout the passage that the music is unique. *Unusual* is closest in meaning to unique. Also, note that in the next sentence, the author states that the *bailes* had unusual melodic structures and the players had unique methods of bowing and tuning their instruments.

104. d. The passage does not explicitly state that European culture was imposed on native traditions. Rather, it states that the cultures mixed to give rise to the music.

105. c. The passage clearly states that both ceremonies used improvised verses. The New Year's celebration included improvised couplets, composed on the spot, and the verses of the song of the wedding ceremony, played to a lively waltz, were improvised. Each of the other choices is true for one of the ceremonies but not both.

106. a. The sentence following the first mention of the ceremony states its purpose: *the community would gather to sanction the new couple.* It is stated that the guests file past to bless the couple. Choices **b**, **d**, and **e** are all part of the ceremony but not its main purpose. Choice **c** is not explicitly supported by the text.

107. e. This title indicates that the passage covers both popular and ceremonial music and introduces the main theme of the passage: the unique (extraordinary) musical tradition of the Rio Grande region. The other choices are all too narrow (choice **d**) or are totally inappropriate (choice **c**).

108. b. The introductory and final paragraphs of the passage reveal the author's admiration for the music. The author describes the musical tradition as unique, rich, and he or she calls the ceremonial music "some of the most extraordinary . . . in the Hispanic world." The author describes the *indita* as extraordinary. Although he or she describes the tradition in positive terms, *awe* overstates the case.

109. c. The Lewis and Clark expedition did not have a military goal and did not have any violent encounters except the one described in lines 26–28.

110. b. Jefferson and his representatives wanted Native Americans to acknowledge American sovereignty and to see themselves as children to his role as their "father."

111. c. One meaning of *protocol* is a code that demands strict adherence to etiquette.

112. d. The passage states that Lewis and Clark sought to impose their own notions of hierarchy on Native Americans by "making chiefs" with medals, printed certificates, and gifts.

113. c. Placing a peace medal around the neck of a man killed by the expedition makes an ironic statement about the meaning of "peace."

114. b. To the Plains Native Americans, the pipe ceremony meant that those who participated accepted sacred obligations to share wealth, aid in war, and revenge injustice. The passage suggests that Lewis and Clark most likely did not understand the significance of the ceremony.

115. e. One meaning of *adopt* is to take by choice into a relationship. In this context, adopt has another meaning: to take up and practice or use.

116. e. By giving manufactured goods to Native Americans, Lewis and Clark were promoting Euro-American culture. Jefferson hoped that these free samples would introduce the Native Americans to mechanized agriculture as part of his plan to "civilize and instruct" them.

117. a. The passage compares different abstract principles, or organizing principles of

Euro-American society versus that of tribal societies. For example, it explores the principles of hierarchy and kinship.

118. b. Choice **a** is too general to be the primary purpose of the passage, whereas choices **c** and **e** are too specific. Choice **d** is not supported by the passage.

119. a. The narrator of Passage 1 mentions, *At sea we do meet with rough weather at times.* In Passage 2, the boy recounts that his boat ran into a vicious Atlantic storm, and the waves tossed the *Alba* around like it was a tiny raft. Choice **d** may seem like an attractive answer, but there is only evidence that the *Alba* leaks, not the yacht, and the question requires support from both passages.

120. c. In the last sentence of Passage 2, the narrator questions his decision to take the voyage aboard the Alba by asking himself *What have I gotten myself into?* This self-doubt indicates that he believed his decision may have been a mistake. This choice best answers the question.

121. d. The author of Passage 1 tells of the beautiful property belonging to the Earl of Mount Edgcumbe and implores the reader to visit Plymouth if they ever get the chance. He then goes on to describe the bustling harbor at Plymouth and finishes with: There is a great deal to see at Plymouth besides the sea itself. In short, he describes all the interesting sights to behold at Plymouth. All the other choices either do not make sense or are not specifically supported by details from the text.

122. b. In Passage 1, the narrator states that the yacht is a particular type of ship known as a cutter. In Passage 2, the captain explains to his nephew that the *Alba* is a cutter, as well. In that same conversation, the nephew learns that all cutters share a similar trait: They possess only a single mast. Therefore, choice **b** is the correct answer.

123. d. When you answer this question, the key is to be sure to find the only choice that is supported by specific examples from the text. Nowhere in the text of Passage 1 does it state that the yacht carries cargo, but on the other hand it never mentions the fact that it does not. The same reasoning goes for choices **b**, **c**, and **e**. The yacht may be bigger and faster than the *Alba*, and the *Alba* may carry only crew, but these facts are never mentioned in the texts so we can't know for sure. That leaves only one possible answer: choice **d**. The yacht is most certainly more luxurious than the *Alba*, and this statement is backed by both narrators' descriptions of their respective vessels.

124. e. The captain knew it was important that the crew understood the boy was no more privileged than anyone else aboard the *Alba*. Evidence for this choice is found in the narrator's statement: *because I was his nephew, I would probably have to work twice as hard as the others to prove my worth.* All the other choices do not make sense or are not backed by specific examples from the text.

125. a. As used in Passage 1, the verb *repair* most closely means take themselves, or more simply, go. Today, *repair* is most commonly used as a verb that means to fix something (choice **b**). However, in the context of the sentence, this makes no sense. The easiest way to answer this question is to replace *repair* in the sentence with each the answer choices, and see which one fits best in context. By doing this, you should narrow down your choice to just one: choice **a**.

126. c. The narrator's familiarity with yachts and the harbor at Plymouth in Passage 1 seems to indicate that he is an experienced yachtsman. He reveals his passion for yachting when he declares, *Of all amusements, give me yachting.* All the other answer choices either do not make sense or are not supported by specific examples from the text.

127. e. Nigel probably had rotten or missing teeth. The narrator of Passage 2 chose to describe Nigel's smile as *a graveyard of yellow sincerity*, describing his yellow teeth as tombstones in a graveyard. When a writer uses a descriptive word or phrase in place of another to suggest a similarity between the two, this figure of speech is called a metaphor (choice **e**). If the boy had instead said, Nigel's smile was "like a graveyard of yellow sincerity," it would have been a simile, choice **b**.

128. a. Both passages are basically concerned with a similar situation—life aboard a cutter. The author of Passage 1 sets a pleasurable tone in the first paragraph by describing the idyllic scene at Plymouth and the anchored yacht. He later describes the yacht as elegant, tasteful, and luxurious, and the smell of the food delightful. In stark contrast, the boy narrator in Passage 2 begins the passage by describing the menacing facade of his uncle and the immediate reality check the boy receives when he steps aboard. His description of the heat and smell below deck, and the horrible food, effectively sets the dark and oppressive tone of the passage. Together, these two very different descriptions prove that the reality of two seemingly similar situations can often be extremely different, choice **a**.

129. b. The word *berth*, when used as a noun, often refers to the sleeping quarters aboard a boat or a train. The boy describes his berth as the place where he could stow his clothes, and at night string up his hammock.

130. e. The three examples in the first paragraph show that there is a wide range of styles of public art in New York City and that public art can be found in a variety of places, including more mundane locations such as the subway and post office.

131. a. *Inherently* is an adverb that describes the essential nature of something. The context clue to answer this question is found in the same sentence. All art is inherently public because it is created in order to convey an idea or emotion to others. The author is saying that an essential characteristic of art is that it is created for others.

132. b. Public art is defined as the kind of art created for and displayed in public spaces, and it is specifically designed for a public arena where the art will be encountered by people in their normal day-to-day activities. This is in contrast to private art, which is less accessible because it is kept in specific, non-public places such as museums and galleries.

133. b. To sequester is to seclude or isolate. Thus, the use of this word suggests that the author feels private art is too isolated and cut off from the public.

134. d. The seven functions are listed in the fifth paragraph: educating, place making, stimulating the public, promoting community, beautifying, and regenerating. While promoting good citizenship may be a side benefit of public art, it is not discussed in the passage.

135. a. After defining public art, the passage discusses the functions of public art and its impact on the city.

136. d. The examples in the first paragraph and the list of different kinds of public art (e.g., ornamental benches) will make readers more aware of public art; paragraphs 2 and 3 explain the difference between public and private art; paragraph 5 explains how public art affects the community; and paragraph 6 discusses how public art should be created. A few readers may be inspired to create public art after reading this passage, but that is not one of its goals.

137. a. Although the passage states that there exists in every city a symbiotic relationship between the city and its art and paragraph 5 explains how public art affects the city, there is no discussion of how the city affects art.

138. b. Because the main purpose is to show what public art is and how public art affects the city, the passage would be best served by an expanded discussion of how public art fulfills each of the important functions in paragraph 5.

139. c. The women refer to each other as "Mrs.," and their conversation reveals that they don't know much about each other. Mrs. Hale, for example, asks Mrs. Peters if she knew Mr. Wright and if she were raised round here.

140. a. Mrs. Peters says *It would be lonesome for me sitting here alone*—to which Mrs. Hale replies, *It would, wouldn't it?* and then expresses her wish that she'd come to see Mrs. Wright. She says *it's a lonesome place and always was* and then says *I can see now*, suggesting that she can understand now how Mrs. Wright must have felt.

141. d. Mrs. Hale describes Mr. Wright as a *hard man* who was *like a raw wind that gets to the bone.* Mrs. Wright's loneliness would be deepened by living with a man who was quiet and cold.

142. b. The punctuation here—the dashes between each word—suggest that Mrs. Wright changed from the sweet, fluttery woman she was to a bitter, unhappy person over the years. The emphasis on her loneliness and the dead husband and bird add to this impression.

143. d. The women decide to take the quilt to Mrs. Wright to keep her busy; it would give her something to do, something familiar and comforting.

144. c. Because her house was so lonely, Mrs. Wright would have wanted the company of a pet—and a pet that shared some qualities with her (or with her younger self) would have been particularly appealing. She would have liked the bird's singing to ease the quiet in the house, and she also used to sing real pretty herself and would have felt a real connection with the bird.

145. b. The clues in the passage—the violently broken birdcage, the dead bird lovingly wrapped in silk and put in a pretty box, the description of John Wright as a hard and cold man—suggest that he killed the bird and that Mrs. Wright in turn killed him for destroying her companion.

146. d. The fact that Mrs. Hale slips box under quilt pieces suggests that she will not share her discovery with the men.

147. d. Choices **a**, **b**, and **e** are too specific to be the primary purpose of the passage, whereas choice **c** is too general. The passage focuses on the importance of the first official report to name smoking a serious health hazard.

148. c. One meaning of *preoccupied* is lost in thought; another is engaged or engrossed. In this case, *absorbed* is nearest in meaning.

149. a. The debate over the hazards and benefits of smoking that continued since the sixteenth century points to a long-standing controversy.

150. e. An alliance of prominent private health organizations gave the push for an official report on smoking.

151. d. The quotation illustrates the response to the report, describing its effect on the country as *a bombshell* (lines 31–32).

152. b. *Hedged* can mean hindered or hemmed in, but in this instance, it most nearly means *evaded.* The author suggests that the report evaded a risk by calling smoking a habit rather than an addiction.

153. b. The author's statement implies that the report could have suggested specific actions to confront the health problem of smoking, but that it did not.

154. b. The author describes the influence of the report in positive terms except to mention that it did not give recommendations for remedial actions.

155. d. In the first paragraph, where the theme is typically introduced, it states that members of Congress have decided they need to do something about the obesity epidemic.

156. e. What they are also getting could be, in one meal, more than the daily recommended allowances of calories, fat, and sodium.

157. c. Clues for this question are found in the first paragraph, in which the obesity problem is called an epidemic, and the staggering cost of the problem is mentioned.

158. b. Paragraph 5 states that the restaurant industry has responded to the bill by pointing out that diet alone is not the reason for America's obesity epidemic. A lack of adequate exercise is also to blame.

159. c. The chicken breast sandwich contains more than twice the recommended daily amount of sodium.

160. a. Paragraph 6 explains that those who support menu-labeling believe nutritional information must be provided where they are selecting their food.

161. b. Menu-labeling would result in menus that look like the nutrition facts panels found on food in supermarkets.

162. c. Isabella Beecher Hooker invokes the Constitution and recites the Preamble in order to appeal to and persuade her audience.

163. a. Isabella Beecher Hooker plays on the two meanings suggested by the phrase *learn it by heart as well as by head*. She asks her audience to not only memorize the Constitu-

tion's Preamble, but to use both emotion and intellect to understand its meaning.

164. e. One meaning of *anxious* is extreme uneasiness or dread. An alternative meaning applies to this context—that of ardently or earnestly wishing.

165. c. Passage 1 argues that the foremothers of the nation were patriotic and did their full share of contributing to the early republic.

166. b. The passage anticipates the arguments of those in favor of women's right to vote and refutes them.

167. c. *Novel* means new and not resembling something known or used in the past. Choice **b**, *original*, could fit this definition but its connotation is too positive for the context.

168. a. Passage 2 describes woman-suffrage societies as thoroughly organized, with active and zealous managers. Choice **b**, *courageous*, is too positive for the context of the passage.

169. a. Passage 2 states that *every one . . . knows that without female suffrage, legislation for years has improved and is still improving the condition of women.*

170. d. Passage 2 emphasizes how well women are served by judges. Passage 1 does not refer to this issue at all.

171. b. Passage 1 describes men as fighters by nature, but not women. Passage 2 describes women as incapable of performing military duty.

172. d. Passage 1 addresses its audience in the second person, whereas Passage 2 does not. Passage 1 also refers to its audience as friends and brothers.

173. b. The author uses the phrase *going gray* as a metaphor for growing older. It describes the phenomenon of a large segment of a population growing older.

174. c. The passage makes an argument for more geriatric training based on statistical information and studies.

175. d. The passage emphasizes the need for age-specific care.

176. a. In this context, *address* most nearly means *manage*, or treat. The sentence implies that some kind of action is taken after the problem has first been identified, analyzed, and dissected.

177. c. Although choices **a** and **b** may be correct statements, they do not reflect the author's purpose in citing the example of untreated depression in the elderly. Choice **d** is incorrect and choice **e** is not supported by the passage.

178. c. According to the passage, geriatric training improves a healthcare provider's ability to distinguish between "normal" characteristics associated with aging and illness.

179. b. The author states that healthcare providers should consider not only the physical but mental, emotional, and social changes of the aging process.

180. d. The author's sense of urgent recommendation is expressed through the use of the helping verbs *must* and *should*.

181. b. The passage illustrates several protest strategies used in the Civil Rights movement. Choices **c** and **e** are true statements but are too specific to be the primary focus of the passage. Choices **a** and **d** are not described in detail in the passage.

182. c. The passage states that Rosa Park's actions and arrest set off a train of events that generated a momentum the Civil Rights movement had never before experienced.

183. e. In this context, *test* refers to putting something to a test or challenging something.

184. d. The protest at the Greensboro Woolworth lunch counter inspired others. Two weeks later similar demonstrations had spread to several cities, within a year similar peaceful demonstrations took place in over a hundred northern and southern cities.

185. b. The passage implies that the 1963 March on Washington was a very successful demonstration: It attracted more than twice the number of people that organizers expected and riveted the nation's attention, drawing attention to the issues that the march promoted.

186. c. One meaning of *refrain* is a regularly recurring verse in a song. In this context, *refrain* refers to the recurring phrase *I have a dream*, which Reverend Martin Luther King, Jr. used in his famous speech.

187. d. The term *second-class citizen* is not a legal state of citizenship, rather it is a descriptive term that refers to a condition in which citizens of a nation are denied the rights and privileges that other citizens enjoy.

188. e. The passage does not speculate about the future nor does it describe the racial discrimination that occurs today in the United States.

189. e. Chick Gandil first approached the gambler with his scheme, and then recruited the seven other players.

190. b. *Parsimonious* is a word used to describe someone who is frugal to the point of stinginess. Comiskey's pay cuts, bonus of cheap champagne, refusal to launder uniforms, and his benching of Eddie Ciccotte are all clues that should help you deduce the answer from the given choices.

191. b. Answering this question involves a bit of deductive reasoning. Though the actual name of the ballpark is never given in the passage, the passage states that the 1917 White Sox won the World Series playing in a park named for their owner.

192. a. As it is used in the passage, *thrown* means to have lost intentionally. For $100,000 Chick Gandil would make sure the Sox lost the Series.

193. c. The passage states between the years of 1900 and 1915, the White Sox had won the World Series only once, and then it tells us they won it again in 1917. Be careful not to mistakenly select choice **d**, three; the question asks for the number of World Series the Sox won, not the number of series played.

194. d. The author states that after Ciccotte won his 29th game he was benched by Comiskey for the rest of the season. Choice **d** asks for the number of games he pitched. It is stated that he pitched and won 29 games in 1919, but the passage doesn't mention the number of games he pitched in which he lost, so you can't know for sure.

195. b. *Ignominious* is a word used to describe something marked with shame or disgrace, something *dishonorable*. The ignominious label referred to is Black Sox—the nickname the Chicago press took to calling the scandalized and disgraced White Sox team.

196. c. It is stated throughout the passage Comiskey was a frugal man, yet it says that he paid for the players' defense lawyers. Why? The answer to that and the biggest clue to answering this question lies in the last sentence of the passage: Comiskey's once mighty team was decimated by the loss of its most talented players, and the 1921 White Sox finished the season in seventh place.

197. b. The passage states that gamblers would often target with the lower-paid athletes because the money with which these gamblers tempted the players was hard to refuse. The passage tells that because of Charles Comiskey's stinginess with his players, there were many underpaid players on the White Sox who were dissatisfied and they were the most discontented team in baseball. These factors suggest that if Charles Comiskey had treated his players better, perhaps they might not have been so eager to betray him.

198. d. In the first few lines, the narrator states that Miss Temple was the superintendent of the seminary and that she received both instruction and friendship from Miss Temple, who was also like a mother to her (*she had stood me in the stead of mother*).

199. a. The narrator states that with Miss Temple, *I had given in allegiance to duty and order; I was quiet; I believed I was content.*

200. d. The context here suggests existence or habitation, not captivity or illness.

201. c. We can assume that the narrator would go home during vacations, but she spent all of her vacations at school because *Mrs. Reed had never sent for me to Gateshead*. Thus, we can infer that Mrs. Reed was her guardian, the one who sent the narrator to Lowood in the first place.

202. b. The narrator describes her experience with school-rules and school-duties and how she tired of the routine after Miss Temple left. She also contrasts Lowood with the real world of hopes and fears, of sensations and excitements and that the view from her window seemed a prison-ground, exile limits. Thus, it can be inferred that Lowood is both a structured and isolated place.

203. a. The narrator states that she had undergone a transforming process and that now she again felt *the stirring of old emotions* and remembered that *the real world was wide* and *awaited those who had courage to go forth*. She also looks at the road from Lowood and states how she *longed to follow it further*. More important, she repeats her desire for liberty and prays for a new servitude—something beyond Lowood.

204. e. The narrator states that with Miss Temple at Lowood, she believed she was content, that to the eyes of others, usually even to my own, I appeared a disciplined and subdued character. This suggests that in her natural element she is not so disciplined or subdued. Her desire for freedom and to explore the world are also evident in this passage; she longs to follow the road that leads away from Lowood and she is half desperate in her cry for something new, something beyond Lowood.

205. d. Because Lowood had been the narrator's home for eight years and all she knew of existence was school rules, duties, habits, faces, etc., it is likely that she feels her initial prayers were unrealistic. At least a new servitude would provide some familiar territory, and it, therefore, seems more realistic and attainable than liberty or change.

206. c. The author does not have a bite to his argument, as required by satire, cynicism, and sarcasm. He is also not speaking to two audiences, one that *gets it* and one that doesn't, as with irony. He is simply trying to be funny, saying that once a boy becomes a man, he will compete for cash on an island.

207. d. This is the only statement made by both authors. Don't be tricked by the choices that are true, such as **a**, **b**, and **e**. They need to be believed by both authors to be correct.

208. a. Passage 2 repeats a number of times its first question: *Why does reality TV get such a bad rap?* Lines 2 and 3 explain the argument further, saying its popularity is blamed on degenerate morals and a decreasing attention span. The first lines of paragraph 2 again question the argument against reality TV, and the last paragraph repeats the questioning. There are no outcomes or any need for change mentioned. A brief history is given, and the subject of getting famous through exposure on reality TV is brought up, but neither is the primary purpose of the passage.

209. b. Passage 1 centers on a problem with reality TV, and while Passage 2 does mention some problems, they are not what he or she feels, but rather the opinion of some people. Choice **a** is incorrect because Passage 1 does not defend reality TV. Choice **c** is incorrect because the author of Passage 2 acknowledges that some people have a problem with reality TV. Choice **d** is incorrect because Passage 2 does not say anything about variety in TV programming. Choice **e** is wrong because Passage 2 doesn't mention the cost of producing TV shows.

210. a. Ratings refers to how many people watch the show. A homerun is the best possible kind of hit, so a *ratings homerun* is a symbolic term meaning that many people watch the show. Choices **b**, **c**, and **e** reference ball games literally, but the author used the term figuratively, so those choices are incorrect. Nielsen is the company that gathers TV ratings, but high ratings have nothing to do with whether they like a show.

211. e. Both passages show that there is a debate about reality TV. In Passage 1, the author is against it but notes that it is popular. The author of Passage 2 likes it and also recognizes that it gets a bad rap. Although most of the other choices are factual, they do not appear in both passages and are not illustrated by them.

212. c. The clue comes in Passage 1, which describes the swathing and flower gluing as crimes against defenseless walls. Swathing is, therefore, something done to a wall. The only choice that makes sense is **c**, *to cover.*

213. d. While there is evidence for the other choices, they are not the most troublesome. The author repeats in every paragraph the idea that reality TV isn't real.

214. b. *Discrete* means distinct, and as used in the passage, it is paired with *specialized*, a context clue. Choices **a**, **c**, **d**, and **e** are all synonyms for the homophone, *discreet*.

215. d. Choice **b** is not covered in the passage. Choices **a**, **c**, and **e**, while mentioned, are too specific to be viable titles. Choice **d** is broad-ranging enough to encompass the entire passage.

216. c. *Scrimshawed* means carved. The word is often associated with whaling and seafaring, so answer choices **a**, **d**, and **e** are all distracters stemming from that confusion regarding context. Because scrimshaw and enamel are wax-like substances, a less careful reader may choose **b**.

217. d. According to the passage, choices **a**, **b**, **c**, and **e** are all parts of the physical structure of teeth. Choice **d**, *tusk*, is not a component of teeth, but rather a type of tooth found in some mammals.

Short-Passage Questions

For short-passage questions, you will need to read the short passages thoroughly and answer multiple questions that follow each passage. These questions tend to center on crucial ideas in the passage, such as key phrases, main ideas, and the author's point of view. Use the following 44 practice questions to familiarize yourself with this type of Critical Reading question.

SHORT-PASSAGE QUESTIONS

1. ⓐ ⓑ ⓒ ⓓ ⓔ	16. ⓐ ⓑ ⓒ ⓓ ⓔ	31. ⓐ ⓑ ⓒ ⓓ ⓔ
2. ⓐ ⓑ ⓒ ⓓ ⓔ	17. ⓐ ⓑ ⓒ ⓓ ⓔ	32. ⓐ ⓑ ⓒ ⓓ ⓔ
3. ⓐ ⓑ ⓒ ⓓ ⓔ	18. ⓐ ⓑ ⓒ ⓓ ⓔ	33. ⓐ ⓑ ⓒ ⓓ ⓔ
4. ⓐ ⓑ ⓒ ⓓ ⓔ	19. ⓐ ⓑ ⓒ ⓓ ⓔ	34. ⓐ ⓑ ⓒ ⓓ ⓔ
5. ⓐ ⓑ ⓒ ⓓ ⓔ	20. ⓐ ⓑ ⓒ ⓓ ⓔ	35. ⓐ ⓑ ⓒ ⓓ ⓔ
6. ⓐ ⓑ ⓒ ⓓ ⓔ	21. ⓐ ⓑ ⓒ ⓓ ⓔ	36. ⓐ ⓑ ⓒ ⓓ ⓔ
7. ⓐ ⓑ ⓒ ⓓ ⓔ	22. ⓐ ⓑ ⓒ ⓓ ⓔ	37. ⓐ ⓑ ⓒ ⓓ ⓔ
8. ⓐ ⓑ ⓒ ⓓ ⓔ	23. ⓐ ⓑ ⓒ ⓓ ⓔ	38. ⓐ ⓑ ⓒ ⓓ ⓔ
9. ⓐ ⓑ ⓒ ⓓ ⓔ	24. ⓐ ⓑ ⓒ ⓓ ⓔ	39. ⓐ ⓑ ⓒ ⓓ ⓔ
10. ⓐ ⓑ ⓒ ⓓ ⓔ	25. ⓐ ⓑ ⓒ ⓓ ⓔ	40. ⓐ ⓑ ⓒ ⓓ ⓔ
11. ⓐ ⓑ ⓒ ⓓ ⓔ	26. ⓐ ⓑ ⓒ ⓓ ⓔ	41. ⓐ ⓑ ⓒ ⓓ ⓔ
12. ⓐ ⓑ ⓒ ⓓ ⓔ	27. ⓐ ⓑ ⓒ ⓓ ⓔ	42. ⓐ ⓑ ⓒ ⓓ ⓔ
13. ⓐ ⓑ ⓒ ⓓ ⓔ	28. ⓐ ⓑ ⓒ ⓓ ⓔ	43. ⓐ ⓑ ⓒ ⓓ ⓔ
14. ⓐ ⓑ ⓒ ⓓ ⓔ	29. ⓐ ⓑ ⓒ ⓓ ⓔ	44. ⓐ ⓑ ⓒ ⓓ ⓔ
15. ⓐ ⓑ ⓒ ⓓ ⓔ	30. ⓐ ⓑ ⓒ ⓓ ⓔ	

Questions 1–4 are based on the following passage.

Line

Although it is called Central Park, New York City's great green space has no "center"—no formal walkway down the middle of the park, no central monument or body of water, no single orienting feature. The paths wind, the landscape constantly shifts and changes, the sections spill into one another in a seemingly random manner. But this "decentering" was precisely the intent of the park's innovative design. Made to look

(5)   as natural as possible, Frederick Law Olmsted's 1858 plan for Central Park had as its main goal the creation of a democratic playground—a place with many centers to reflect the multiplicity of its uses and users. Olmsted designed the park to allow interaction among the various members of society, without giving preference to one group or class. Thus, Olmsted's ideal of a "commonplace civilization" could be realized.

1. In lines 2–4, the author describes specific park features in order to
   a. present both sides of an argument.
   b. suggest the organization of the rest of the passage.
   c. provide evidence that the park has no center.
   d. demonstrate how large the park is.
   e. show how well the author knows the park.

2. The main idea of this passage is that
   a. New York City is a democratic city.
   b. Olmsted was a brilliant designer.
   c. more parks should be designed without centers.
   d. Central Park is used by many people for many different purposes.
   e. Central Park is democratic by design.

3. The passage suggests that Olmsted's design
   a. was like most other parks being designed at the time.
   b. was radically different from other park designs.
   c. was initially very unpopular with New Yorkers.
   d. was inspired by similar parks in Europe.
   e. did not succeed in creating a democratic playground.

4. The word *commonplace* as used in line 8 most nearly means
   a. inclusive.
   b. ordinary.
   c. mediocre.
   d. normal.
   e. trite.

Questions 5–8 are based on the following passage.

In this excerpt from Toni Morrison's 1970 novel The Bluest Eye, *Pauline tries to ease her loneliness by going to the movies.*

Line

One winter Pauline discovered she was pregnant. When she told Cholly, he surprised her by being pleased. [. . .] They eased back into a relationship more like the early days of their marriage, when he asked if she were tired or wanted him to bring her something from the store. In this state of ease, Pauline stopped doing day work and returned to her own housekeeping. But the loneliness in those two rooms had not gone away.

(5) When the winter sun hit the peeling green paint of the kitchen chairs, when the smoked hocks were boiling in the pot, when all she could hear was the truck delivering furniture downstairs, she thought about back home, about how she had been all alone most of the time then too, but this lonesomeness was different. Then she stopped staring at the green chairs, at the delivery truck; she went to the movies instead. There in the dark her memory was refreshed, and she succumbed to her earlier dreams. Along with the

(10) idea of romantic love, she was introduced to another—physical beauty. Probably the most destructive ideas in the history of human thought. Both originated in envy, thrived in insecurity, and ended in disillusion.

5. Lines 1–3 suggest that just prior to Pauline's pregnancy, Cholly had
   a. loved Pauline dearly.
   b. begun to neglect Pauline.
   c. worked every day of the week.
   d. cared about Pauline's dreams.
   e. graduated from college.

6. Pauline's loneliness is different from the loneliness she felt back home (lines 6–8) because
   a. she's more bored than lonely.
   b. her family has abandoned her.
   c. she wants Cholly to be more romantic.
   d. she's a mother now.
   e. she shouldn't feel lonely with Cholly.

7. Pauline's earlier dreams (line 9) were of
   a. romance.
   b. being beautiful.
   c. having many children.
   d. being a famous actress.
   e. owning her own store.

8. The passage suggests that going to the movies will
   a. inspire Pauline to become an actress.
   b. inspire Pauline to demand more respect from Cholly.
   c. only make Pauline more unhappy with her life.
   d. encourage Pauline to study history.
   e. create a financial strain on the family.

Questions 9–13 are based on the following passages.

Line

Passage 1

Although cosmetic surgery (and non-surgical cosmetic procedures, such as Botox injections) sometimes produce negative outcomes—the media often highlights surgery "disasters"—for the most part, the health risk for cosmetic procedures is low and patient satisfaction is high. Often, people who have been hobbled by poor body image all of their lives, walk away from cosmetic surgery with confidence and the
(5)   motivation to lead healthier lives. In addition, reconstructive surgery for burn and accident victims or to those disfigured from disease restores self-esteem and well-being in a way that other therapies cannot. In my professional opinion, it is time for members of the medical community to examine the benefits and results of cosmetic surgery without prejudice or jealousy.

Passage 2

In 2002, more than 1.1 million Americans had Botox injections—a not entirely risk-free procedure that
(10) erases wrinkles by paralyzing facial muscles. For myself, I find the idea of paralyzing my facial muscles somewhat repellent and a betrayal of the emotions I have experienced—the joys and losses of a lifetime—that are written in those "crow's feet" and "worry lines." I'm not immune to the cultural pressures to look young, but for my money, a truly youthful appearance comes from a joy of life that shines through the ravages of time.

9. Which statement best characterizes the relationship between Passage 1 and Passage 2?
- **a.** Passage 1 praises medical techniques that Passage 2 derides.
- **b.** Passage 1 discusses positive applications of cosmetic procedures, while Passage 2 discusses negative outcomes of cosmetic procedures.
- **c.** Passage 1 informs while Passage 2 debates.
- **d.** Passage 1 discusses medicinal benefits of cosmetic procedures, while Passage 2 discusses societal benefits of cosmetic procedures.
- **e.** Passage 1 introduces a concept upon which Passage 2 elaborates.

10. Which aspect of the cosmetic procedure trend is discussed in Passage 1, but not in Passage 2?
- **a.** the possibility that cosmetic procedures will have negative outcomes
- **b.** non-surgical techniques like Botox injections
- **c.** the high cost of cosmetic procedures
- **d.** the personal satisfaction felt by those who have had cosmetic procedures
- **e.** reasons that people might have cosmetic procedures performed

11. The two authors would most likely agree with which statement?
  a. Cosmetic surgery takes away individuality.
  b. One's concept of beauty has an effect on one's sense of self-worth.
  c. Reconstructive surgery is beneficial to burn and accident victims.
  d. Cosmetic procedures help people maintain a youthful appearance.
  e. The benefits of plastic surgery outweigh the risks.

12. The approaches of the two passages to the topic are similar in that they both use
  a. the first-person point of view.
  b. the second-person address to the reader.
  c. references to other sources on the subject.
  d. a summary of types of plastic surgery.
  e. an array of opinions on the subject.

13. What is the main difference between Passage 1 and Passage 2?
  a. Passage 1 is an informed position, while Passage 2 is an uninformed position.
  b. Passage 1 uses statistics to further its argument, while Passage 2 uses common knowledge.
  c. Passage 1 argues that cosmetic procedures should increase, while Passage 2 argues that cosmetic procedures should decrease.
  d. Passage 1 argues a specific point, while Passage 2 presents a more universal argument.
  e. Passage 1 is mainly about the benefits of cosmetic procedures, while Passage 2 is mainly a personal view of beauty.

Questions 14–17 are based on the following passage.

In this excerpt from Book One of his Nicomachean Ethics, *Aristotle expands his definitions of "good" and "happiness."*

Line

Good things are commonly divided into three classes: (1) external goods, (2) goods of the soul, and (3) goods of the body. Of these, we call the goods pertaining to the soul goods in the highest and fullest sense. But in speaking of "soul," we refer to our soul's actions and activities. Thus, our definition [of good] tallies with this opinion which has been current for a long time and to which philosophers subscribe. We
(5)   are also right in defining the end as consisting of actions and activities; for in this way the end is included among the goods of the soul and not among external goods.

Also the view that a happy man lives well and fares well fits in with our definition: for we have all but defined happiness as a kind of good life and well-being.

Moreover, the characteristics which one looks for in happiness are all included in our definition. For
(10)   some people think that happiness is a virtue, others that it is practical wisdom, others that it is some kind of theoretical wisdom; others again believe it to be all or some of these accompanied by, or not devoid of, pleasure; and some people also include external prosperity in its definition.

14. According to the passage, the greatest goods are those that
   a. are theoretical.
   b. are spiritual.
   c. are intellectual.
   d. create happiness.
   e. create prosperity.

15. The word *tallies* in line 4 means
   a. keeps count.
   b. records.
   c. labels.
   d. corresponds.
   e. scores.

16. The author's definition of happiness in lines 7–8 is related to the definition of good in that
   a. living a good life will bring you happiness.
   b. happiness is the same as goodness.
   c. happiness is often sacrificed to attain the good.
   d. all things that create happiness are good things.
   e. happiness is a virtue.

17. In lines 9–12, the author's main purpose is to
   a. show that different people have different definitions of happiness.
   b. define virtue.
   c. prove that his definition of happiness is valid.
   d. explain the relationship between happiness and goodness.
   e. provide guidelines for good behavior.

Questions 18–20 are based on the following passage.

Line

Many studies make it clear that sleep deprivation is dangerous. Sleep-deprived people who are tested by using a driving simulator or by performing a hand-eye coordination task perform as badly as or worse than those who are intoxicated. Sleep deprivation also magnifies alcohol's effects on the body, so a fatigued person who drinks will become much more impaired than someone who is well rested. Driver fatigue is
(5)   responsible for an estimated 100,000 motor vehicle accidents and 1,500 deaths each year, according to the National Highway Traffic Safety Administration. Since drowsiness is the brain's last step before falling asleep, driving while drowsy can—and often does—lead to disaster. Caffeine and other stimulants cannot overcome the effects of severe sleep deprivation. The National Sleep Foundation says that if you have trouble keeping your eyes focused, if you can't stop yawning, or if you can't remember driving the
(10)   last few miles, you are probably too drowsy to drive safely.

18. The author seems to view sleep deprivation with
   a. obliviousness.
   b. anticipation.
   c. derision.
   d. impassivity.
   e. wariness.

19. The primary purpose of the passage is to
   a. offer preventive measures for sleep deprivation.
   b. explain why sleeplessness has become a common state in Western cultures.
   c. recommend the amount of sleep individuals need at different ages.
   d. alert readers to the risks of not getting enough sleep.
   e. discuss the effects of alcohol on a sleep-deprived person.

20. Why does the author refer to the National Highway Traffic Safety Administration and the National Sleep Foundation?
   a. to enhance his or her argument with information from reputable organizations
   b. to show the wide variety of organizations that are concerned with sleep deprivation
   c. to give the reader a reference point with which he or she would be familiar
   d. to balance the perspective by showing differing points of view on the same subject matter
   e. to present commonly held viewpoints with which the author disagrees

Questions 21–25 are based on the following passages.

Line

Passage 1

At Wal-Mart, we're concerned about more than just the bottom line. Our commitment to community improvement is unparalleled among national retailers—last year alone, we gave over $170 million dollars in cash contributions to more than 100,000 organizations. In addition, our Community Grant Program distributes resources to thousands of local charities around the country. And, of course, our everyday low
(5)   prices are saving customers billions of dollars each year.

Passage 2

Despite ongoing attempts to counteract negative publicity, Wal-Mart continues to harm employees and the communities around them with their cutthroat, "profit at any cost" mentality. The average Wal-Mart employee earns a paltry $8.23 per hour, far below the national average of $10.35 for supermarket employees. Hiring of full-time workers is routinely discouraged in favor of part-time employees who are ineligi-
(10)   ble for healthcare. Wal-Mart's immense purchasing power allows them to set their prices lower than other stores in the community, forcing local, mom-and-pop stores out of business. Even Wal-Mart's famously low prices are nothing but a shell game; although consumers may see immediate savings, the combined effect of replacing local businesses with a national retailer who pays lows wages and does not provide healthcare will inevitably cripple local economies.

21. The author of Passage 1 would most likely describe Wal-Mart's community involvement as
  a. cost-effective.
  b. significant.
  c. reprehensible.
  d. overblown.
  e. preventative.

22. The phrase *the bottom line* in Passage 1 refers to
  a. savings.
  b. the community.
  c. the final point.
  d. healthcare.
  e. profit.

23. Like Passage 1, Passage 2 does which of the following?
  a. requests an explanation
  b. contradicts a popular notion
  c. takes a side in an argument
  d. comes to a solution
  e. responds to an accusation

24. Both authors would most likely agree with which of the following statements?
  a. Wal-Mart is an important financial force in America.
  b. Wal-Mart contributes large amounts of money to charitable organizations.
  c. Wal-Mart's employees are not allowed to contest their low wages.
  d. Wal-Mart is actively trying to improve its local communities.
  e. Wal-Mart's prices may be low, but its costs to a community are not.

25. Both passages are primarily concerned with
  a. fighting negative stereotypes of national retailers.
  b. Wal-Mart's commitment to charity.
  c. the effects Wal-Mart has on the economy.
  d. Wal-Mart's local impact.
  e. Wal-Mart's relationship to its employees.

Questions 26–28 refer to the following passage.

Line

The history of microbiology begins with a Dutch haberdasher named Antoni van Leeuwenhoek, a man of no formal scientific education. In the late 1600s, Leeuwenhoek, inspired by the magnifying lenses used by drapers to examine cloth, assembled some of the first microscopes. He developed a technique for grinding and polishing tiny, convex lenses, some of which could magnify an object up to 270 times. After
(5)   scraping some plaque from between his teeth and examining it under a lens, Leeuwenhoek found tiny squirming creatures, which he called "animalcules." His observations, which he reported to the Royal Society of London, are among the first descriptions of living bacteria. Leeuwenhoek discovered an entire universe invisible to the naked eye. He found more animalcules—protozoa and bacteria—in samples of pond water, rainwater, and human saliva. He gave the first description of red corpuscles, observed plant
(10)   tissue, examined muscle, and investigated the life cycle of insects.

Nearly 200 years later, Leeuwenhoek's discovery of microbes aided French chemist and biologist Louis Pasteur to develop his "germ theory of disease." This concept suggested that disease derives from tiny organisms attacking and weakening the body. The germ theory later helped doctors fight infectious diseases including anthrax, diphtheria, polio, smallpox, tetanus, and typhoid.

26. According to the passage, Leeuwenhoek would be best described as a
   a. bored haberdasher who stumbled upon scientific discovery.
   b. trained researcher with an interest in microbiology.
   c. proficient hobbyist who made microscopic lenses for entertainment.
   d. inquisitive amateur who made pioneer studies of microbes.
   e. talented scientist interested in finding a cure for disease.

27. In line 2, *inspired* most nearly means
   a. introduced.
   b. invested.
   c. influenced.
   d. indulged.
   e. inclined.

28. The author's attitude toward Leeuwenhoek's contribution to medicine is one of
   a. ecstatic reverence.
   b. genuine admiration.
   c. tepid approval.
   d. courteous opposition.
   e. antagonistic incredulity.

Questions 29–32 are based on the following passage.

Line

Almost 50% of American teens are not vigorously active on a regular basis, contributing to a trend of sluggishness among Americans of all ages, according the U.S. Centers for Disease Control (CDC). Adolescent female students are particularly inactive—29% are inactive compared with 15% of male students. Unfortunately, the sedentary habits of young "couch potatoes" often continue into adulthood. Inactivity can be

(5)   a serious health risk factor, setting the stage for obesity and associated chronic illnesses. The benefits of exercise include building bone, muscle, and joints, controlling weight, and preventing the development of high blood pressure.

Some studies suggest that physical activity may have other benefits as well. One CDC study found that high school students who take part in team sports or are physically active outside of school are less

(10)   likely to engage in risky behaviors, like using drugs or smoking. The CDC recommends moderate, daily physical activity for people of all ages, such as brisk walking for 30 minutes or 15 to 20 minutes of more intense exercise. A survey conducted by the National Association for Sport and Physical Education questioned teens about their attitudes toward exercise and about what it would take to get them moving. Teens chose friends (56%) as their most likely motivators for becoming more active, followed by parents (18%)

(15)   and professional athletes (11%).

29. The first paragraph (lines 1–7) of the passage serves all of the following purposes EXCEPT to

    a. provide statistical information to support the claim that teenagers do not exercise enough.

    b. list long-term health risks associated with lack of exercise.

    c. express skepticism that teenagers can change their exercise habits.

    d. show a correlation between inactive teenagers and inactive adults.

    e. highlight some health benefits of exercise.

30. In line 4, *sedentary* most nearly means

    a. slothful.

    b. apathetic.

    c. stationary.

    d. stabilized.

    e. inflexible.

31. Which of the following techniques is used in the last sentence of the passage (lines 13–15)?

    a. explanation of terms

    b. comparison of different arguments

    c. contrast of opposing views

    d. generalized statement

    e. illustration by example

32. The primary purpose of the passage is to

    a. refute an argument.

    b. make a prediction.

    c. praise an outcome.

    d. promote a change.

    e. justify a conclusion.

Questions 33–37 are based on the following passage.

The following passage is from Frank McCourt's 1996 memoir Angela's Ashes. *The author describes what it was like to go to school as a young boy.*

Line

    We go to school through lanes and back streets so that we won't meet the respectable boys who go to the Christian Brothers' School or the rich ones who go to the Jesuit school, Crescent College. The Christian Brothers' boys wear tweed jackets, warm woolen sweaters, shirts, ties, and shiny new boots. We know they're the ones who will get jobs in the civil service and help the people who run the world. The Cres-

(5)   cent College boys wear blazers and school scarves tossed around their necks and over their shoulders to show they're cock o' the walk. They have long hair which falls across their foreheads and over their eyes so that they can toss their quaffs like Englishmen. We know they're the ones who will go to university, take over the family business, run the government, run the world. We'll be the messenger boys on bicycles who deliver their groceries or we'll go to England to work on the building sites. Our sisters will mind their chil-

(10)   dren and scrub their floors unless they go off to England, too. We know that. We're ashamed of the way we look and if boys from the rich schools pass remarks we'll get into a fight and wind up with bloody noses or torn clothes. Our masters will have no patience with us and our fights because their sons go to the rich schools and, Ye have no right to raise your hands to a better class of people so ye don't.

33. The *we* the author uses throughout the passage refers to
   a. his family.
   b. the poor children in his neighborhood.
   c. the children who attend rich schools.
   d. the author and his brother.
   e. the reader and writer.

34. The passage suggests that the author goes to school
   a. in shabby clothing.
   b. in a taxi cab.
   c. in warm sweaters and shorts.
   d. on a bicycle.
   e. to become a civil servant.

35. The word *pass* as used in line 11 means to
   a. move ahead of.
   b. go by without stopping.
   c. be approved or adopted.
   d. utter.
   e. come to an end.

36. The author quotes his school masters saying *Ye have no right to raise your hands to a better class of people so ye don't* (lines 12–13) in order to
   a. demonstrate how strict his school masters were.
   b. contrast his school to the Christian Brothers' School and Crescent College.
   c. show how his teachers reinforced class lines.
   d. prove that the author was meant for greater things.
   e. show how people talked.

37. The passage implies that
   a. the author was determined to go to England.
   b. the author was determined to be someone who will run the world.
   c. the author often got into fights.
   d. the author didn't understand the idea of class and rank in society.
   e. one's class determined one's future.

Questions 38–40 are based on the following passage.

Line

The seemingly simple question of "What defines a sport?" has been the fodder for argument and conversation for years, among professional and armchair athletes alike. There seems to be no doubt that vigorous and highly competitive activities such as baseball, football, and soccer are truly "sports," but when the subject of other activities such as darts, chess, and shuffleboard is broached we find ourselves
(5) at the heart of a controversy.
    To help resolve this dispute, the first text to consult would have to be the dictionary. According to one dictionary, a sport is defined as "a diversion" or "a recreation." Assuming one strictly adheres to the simple guidelines laid out in that definition, it would seem that almost any activity that provides enjoyment could be classified as a sport. And if, according to the dictionary, watching a sport on television is
(10) a sport itself, I guess that would make a couch potato an athlete. Play ball!

38. The author's tone in this passage could be
described as
   a. serious.
   b. light-hearted.
   c. confrontational.
   d. dark.
   e. romantic.

39. The word *vigorous* in line 3 most nearly means
   a. languorous.
   b. boring.
   c. intricate.
   d. ancient.
   e. strenuous.

40. The author would agree that
   a. watching TV should be seen as a sport.
   b. true sports involve some sort of physical activity.
   c. the dictionary definition of sports is misleading.
   d. shuffleboard should not be considered a sport.
   e. the dictionary definition of sports is wider
   than many might think.

Questions 41–44 are based on the following passages.

The following two passages discuss the role of affirmative action in the American university.

Line

Passage 1
Since the 1960s, there has been a sea change in university admissions. Key Supreme Court decisions and federal laws made equal opportunity the law of the land, and many institutions of higher learning adopted policies of affirmative action. The term *affirmative action* was first used in the 1960s to describe the active recruitment and promotion of minority candidates in both the workplace and in colleges and universi-
(5)   ties. President Lyndon Johnson, speaking at Howard University in 1965, aptly explained the reasoning behind affirmative action. As he said, "You do not take a man who, for years, has been hobbled by chains and liberate him, bring him to the starting line in a race and then say, 'You are free compete with all the others,' and still believe that you have been completely fair."

Passage 2
Some may argue that affirmative action had its place in the years following the Civil Rights movement, but
(10)   that it is no longer necessary on college campuses. To assume that all students are now on a level playing field is naïve. When all things are equal, choosing the minority candidate not only gives minorities fair access to institutions of higher learning, but it ensures diversity on our campuses. Exposing all students to a broad spectrum of American society is a lesson that may be the one that best prepares them to participate in American society and succeed in the future.

41. In Passage 1, the expression *sea change* means
   a. increase.
   b. storm.
   c. decrease.
   d. wave.
   e. transformation.

42. The author uses the quote from President Lyndon Johnson in Passage 1 to
   a. provide an example of discrimination in the past.
   b. show how Howard University benefited from affirmative action policies.
   c. make the passage more interesting.
   d. explain the rationale for affirmative action.
   e. prove that affirmative action has been effective at promoting diversity.

43. The argument for affirmative action in the workplace that most closely mirrors the reasoning in Passage 2 about affirmative action in college admissions is
   a. it is the law of the land.
   b. diversity in the workplace better prepares a company to compete in the marketplace.
   c. a diverse workforce is more efficient.
   d. a less qualified minority candidate is still a great asset to a company.
   e. it is the right thing to do.

44. The author of Passage 2 would agree that
   a. the Civil Rights movement impeded the progress of affirmative action.
   b. affirmative action should be phased out gradually.
   c. university culture can teach societal behavior.
   d. special preference should not be given based on skin color.
   e. most Americans no longer support affirmative action.

▶ Answers

1. c. The description of the winding paths, shifting landscape, and sections that spill into one another support the assertion that the park lacks a center.

2. e. The passage states that Olmsted wanted to create a democratic playground, so he designed the park to have many centers that would allow interaction among the various members of society.

3. b. The passage states that the park's design was innovative, suggesting it was very different from other park designs.

4. a. Olmsted's goal of creating a democratic park with many centers that would allow interaction among everyone without giving preference to one group or class shows his philosophy of inclusion.

5. b. The passage states that after Pauline became pregnant, Cholly had acted like the early days of their marriage when he would ask if she were tired or wanted him to bring her something from the store. This statement suggests that Cholly had not done that for a while and, therefore, had begun to neglect Pauline.

6. e. Although there is a state of ease in the relationship between Pauline and Cholly, there is intense loneliness for Pauline. There may be less tension in this state of ease, but there does not appear to be more intimacy, because the loneliness prevails. We can infer that back home she was living with her family, not Cholly, and that Pauline would expect her husband to fulfill her need for companionship.

7. a. At the end of the passage, Pauline rediscovers her dreams of romance. The passage tells us she succumbed to her earlier dreams, and the following sentence tells us what whose dreams were about: romantic love.

8. c. Because the narrator states that romantic love and physical beauty are probably the most destructive ideas in the history of human thought because they both *originated in envy, thrived in insecurity, and ended in disillusion,* and because these are the two ideas Pauline was introduced to in the theater, we can infer that she will only become more unhappy as a result of going to the movies.

9. a. The two passages present opposing points of view. Passage 1 argues that cosmetic procedures can be beneficial, while the author of Passage 2 explains her negative feelings toward cosmetic procedures. The author of Passage 1, therefore, praises the cosmetic procedures that the author of Passage 2 derides.

10. d. The author of Passage 2 describes Botox as "not entirely risk-free," so **a** is not a possibility. Non-surgical techniques are discussed in both passages, neither passage discusses the high cost of cosmetic procedures, and both mention reasons people might feel the need to have cosmetic procedures performed. Only Passage 1 discusses the personal satisfaction felt by those who have had cosmetic surgery or procedures.

11. b. Although they came to different conclusions, both arguments tie a sense of self-worth to feeling attractive.

12. a. Both passages use first-person points of view to build an argument.

13. e. Of the five answer choices, the trickiest one is choice **c**. However, looking at the arguments closely, neither author is necessarily arguing that the amount of cosmetic procedures should change. The essential argument of the two passages is different—Passage 1 is arguing for cosmetic surgery and procedures, while Passage 2 is mainly discussing the author's reasons for not having cosmetic procedures performed.

14. b. The passage states that the goods pertaining to the soul are called goods in the highest and fullest sense.

15. d. Aristotle notes that the definition of good *corresponds* with the current opinion about the nature of the soul.

16. a. In the second paragraph, Aristotle states that we have all but defined happiness as a kind of good life and well-being. Thus, the definitions of happiness and goodness are intertwined; living a good life will bring happiness.

17. c. In the third paragraph, Aristotle lists several different ways that people define happiness to show that they all fit into the broad definition of a kind of good life and well-being.

18. e. The passage provides a warning about sleep deprivation; therefore, the author's views sleep deprivation with wariness.

19. d. The passage mainly deals with the dangers of not getting enough sleep. Choices **b** and **e** are too specific to be the passage's primary purpose. Choices **a** and **c** are not supported by the passage.

20. a. The author provides information from the two professional organizations to enhance his or her argument. Although this information does show that different organizations are concerned with sleep deprivation, this is not the primary purpose of discussing the organizations. The reader may or may not be familiar with the two organizations, so choice **c** is incorrect. Choices **d** and **e** are incorrect because the information from the organizations does not contradict with the author's opinion or anything in the passage.

21. b. The author details the large amounts of money Wal-Mart gives to charitable organizations. The author would most likely describe this amount as *significant.*

22. e. The author of Passage 1 states that Wal-Mart cares about *more than just the bottom line.* He or she is making the argument that Wal-Mart is concerned with doing good works for the betterment of society and not merely with making a profit.

23. c. Passage 1 argues that Wal-Mart is beneficial to society, while Passage 2 argues that the store is detrimental; therefore, each of the passages takes a side in an argument.

24. a. Choice **b** and **d** are points presented in Passage 1, choice **e** is an argument presented in Passage 2, and choice **c** is not presented in either passage. The only choice with which both authors would agree is choice **a**.

25. d. Both authors discuss the impact Wal-Mart has on a community, so it is fair to say that both passages are concerned with Wal-Mart's local impact.

26. d. Although he was a man of no formal scientific education, Leeuwenhoek demonstrated a craving of knowledge. The phrase *stumbled upon* in choice **a** is too accidental to describe Leeuwenhoek's perseverance. The words *proficient* and *entertainment* in choice **c** do not accurately describe Leeuwenhoek's skill and drive depicted in the passage. Choices **b** and **e** are incorrect; Leeuwenhoek was not trained nor did he know that his discoveries would later help to cure disease.

27. c. *Inspired* means to exert an animating or enlivening influence on. In the context of the passage, Leeuwenhoek's creation of microscope lenses were influenced by the lenses used by drapers.

28. b. The tone of the passage is positive. However, *ecstatic reverence* (choice **a**) is too positive, and *tepid approval* (choice **c**) is not positive enough.

29. c. Nowhere in the passage does the author speculate about whether teenagers can change their exercise habits.

30. c. One meaning of *sedentary* is settled; another meaning is doing or requiring much sitting. *Stationary*, defined as fixed in a course or mode, is closest in meaning.

31. e. The last sentence illustrates factors that motivate teenagers to exercise by using the results of a national survey to provide specific examples.

32. d. The passage promotes change in teenagers' exercise habits by emphasizing the benefits of exercise, the moderate amount of exercise needed to achieve benefits, and some factors that may encourage teenagers to exercise.

33. b. The *we* go to school, so the reference must be to school-aged children. In addition, the passage contrasts the *we*'s with the respectable boys and the rich ones, so the *we*'s are neither wealthy nor respected.

34. a. The author and his classmates go to school through lanes and back streets to avoid the students who go to school dressed in warm and respectable clothing. He also states that they are ashamed of the way they look, implying that they are poorly dressed.

35. d. The boys would get into fights if the rich boys were to utter derogatory words or pass remarks.

36. c. Although the quote here does show how the author's school masters talked, it has a more important function: to show that his school masters reinforced the class system by telling the author and his classmates to stay in their place and not challenge the existing class structure.

37. e. The author "knows," based only on the fact of which school the boys attend, what they will be when they grow up—the respectable boys will have the administrative jobs while the rich boys will run the government, run the world. The author and those in his socioeconomic class will be laborers. The author emphasizes the certainty of this knowledge with the repetition of the phrase *we know* and the sentence *We know that.* Thus, he demonstrates that their future was already set based upon their socioeconomic standing.

38. b. The author's tone in this passage could only be described as light-hearted. The subject of the passage itself is not of a particularly serious nature, and the author's deduction that watching a sport on television would technically characterize couch potatoes as athletes is humorous and subtly mocks those who would argue over what is a "true" sport.

39. e. *Vigorous,* as it is used in the passage, is an adjective that describes an activity carried out forcefully or energetically. This type of activity is best described as *strenuous,* choice **e.**

40. e. The author discusses the dictionary definition of *sport,* and admits that activities such as darts, chess, and shuffleboard match this definition. He also says that there is an argument over what constitutes a sport. The choice that most accurately states the author's opinion is choice **e.**

41. e. A *sea change* is a *transformation.* This can be inferred from the next sentence, which states that colleges adopted policies of affirmative action. Affirmative action is a transformation in college admissions.

42. d. The author clearly states that President Johnson aptly explained the reasoning behind affirmative action.

43. b. The author's main argument for affirmative action is that the student body benefits from diversity. His final point is that students who have been exposed to a broad spectrum of American society are better prepared for their futures. The idea that diversity benefits a company and makes it better prepared to compete in marketplace most closely mirrors this reasoning.

44. c. The author argues that affirmative action on campus encourages good societal behavior, so it is reasonable to assume that the author believes university culture can teach societal behavior.

Posttest ▶

Now that you have completed the different types of practice questions in this book, it's time to take the posttest. This posttest will help establish how much you have learned and where you may need additional practice.

This posttest is not timed, but try and complete it as fast as you can. On the official test, you will only have 35 minutes to do 60 questions. At that rate, this one should only take you about 15 minutes or less. Be sure to check your answers after you finish.

POSTTEST

1.	ⓐ	ⓑ	ⓒ	ⓓ	ⓔ
2.	ⓐ	ⓑ	ⓒ	ⓓ	ⓔ
3.	ⓐ	ⓑ	ⓒ	ⓓ	ⓔ
4.	ⓐ	ⓑ	ⓒ	ⓓ	ⓔ
5.	ⓐ	ⓑ	ⓒ	ⓓ	ⓔ
6.	ⓐ	ⓑ	ⓒ	ⓓ	ⓔ
7.	ⓐ	ⓑ	ⓒ	ⓓ	ⓔ
8.	ⓐ	ⓑ	ⓒ	ⓓ	ⓔ
9.	ⓐ	ⓑ	ⓒ	ⓓ	ⓔ
10.	ⓐ	ⓑ	ⓒ	ⓓ	ⓔ

11.	ⓐ	ⓑ	ⓒ	ⓓ	ⓔ
12.	ⓐ	ⓑ	ⓒ	ⓓ	ⓔ
13.	ⓐ	ⓑ	ⓒ	ⓓ	ⓔ
14.	ⓐ	ⓑ	ⓒ	ⓓ	ⓔ
15.	ⓐ	ⓑ	ⓒ	ⓓ	ⓔ
16.	ⓐ	ⓑ	ⓒ	ⓓ	ⓔ
17.	ⓐ	ⓑ	ⓒ	ⓓ	ⓔ
18.	ⓐ	ⓑ	ⓒ	ⓓ	ⓔ
19.	ⓐ	ⓑ	ⓒ	ⓓ	ⓔ
20.	ⓐ	ⓑ	ⓒ	ⓓ	ⓔ

21.	ⓐ	ⓑ	ⓒ	ⓓ	ⓔ
22.	ⓐ	ⓑ	ⓒ	ⓓ	ⓔ
23.	ⓐ	ⓑ	ⓒ	ⓓ	ⓔ
24.	ⓐ	ⓑ	ⓒ	ⓓ	ⓔ
25.	ⓐ	ⓑ	ⓒ	ⓓ	ⓔ

▶ Sentence Completion

In each of the following sentences, one or two words have been omitted (indicated by a blank). Choose the word(s) from the answer choices provided that makes the most sense in the context of the sentence.

1. The villagers' only connection to the modern world was a 15-year-old computer that seemed _____ compared to today's technology.
   a. brash
   b. elicit
   c. pertinent
   d. retrograde
   e. archaic

2. When the author's memoir was found to be completely _____, he was publicly _____ by his irate publisher.
   a. audacious . . . apprehended
   b. pertinent . . . exulted
   c. fallacious . . . denounced
   d. ersatz . . . lauded
   e. conventional . . . castigated

3. Although the siege lasted for hours, the fortress was so well defended, the opposing army found it absolutely _____.
   a. resilient
   b. unassailable
   c. resourceful
   d. intangible
   e. unconscionable

4. Bobby refused to do his homework, which the teacher took to be a _____ display of _____.
   a. distressing . . . certitude
   b. persistent . . . impertinence
   c. resilient . . . arrogance
   d. contemptuous . . . insolence
   e. tenacious . . . admiration

5. Terri adores the new Aerostar CD; she's been _____ its virtues for weeks.
   a. amassing
   b. ensuring
   c. decrying
   d. assuring
   e. extolling

6. I felt _____ and _____ when I awoke in the hospital after my surgery; however, once I realized where I was, I no longer felt confused.
   a. disconcerted . . . discombobulated
   b. deranged . . . defiant
   c. addled . . . amicable
   d. exhausted . . . exalted
   e. reticent . . . reproachful

7. The time we eat dinner is _____ upon the length of the movie we see beforehand.
   a. contingent
   b. exacted
   c. predetermined
   d. insistent
   e. complicit

► Short-Passage Questions

Read the following passage and the questions that follow it. As you form your answers, be sure to base them on what is stated in the passage or the inferences you can make from the passage.

Line

Jazz, from its early roots in slave spirituals and the marching bands of New Orleans, had developed into the predominant American musical style by the 1930s. In this era, jazz musicians played a lush, orchestrated style known as swing. Played in large ensembles, also called big bands, swing filled the dance halls and night-clubs. Then came bebop. In the mid-1940s, jazz musicians strayed from the swing style and developed a
(5)   more improvisational method of playing known as bebop. Jazz was transformed from popular music to an elite art form.

The soloists in the big bands improvised from the melody. The young musicians who ushered in bebop expanded on the improvisational elements of the big bands. They played with advanced harmonies, changed chord structures, and made chord substitutions. These young musicians got their starts with the
(10)   leading big bands of the day, but during World War II, they started to play together in smaller groups.

These pared-down bands helped foster the bebop style. Rhythm is the distinguishing feature of bebop, and in small groups the drums became more prominent. Setting a driving beat, the drummer interacted with the bass, piano, and the soloists, and together the musicians created fast, complex melodies.

8. The swing style can be most accurately characterized as
  a. complex and inaccessible.
  b. appealing to an elite audience.
  c. lively and melodic.
  d. lacking in improvisation.
  e. played in small groups.

9. According to the passage, one of the most significant innovations of the bebop musicians was
  a. to shun older musicians.
  b. to emphasize rhythm.
  c. to use melodic improvisation.
  d. to play in small clubs.
  e. to ban dancing.

10. The main purpose of the passage is to
  a. mourn the passing of an era.
  b. condemn bebop for making jazz inaccessible.
  c. explain the development of the bebop style.
  d. celebrate the end of the conventional swing style of jazz.
  e. instruct in the method of playing bebop.

► Passage-Length Questions

Read the passage and the questions that follow it. As you form your answers, be sure to base them on what is stated in the passage or the inferences you can make from the passage.

The following passage from the Lowell National Historical Park Handbook *describes the advent of American manufacturing, imported from England in the 1790s. The Arkwright system mentioned in the passage refers to a water frame, a water-powered spinning machine that was used to make cloth.*

Line

The mounting conflict between the colonies and England in the 1760s and 1770s reinforced a growing conviction that Americans should be less dependent on their mother country for manufactures. Spinning bees and bounties encouraged the manufacture of homespun cloth as a substitute for English imports. But manufacturing of cloth outside the household was associated with relief of the poor. In Boston and
(5)   Philadelphia, Houses of Industry employed poor families at spinning for their daily bread.

Such practices made many pre-Revolutionary Americans dubious about manufacturing. After independence, there were a number of unsuccessful attempts to establish textile factories. Americans needed access to the British industrial innovations, but England had passed laws forbidding the export of machinery or the emigration of those who could operate it. Nevertheless, it was an English immigrant, Samuel
(10)   Slater, who finally introduced British cotton technology to America.

Slater had worked his way up from apprentice to overseer in an English factory using the Arkwright system. Drawn by American bounties for the introduction of textile technology, he passed as a farmer and sailed for America with details of the Arkwright water frame committed to memory. In December 1790, working for mill owner Moses Brown, he started up the first permanent American cotton spinning mill
(15)   in Pawtucket, Rhode Island. Employing a workforce of nine children between the ages of seven and 12, Slater successfully mechanized the carding and spinning processes.

A generation of millwrights and textile workers trained under Slater was the catalyst for the rapid proliferation of textile mills in the early nineteenth century. From Slater's first mill, the industry spread across New England to places like North Uxbridge, Massachusetts. For two decades, before Lowell mills
(20)   and those modeled after them offered competition, the "Rhode Island System" of small, rural spinning mills set the tone for early industrialization.

By 1800, the mill employed more than 100 workers. A decade later, 61 cotton mills turning more than 31,000 spindles were operating in the United States, with Rhode Island and the Philadelphia region the main manufacturing centers. The textile industry was established, although factory operations were
(25)   limited to carding and spinning. It remained for Francis Cabot Lowell to introduce a workable power loom and the integrated factory, in which all textile production steps take place under one roof.

As textile mills proliferated after the turn of the century, a national debate arose over the place of manufacturing in American society. Thomas Jefferson spoke for those supporting the "yeoman ideal" of a rural republic, at whose heart was the independent, democratic farmer. He questioned the spread
(30)   of factories, worrying about factory workers' loss of economic independence. Alexander Hamilton led those who promoted manufacturing and saw prosperity growing out of industrial development. The debate, largely philosophical in the 1790s, grew more urgent after 1830 as textile factories multiplied and increasing numbers of Americans worked in them.

11. The primary purpose of the passage is to
  a. account for the decline of rural America.
  b. contrast political views held by the British and the Americans.
  c. summarize British laws forbidding the export of industrial machinery.
  d. describe the introduction of textile mills in New England.
  e. make an argument in support of industrial development.

12. The passage refers to Houses of Industry (line 5) to illustrate
  a. a highly successful and early social welfare program.
  b. the perception of cloth production outside the home as a social welfare measure.
  c. the preference for the work of individual artisans over that of spinning machines.
  d. the first textile factory in the United States.
  e. the utilization of technological advances being made in England at the time.

13. The first paragraph (lines 1–5) of the passage implies that early American manufacturing was
  a. entirely beneficial.
  b. politically and economically necessary.
  c. symbolically undemocratic.
  d. environmentally destructive.
  e. spiritually corrosive.

14. The description of Slater's immigration to the American colonies (lines 12–15) serves primarily to
  a. demonstrate Slater's craftiness in evading British export laws.
  b. show the attraction of farming opportunities in the American colonies.
  c. explain the details of British manufacturing technologies.
  d. illustrate American efforts to block immigration to the colonies.
  e. describe the willingness of English factories to share knowledge with the colonies.

15. Lines 15–16 imply that Slater viewed child labor as
  a. an available workforce.
  b. a necessary evil.
  c. an unpleasant reality.
  d. an immoral institution.
  e. superior to adult labor.

16. The author implies that the *catalyst* (line 17) behind the spread of American textile mills in the early 1800s was
  a. Slater's invention of a water-powered spinning machine.
  b. the decline in the ideal of the self-sufficient American farm family.
  c. the expertise of the workforce trained in Slater's prototype mill.
  d. an increased willingness to employ child laborers.
  e. the support of British manufacturers who owned stock in American mills.

17. In line 20, *modeled* most nearly means
   a. posed.
   b. displayed.
   c. arranged.
   d. illustrated.
   e. fashioned.

18. Which of the following techniques is used in the last paragraph of the passage (lines 27–33)?
   a. explanation of terms
   b. description of consensus reached by historians
   c. contrast of different viewpoints
   d. generalized statement
   e. illustration by example

This passage details the history and reasoning of Daylight Saving Time.

Line

For centuries, time was measured by the position of the sun through the use of sundials. Noon was recognized when the sun was the highest in the sky, and cities would set their clock by this Apparent Solar Time, even though some cities would often be on a slightly different time. "Summer time" or Daylight Saving Time (DST) was instituted to make better use of daylight. Thus, clocks are set forward one hour in the
(5)   spring to move an hour of daylight from the morning to the evening and then set back one hour in the fall to return to normal daylight.

Benjamin Franklin first conceived the idea of daylight saving during his tenure as an American delegate in Paris in 1784 and wrote about it extensively in his essay "An Economical Project." It is said that Franklin awoke early one morning and was surprised to see the sunlight at such an hour. Always the econ-
(10)   omist, Franklin believed the practice of moving the time could save on the use of candlelight, as candles were expensive at the time. In England, builder William Willett (1857–1915), became a strong supporter for Daylight Saving Time upon noticing blinds of many houses were closed on an early sunny morning. Willett believed everyone, including himself, would appreciate longer hours of light in the evenings. In 1909, Sir Robert Pearce introduced a bill in the House of Commons to make it obligatory to adjust the clocks.
(15)   A bill was drafted and introduced into Parliament several times but met with great opposition, mostly from farmers. Eventually, in 1925, it was decided that summer time should begin on the day following the third Saturday in April and close after the first Saturday in October.

The U.S. Congress passed the Standard Time Act of 1918 to establish standard time and preserve and set Daylight Saving Time across the continent. This act also devised five time zones throughout the United
(20)   States: Eastern, Central, Mountain, Pacific, and Alaska. The first time zone was set on "the mean astronomical time of the 75th degree of longitude west from Greenwich" (England). In 1919, this act was repealed. President Roosevelt established year-round Daylight Saving Time (also called "War Time") from 1942–1945. However, after this period each state adopted their own DST, which proved to be disconcerting to television and radio broadcasting and transportation. In 1966, President Lyndon Johnson created the
(25)   Department of Transportation and signed the Uniform Time Act. As a result, the Department of Transportation was given the responsibility for the time laws. During the oil embargo and energy crisis of the 1970s, President Richard Nixon extended DST through the Daylight Saving Time Energy Act of 1973 to conserve energy further. This law was modified in 1986, and Daylight Saving Time was set for beginning on the first Sunday in April (to "spring ahead") and ending on the last Sunday in October (to "fall back").

(30)   Through the years, the U.S. Department of Transportation conducted polls concerning Daylight Saving Time and found that many Americans were in favor of it because of the extended hours of daylight and the freedom to do more in the evening hours. In further studies, the U.S. Department of Transportation also found that DST conserves energy by cutting the electricity usage in the morning and evening for lights and particular appliances. During the darkest winter months (November through February), the advantage of

(35) conserving energy in afternoon daylight saving time is outweighed by needing more light in the morning because of late sunrise. In Britain, studies showed that there were fewer accidents on the road because of the increased visibility resulting from additional hours of daylight.

       Despite these advantages, there is still opposition to DST. One perpetual complaint is the inconvenience of changing many clocks and the adjustment to a new sleep schedule. Farmers often wake at

(40) sunrise and find that their animals do not adjust to the changing of time until weeks after the clock is either moved forward or back. In Israel, Sephardic Jews have campaigned against Daylight Saving Time because they recite prayers in the early morning during the Jewish month of Elul. Many places around the globe still do not observe Daylight Saving Time—such as Arizona (excluding Navajo reservations), five counties in Indiana, Hawaii, Puerto Rico, Japan, and Saskatchewan, Canada. Countries located near

(45) the equator have equal hours of day and night and do not participate in Daylight Saving Time.

19. In line 14, the word *obligatory* most nearly means
  a. approved.
  b. sparse.
  c. aberrant.
  d. requisite.
  e. optional.

20. According to the passage what is the most beneficial effect of DST?
  a. changing sleeping patterns
  b. less car accidents
  c. conservation of energy
  d. additional time for family outings
  e. preferred harvesting time for farmers

21. Who first established the idea of DST?
  a. President Richard Nixon
  b. Benjamin Franklin
  c. Sir Robert Pearce
  d. President Lyndon Johnson
  e. William Willett

22. According to the passage, in which area of the world is DST least useful?
  a. the tropics
  b. Indiana
  c. Navajo reservations
  d. Mexico
  e. Saskatchewan

23. Which of the following statements is true of the U.S. Department of Transportation?
  a. It was created by President Richard Nixon.
  b. It set the standards for DST throughout the world.
  c. It constructed the Uniform Time Act.
  d. It oversees all time laws in the United States.
  e. It established the standard railway time laws.

24. Which of the following statements is the best title for this passage?
  a. The History and Rationale of Daylight Saving Time
  b. Lyndon Johnson and the Uniform Time Act
  c. The U.S. Department of Transportation and Daylight Saving Time
  d. Daylight Saving Time in the United States
  e. Benjamin Franklin's Discovery

25. In which month does the need for more energy in the morning offset the afternoon conservation of energy by DST?
  a. June
  b. July
  c. October
  d. January
  e. March

▶ Answers

1. e. A 15-year-old computer would be considered out-of-date compared to today's technology; the answer choice that means "old and out-of-date" is *archaic*.

2. c. The best clue for determining the correct answer choice to this question is the word *irate*. Based on this knowledge, you can rule out choices **b** and **d**; an irate publisher would not *exult* or *laud* the person who inflamed his or her anger. Most likely, an *audacious* or *conventional* memoir would not be enough to cause someone great anger, so the best answer choice is **c**.

3. b. The sentence implies that the opposing army could not break through the fortress's strong defenses. *Unassailable*, meaning "not subject to seizure," is the best of the five answer choices.

4. d. If a student refused to do his homework, the teacher would most likely be upset. The choices can therefore be narrowed down to **b** and **d**. Of the two answer choices, there is no indication that the student consistently refused to do his homework, so *persistence* can be ruled out, leaving answer choice **d**.

5. e. Because we know that Terri adores the CD, she is most likely speaking highly about it. To extol means to praise highly.

6. a. Based on the second sentence, you can assume that the best answer choice will be synonymous with *confused*. Of the five answer choices, only choice **a** features two synonyms for confused.

7. a. Sentence context indicates that the time of dinner is affected by the length of the movie. The answer choice that implies this connection is choice **a**, *contingent*.

8. c. The passage describes swing as *vibrant*, a synonym for *lively*. It is also stated that soloists in big bands improvised from the melody, indicating that the music was *melodic*.

9. b. The author states that rhythm is the distinguishing feature of bebop.

10. c. The tone of the passage is neutral so only the answers beginning with *explain* or *instruct* are possible choices. The passage does not explain how to play bebop music, so **c** is the best choice.

11. d. The passage describes the introduction of British cotton technology to America, specifically to New England.

12. b. The passage mentions the Houses of Industry in Boston and Philadelphia as examples of the association of cloth manufacturing with relief of the poor.

13. b. The mounting conflict between the colonies and England suggests that America had political and/or economic reasons for developing its own textile industry.

14. a. The description of Samuel Slater's immigration to America shows the deceptive measures necessary to evade British export laws and introduce cotton technology to the colonies. Slater posed as a farmer in order to emigrate to America and committed to memory the cotton technology he learned in English factories.

15. a. The author does not offer Slater's personal viewpoint on child labor, only the fact that Slater hired nine children between the ages of seven and 12 to work in his Rhode Island mill.

16. c. According to the passage, the knowledge and training acquired in Slater's mill of a generation of millwrights and textile workers provided the catalyst for the spread of cotton mills in New England.

17. e. One meaning of *to model* is "to display by means of wearing, using, or posing." In this context, *to model* means "to construct or fashion after a pattern."

18. c. The author contrasts different viewpoints exemplified by the philosophy of Thomas Jefferson, who supported a republic whose heart was the independent, democratic farmer and that of Alexander Hamilton, who promoted manufacturing and industrial development.

19. d. Choices **b** and **c**, meaning scattered and erratic respectively, are not supported in the document. Choice **e** is incorrect because it is an antonym of *obligatory*. Choice **a** may be considered a synonym, but it is not the best choice. The best choice is **d**, *requisite*.

20. c. Choices **b** and **d** are also true but not the best answers. Choices **a** and **e** are not true.

21. b. The passage clearly states that Benjamin Franklin first considered the concept of DST.

22. a. Locations near the equator do not participate in DST because they have equal hours of day and night; therefore, DST, which extends the daylight period, is not useful. Choice **c** is incorrect because Navajo reservations observe DST. Choice **b** is incorrect because parts of Indiana do observe DST. Choice **d** is incorrect because the text doesn't even mention Mexico. Choice **e** is incorrect because Saskatchewan chooses to not observe DST.

23. d. This choice is directly supported by the passage.

24. a. Choices **b–e** are incorrect because they each refer to specific points raised in the passage, but not throughout the passage. Only choice **a** describes the point of the entire passage.

25. d. This choice is directly supported by the passage.

NOTES

NOTES

NOTES

NOTES

NOTES

NOTES

NOTES

Special FREE Online Practice from LearningExpress!

Let LearningExpress help you acquire essential reading comprehension skills FAST

Go to the LearningExpress Practice Center at www.LearningExpressFreeOffer.com, an interactive online resource exclusively for LearningExpress customers.

Now that you've purchased LearningExpress's *411 SAT Critical Reading Questions*, you have **FREE** access to:

- **67 practice questions covering all vital reading comprehension skills** that will test your understanding of passages and how well you read overall
- **Immediate scoring** and **detailed answer explanations**
- Benchmark your skills and focus your study with our **customized diagnostic report**
- **Improve** your **reading comprehension skills** and **overcome SAT anxiety**

Follow the simple instructions on the scratch card in your copy of *411 SAT Critical Reading Questions*. Use your individualized access code found on the scratch card and go to www.LearningExpressFreeOffer.com to sign in. Start practicing your reading comprehension skills online right away!

Once you've logged on, use the spaces below to write in your access code and newly created password for easy reference:

Access Code: _____   Password: _____